PRAISE FOR *THE BEST NEW TRUE CRIME STORIES: SERIAL KILLERS*

"True Crime addicts will devour this book. The portraits of these psychopaths will mesmerize and horrify everyone who reads it."
—Aphrodite Jones, bestselling true crime author

"This compelling collection of serial killer stories is more than its beautifully told parts—it adds up to a clear and startling portrait of murder as an addiction and the very human demons that haunt the lives of killers and victims alike."
—Deborah Blum, author of *The Poisoner's Handbook: Murder and the Birth of Forensic Medicine in Jazz Age New York*

"This is by far the best book about serial killers I've ever read—and I've probably read more than is good for my mental health. The writers each have unique insights—sometimes because they have encountered the killers they describe, always because they can get further into the unfathomable minds of the killers through their sensitivity. Chilling, very moving (those poor victims), but above all, essential reading."
—Peter Guttridge, critic and crime fiction author

The Best New
True Crime Stories:
Serial Killers

The Best New True Crime Stories: Serial Killers

Edited by Mitzi Szereto

Mango Publishing

CORAL GABLES

For permission requests, please contact the publisher at:
Mango Publishing Group
2850 S Douglas Road, 2nd Floor
Coral Gables, FL 33134 USA
info@mango.bz

For special orders, quantity sales, course adoptions and corporate sales, please email the publisher at sales@mango.bz. For trade and wholesale sales, please contact Ingram Publisher Services at customer.service@ingramcontent.com or +1.800.509.4887.

The Best New True Crime Stories: Serial Killers

Library of Congress Cataloging-in-Publication number: 2019944219
ISBN: (print) 978-1-64250-072-1 , (ebook) 978-1-64250-073-8
BISAC category code TRU002010, TRUE CRIME / Murder / Serial Killers

Printed in the United States of America

TABLE OF CONTENTS

Introduction

Mitzi Szereto

S erial killers. They make the headlines. They give you nightmares. They make you afraid to leave your house. Yet, according to statistics, you're more likely to be murdered by someone you know than by a complete stranger. When a murder *is* committed by a stranger, it's usually in connection with a burglary or robbery. But serial killers are a different entity. They're the wild card you never see coming.

Who are these predators who target and kill not just once but again and again, repeating the same horrific pattern until they're caught, meet their own deaths, or decide they've had enough? Are they the result of nature or nurture? Did something trigger this desire to kill, or are they hardwired from birth to hurt and destroy? Have they been warped by society, or do they simply get off on killing? We can find examples of serial killers who fit any of these templates and, in some cases, more than one.

Countless studies have been done on criminal behavior. Going by the scientists, psychologists, behaviorists, and neurological studies, there can be many reasons for why someone becomes a murdering-for-pleasure machine. Theories abound, though there doesn't seem to be a one-size-fits-all answer. Nevertheless, the one thing serial killers all seem to have in common is the need for power, the need to control. When they kill, they get to play God. In the words of Richard Ramirez

(California's "Night Stalker"), "We've all got the power in our hands to kill, but most people are afraid to use it. The ones who aren't afraid, control life itself."

Serial killers have been around for a long time and can be found in every corner of the globe. Most tend to be men, but plenty of women have also joined this notorious group. Although serial killers typically start on their murderous paths at a young age, there are exceptions. The belief that these dangerous individuals possess high levels of intelligence as evidenced in bestselling novels and slick Hollywood films is another characteristic that's not always the case. Although sexual gratification, however warped, is often the main impulse that drives these people to kill, it's by no means the only one. Perhaps those who commit serial murder are like a jigsaw puzzle that leaves you with some missing pieces.

According to the US Federal Bureau of Investigation, 67 percent of serial killers are American grown. The 1980s was considered a "peak" era for American serial killers. In fact, the serial killer database compiled by Virginia's Radford University and Florida Gulf Coast University indicates a decline in identified serial killers in the United States since then. There can be many reasons for this: better forensics, changes in the criminal justice system, and people living more cautious lifestyles. However, there's really no way of knowing how many serial killers have gone unidentified. When you take into account historical record-keeping systems that weren't always accurate, who knows how many serial killers have been overlooked? Add in countries that don't share their statistics outside their borders, let alone within, it's possible the numbers are higher than believed.

The intention of this book is not to glorify or glamorize serial killers nor to sensationalize their crimes or further victimize their victims. But the fact remains: people are interested in and fascinated by this subject matter. We want to know what happened and, if possible, why it happened. Crime, particularly serial murder, is at the extreme end of the human experience.

Our interest in true crime isn't a new phenomenon—we've been interested in the subject for centuries. One of the best-known examples are the popular crime broadsides or "crime sheets" of eighteenth and nineteenth century England, which were often sold to spectators at public executions. In the old days, people crowded into courtrooms to observe criminal trials firsthand. Newspapers even published extra editions, though it's unlikely much in the way of analysis was provided. It was more about sensationalism and cheap entertainment for the masses.

So how does today's true crime writing differ from yesterday's? Although you can still find examples that have more in common with the past than the present, the readership has changed, thereby raising the bar for contemporary true crime writers. As readers, we expect more than salacious reports. We expect our content to have substance. Like traditional journalism, true crime is reporting on what happened and who it happened to. But it's also providing context and analysis. It's even giving a voice to those who weren't heard or may no longer be able to speak. The reader comes away from the experience with more than just a lurid headline and a few juicy "bytes" of information.

The Best New True Crime Stories: Serial Killers contains accounts from an international group of contributors—from award-winning crime writers and true crime podcasters to journalists and experts in the field. They have researched extensively on their subjects. Some have encountered their subjects personally or peripherally, drawing upon memories and experiences to tell a story only they can tell. So, if you're looking for fascinating and thought-provoking content from some of today's best writers of true crime, you've come to the right place.

Mitzi Szereto

The Quiet Man in the Overalls Struggled to be Heard

STEPHEN WADE

There is an image of Dennis Nilsen that dominates the media and imprints him on the minds of readers, researchers, and criminologists across the globe. He wears blue overalls, and he looks placid, still, and silent. In fact, as is the case with so many biographical profiles of dangerous killers, the image could be of the guy next door who spends time with a wrench or a drill and works on his auto or makes things in wood.

Most of us, perhaps, put these criminals in a special compartment in our minds: a spot with a label reading "Mad and Bad." In other words, we leave out the ongoing debates in criminology about an offense coming from a person who is "Mad or Bad." No, we think, they have lost their court battle to avoid responsibility, and they are destined to be a killer, locked away. One true crime reader at a talk I gave once put it this way: "Look, these guys who scoot around slitting throats…hurl them into a dark hole and piss on 'em."

Now I've worked in jails, so I won't take that angle. But neither would I be soft in the head by making sure their dirty laundry is washed for them and that they have choices of muesli every breakfast alongside fresh eggs and bacon. But I do think about the issue of retribution as opposed to rehabilitation, and I've never yet found an answer to the question about jail: Does prison work?

When I first worked as a writer in a jail, it was a talk and a reading in a top-security British prison, and the audience was made up of terrorists, killers, psychopaths, and all the varieties of *homo sapiens* whom you might want to disqualify from that Latin term that defines us. That day, Nilsen was one of them. I read poems, and I talked about being creative with words. Well, the questions at the end of the talk came thick and fast. One man gave me a copy of their prison writing magazine. It was very impressive. I'm telling you this because, in a certain very restricted way, prison does work. That is, it works for some, and it may only work in minor ways by achieving minor goals. Most would surely think that it only works for psychopaths when it provides a box with no windows. For Nilsen, it worked in the sense that he had wanted company, and by God, now he had it.

I'm writing this now, not long after Nilsen's death, because I have strong memories of meeting him. The second time, he was wearing the overalls, the ones we see on a stock photo of him, used and reused in the media. He was one of a bunch of guys who had found a way to cope with a constricted life, yet a life that was, for them, "safe." This seems to say that we have to keep serial killers like wasps in a bottle as if we torment them. Maybe we do.

They were articulate, well-read men, with brains on full throttle. One man who asked questions afterward was Nilsen. He said my poems were "honest and made you listen." Now, I have had critiques in my writing career from professors, lecturers, and reviewers, but only the one time did I have comments from a serial killer.

The second time I met him was in a jail workshop, and he was working on Braille translations for children in African villages. I recall his stare more than his words. I had a sense that the thirty or so people sitting on the benches, occupied with what the jail would term "purposeful behavior," were somehow operating at a bottom level. By that, I mean that they would maybe fit Aldous Huxley's *Brave New World* Delta class—but that makes them sound like airplanes. No, the point is that the serial killer, the dangerous person loose in society, will be able to function as Huxley's Alpha. Such an individual can employ his or her intelligence, or animal cunning, if you like, without obstruction. A top-security prison reduces activity to that of the wasp in a bottle. Now, that might hint at rage, frustration, and a build-up of spite, hatred, and every emotion that, when held in, tends to wait for an explosion. But no, we administer drugs. We supervise. We watch and watch and take no chances.

Who was this mystery man in the overalls with the stare, then? I wish there was a simple and short answer. I still see his face and hear his voice, and the answer to the question seems to change every time I put pen to paper and write about the man.

I have been thinking about him ever since those two brief meetings. In my life as a crime writer, I reflect at length on murder. For six years, I worked as a writer in a number of British prisons, and I met hundreds of people who had killed. The vast majority of these offenders had taken lives during the normal course of human life, often in a context of alcohol or drugs and often in tragic circumstances when mistakes were made. But a person who plans to kill and who takes pleasure in taking a life is of special interest to writers such as I. Nilsen fits a template, and that is why I'm writing about him yet again.

When Nilsen died, surely many rejoiced. He left a trail of misery. Was he misunderstood or overlooked by some healthcare professional? "Who knows?" is the short answer. But one powerful piece of writing in Peter Shaffer's play, *Equus*, explains our puzzle. Shaffer writes about a chance fusion of influences, undefined and unknown, forming a mindset in a child. This is the root of that dark interior of the killer and serial killer. The result of this random, profound event is a "blackout." It is a blackout of "normal" sensibility and empathy. It might be wrong to simply say that a predator has been created. That could be an insult to the lion or the hawk.

But Nilsen wanted to speak—or, at least, to write. Maybe his words would have explained the mystery, elucidate the motivations. He tried to have his words in print, and he failed. The second day I met him, the look was blank, but there was the feeling that his being was like a lonely tarn in the hills, a deep pool, away from others, static, undisturbed, and lethal if you came to take a drink.

The facts of his life and crimes are well-known and in all the reference works. He started out in the world of work in the armed forces; he served abroad in the Catering Corps. Back home, he made a career switch by joining the civil service. Then came the first killing—of Stephen Holmes. This was the beginning of a succession of fifteen murders, all of young men, and these offenses covered the years from 1978 to 1983. We look for "signatures," and in these cases we are faced with the repulsive fact that he mutilated the bodies and tried to dispose of the body parts wherever he could around his own property.

We are not talking about midnight excursions to lonely spots, digging holes in the twilight hours, and furtive looks to see if others observe the disposal. No, the rarity of Nilsen's psychosis is that it involved a strange concealment with the dead just yards from his movements in daily life. *The Times* reported that "Nilsen admitted not knowing how many bodies there were under the floor because he had not done a 'stock-take.' He told the police that he had killed the victims with his own ties, adding 'I started with about fifteen ties. I have only got one left.' "

The issues regarding the nature of Nilsen's double-nature have troubled and baffled many professionals of aberrant psychology. After all, this "double-nature" presents us with something familiar from the biographies of many serial and mass killers: the individuated self and the social self. The individuated self has an ongoing narrative hooked into a counter-reality. In the opposite social self, the domain is a common, shared reality with its rules and regulations. Nilsen, like so many others, operated in both, and "reality" was for him a shifting concept. Perhaps we could say that it never became a concept. It was out of his vision.

Where do we look, then, for the man who notoriously "killed for company"? If we return to the question of his allegedly four-hundred-page autobiography, then that will remain unseen. Despite the insistence from Nilsen that any profits from his writing would be given to charity, the legal point remains. There is no cogent argument for the airing of such extreme deviance in print for general consumption. Seventeen years ago, the last courtroom struggle to have the typescript published ended in failure.

He wrote his autobiography while he was in Whitemoor, and he managed to send it to a publisher. But the manuscript has been seized and kept from him. The case is whether or not he has the right to publish the book, and, in the high court in 2001, Mr. Justice Elias said that Nilsen could challenge the decision to withhold the book from him which prevented publishing. Rather than who would receive the profits, the issue is the contents of the narrative, including its treatment of the crimes.

Generally, the serial killer wants attention. There is a need to be seen and heard. When a writer gets to work behind bars, the golden rule is not to have the clients write about their transgressions. They want to. Some are imbued with the notion that they are a celebrity. There is the thought that tales of horrible murderers have a twisted glamour or that there is *cred* or respect to be won on the wings of the jail. With Nilsen, I guess it was that his life had to be told. He set to work on his memoir.

In March 2002, he lost the legal battle. The high court decided that the Prison Service had the right to seize and keep the typescript and to work on it to censor material.

Now, a memoir to a serious offender is like a beam of light through the dark cell. Inside, with the media circus packed up and gone away, nobody notices them. They are a cell number and a body with a suit of garish prison clothes on them.

Creative writing in prisons provides the opportunity for prisoners to express themselves in a variety of ways: they may choose to join drama groups or poetry workshops. But one tempting option is to write their autobiography. Many dream of writing a bestseller, thinking that their life of crime would have the same kind of appeal as true crime books on the shelves concerned with gangland and hitmen, drug trafficking and bare-knuckle fighting. Recent successes in publishing crime memoirs have increased that interest. But the Prison Service is ordered to prevent prisoners from publishing their writing if it's for profit or deals with offenses the person committed. Nilsen was up against the latter.

Nilsen's legal counsel, Flo Krause, insisted that the government, in suppressing the book, was breaching Nilsen's human rights under Article 8 of the European Convention on Human Rights. The breach was arguably against his "family life, home, and correspondence" as it is worded in the Act. She also argued the government was breaching Article 10, concerning freedom of expression. Justice Crane rejected the plea, saying that "The Home Secretary is fully entitled to require that the manuscript be stopped and read." The only argument the lawyer could try was that the book spoke with importance about his life in and out of prison. But his case had not been helped by the fact that, when the manuscript was completed, Nilsen's lawyer had taken it out of the prison.

THE QUIET MAN IN THE OVERALLS STRUGGLED TO BE HEARD

Even dangerous serial killers, some would argue, deserve to be heard, to be read. Well, that remains a debate. In my time working in prisons, the rule was always that inmates must not write about their offenses; they must never return to the plaguing, tormenting memories they hold. Freeing their imaginations in workshops and performances plays a part in the rethink they all need. Such activities might, one hopes, clear a way toward a sort of redemption, if and when a change occurs, and the "real" of the reality they live in finally hits home.

In 2004, the topic was in the news again. At the Court of Appeal, the case was turned down, as judges said the book, "glorifies the pleasure that his crime caused him." They added, "We do not believe that any penal system could readily contemplate a regime in which a rapist or murderer would be permitted to publish an article glorifying the pleasure that his crime had caused him." The general opinion for some time had been that the memoir did not offer serious comment about imprisonment, but was an indulgence in the nefarious past of the man.

Then, in 2006, there was more to come from Dennis Nilsen. He wrote a letter that reached the press, and in that he wrote about his crimes and about the autobiography. It was sent to Tim Barlass of the *Evening Standard*, because Barlass had been in touch with Nilsen for a while. Nilsen wrote about his book: "My own autobiographies have been obstructed and banned by the Home Office…every inch of the way. A whole list of writers, journalists, and independent academics (some from the US) have wished to visit me in prison, but all such applications have been rejected by the (mostly) Labour administration…under Straw, Blunkett, Clark and (now) Reid, as the Stalinist 'reg flag' keeps flying…if not in their pasts, then presently in their minds when it comes to censorship."

Nilsen explained the situation and gave details about his book: "Even my lawyers have been denied access to four volumes of autobiography…which are not allowed to be sent outside of Home Office control and containment. These banned works amount to four-thousand typewritten pages of first-draft unedited script. Well, that's another story which will unfold through legal events in the fullness of time."

When we recall the nature of his crimes, the reasons for the ban on his publication become clear. Between January 1978 and February 1983, he killed fifteen men in London—twelve at his home in Melrose Avenue, and three in his Cranley Gardens apartment. One victim escaped: he had been taken back to the house, then to bed with Nilsen; when he woke the next day, he felt very ill and had a severe headache. When he checked himself out, he saw he was bruised at the neck and his eyes were red. Nilsen had attempted to strangle him, but he was told that he had caught the flesh of his neck in a sleeping bag.

Nilsen had stated earlier on arrest that he was determined to have some company, even if that was with corpses. I suggest some lines from the Elvis song "Let It Be Me" sum it up: "Tell me you love me only…so never leave me lonely." His first victim was buried under the floorboards, left there for several months, and then taken to the garden to be burned. Nilsen was found out when Dyno-Rod came to clear drains and discovered human remains in the plumbing.

Even if his book analyzed and responded to feelings about the killings, such topics are illegal for a prisoner to disseminate. After all, the works in print about him already offer plenty of bloody details about the *modus operandi* of his murders. His efforts to hide the bodies filled up so much space in his home that he had resorted to storing one victim under the kitchen sink. When Detective Chief Inspector Jay arrived at the home, he reported that there was a noxious smell, and, when asked to explain, Nilsen said, with no sign of emotion, that what the police searched for was, in fact, stored in various plastic bags. The items later found included two severed heads.

Who were his victims? They ranged from a drag artist to a student. Their destinies were to be the source of a stink from the blocked drains of a suburban London apartment in Cranley Gardens, Muswell Hill, or from 195 Melrose Avenue, across the city at Cricklewood. At the latter address, Nilsen confessed to having killed either twelve or thirteen men. The total murdered is fifteen or sixteen. The first victim was an Irishman who was invited to Melrose Avenue in late 1978 after a night's heavy drinking. The Irishman wouldn't stay the night after Nilsen proposed they went to bed. He wanted the company, and the refusal signed the man's death warrant. Disposing of the body was a problem, and so Nilsen wrapped it in plastic and left it in the flat for months. Eventually, he burned the remains in a garden fire.

We know quite a lot about one of the victims: Kenneth Ockenden. He was just twenty-three and from Canada. Again, the two men met in a pub. Ockenden was on his way to Cumbria where he had relatives, but he was never to arrive. Again, there was the offer of a night's sleep from Nilsen. The killer had been a cook in his army days and liked feeding people. He made a meal for his guest, but the young man didn't want a long conversation, which is what Nilsen longed for. Ockenden's fate was to be strangled by a length of flex, and there was the problem of body disposal again. This time, the corpse went under the bed for a while and then was chopped up and placed under the floorboards.

Arguably, the saddest case is that of Malcolm Barlow, killed in September 1981. He was an orphan who, unbelievably for Nilsen, was on his doorstep, claiming illness and in need of help. The killer saw that the young man was epileptic, and he took him to the hospital, but, after release, there he was again, right there on the front steps of the house to thank Nilsen. In no time, Barlow was inside, being fed and then being strangled. The victim's fate was to join all the other cadavers rammed into various nooks and corners of the Nilsen house.

Yet paradoxically, this man, guilty of such repugnant crimes, was the same man whose picture was seen by other officers working at Willesden Green Police Station in London, appearing as just another police constable. The two images clash like a surrealist painting: a police officer in uniform, following orders, and a serial killer stuffing body parts down a drain.

There have been psychological writings about Nilsen, and there is a large volume of biography. As time has gone on, he himself wrote on a range of subjects, no doubt "writing for company." Inside the prison, he works in that Braille workshop, where he has transcribed the texts of complete works into Braille for use in libraries in Africa. In fact, from the time he was arrested, Nilsen wrote. When he was awaiting trial, he wrote copious notes and sketches, compiling fifty notebooks of his memories.

We are left, then, with the man who walked the wings and landings of a jail that had fierce dogs at several doors: a jail in which violence might break out at any time. Tales have been told of the kinds of situations that might arise when dozens of men with these personality mis-fittings have to live together. An ex-inmate told me (it was not confirmed) that he saw one inmate who wrapped copies of thick magazines around his midriff to protect himself from knife attacks. These versions of oral history are passed on in the gangland memoirs that do find print. But my viewpoint on Nilsen's prison life is that he, along with several other men, was almost exclusively cocooned and protected from potentially explosive situations.

He made statements from inside, saying he was "not a violent person" and that, as he told one courtroom, "I killed people over a period of five years, and it got worse." It was as if a part of him "watched" the other part being an alien being.

As a true crime writer, there will always be a paradox every time I reflect on the person who stands there in the overalls, silent and puzzling. The paradox concerns the very nature of prison life for those who will never return to open society. It is an easy matter to fill a page with truisms and clichés such as "a state of limbo" or even "life is forever on hold." Yet the fact is that such killers find that what faces them inside is a high wall of brick—a metaphor of blockage, finality, and the impossibility of progress and change. The same routine for decades will sustain and also kill. Yes, there is purposeful work; yes, there are occasional talks, events, education courses. There is a *duty of care* in every prison service regarding their inmates. But with a serial killer, what is this caring, and how may it be applied? There is no worthwhile cause for self-improvement, but, still, steps have to be taken to provide such opportunities.

What is the result of all this? Why, simply that all prison carers have to enter the limbo and see the high brick wall as well. The psychopaths go on giving problems for others until their last breath. In Nilsen's case, maybe he found company in the next world—but it was more than likely bad company.

An educated guess would be that, in the text of his autobiography, there would be no mention of "false-self syndrome" (one psychologist theorized he had this syndrome that includes schizoid outbreaks), and that would come as no surprise. Perhaps the serial killer cannot stand outside the facts of the reality he or she has stepped into. No, like King Lear, the serial killer "hath ever but slenderly known himself." We cannot expect the empathic ability of "standing outside" a situation that change and redemption needs.

The life of the serial killer has a twisted version of the famous arc of tragedy in classical drama and in much Shakespearean drama:

the course of such a criminal's life begins with a first phase of experimental transgression. This is "dipping the toe" into the great swelling sea of mystery that is serious crime; then at the peak, the first heinous transgression occurs, followed by a realization of a new status—in this case, a status awarded by the media and the salacious paperbacks. The killer becomes a celebrity in today's world. So does the tragic hero. But now, celebrity has transmuted into a wrong-headed glorification of the "art of murder" as it was satirized in the classic text by Thomas De Quincey in his 1827 essay "On Murder Considered as one of the Fine Arts."

Nilsen died in jail on May 12, 2018. He had had plenty of company and for many years, but they were surely not the kind of people he wanted. He will go down in the true crime pantheon of serious serial killers, of course, and chances are that he wouldn't like that. But he did want to see his book in print, and that was never going to happen.

He may well have seen his life as one in which there was "fine art"—meaning that there were reasons for the transgressions. But, as we know only too well, someone has to clear away the bodies and tell the bereaved relatives after the onslaught.

As for me, I still recall that quiet man and the stare. I remember thinking, "Is there something he urgently wants to tell me? Something I need to take away with me, out into the air of freedom, which he will never breathe again?" But no, I think many serial killers have a constant narrative—a story telling something governed by narcissism and the will to be heard and to be validated.

The Accidental Serial Killer

CRAIG PITTMAN

In the mid-1990s and early 2000s, I spent four years covering criminal courts in Florida's most densely populated county. I covered cases involving hit men, con men and one bigamist whose defense was, "I forgot I was married." (It worked—the jury acquitted him.)

I covered about sixty murder trials. I saw crimes of passion, of anger run amok. I saw cases involving drug-gang drive-bys, killing for profit, and robberies gone awry. At first it was exciting, but after a while, I have to admit, many of them blurred together, their details fading as the years rolled on.

A few stick with me, though—particularly the one involving Jimmy Randall. And not just because he winked at me in court, or because of the odd state supreme court ruling on the case.

No, it's mostly because of the dog.

•••

I could start this story with Randall's childhood in Kentucky, his move to Massachusetts, his marriage, or his first stint in prison.

Instead, I think it starts with a waitress named Holly Jean Cote.

Cote, who was twenty-eight, had been married for eleven years to a machinist. They had a six-year-old daughter. Cote worked at a bar called Mahaki in Gardner, Massachusetts. On the night of March

4, 1984, she ended her shift at the Mahaki and went with a group of friends to a different bar, Mr. D's Lounge, which stayed open later.

That was the last time anyone saw her alive. She was supposed to meet some friends at their house for a nightcap, but she never showed up. The next morning her car, a 1969 Pontiac Tempest, was still sitting in the Mr. D's parking lot.

Notified about her vanishing, Massachusetts State Police undertook an extensive search. Her family and friends posted a six thousand dollar reward. Her husband, Joseph, took a month off from work to try to find her. Three months passed with no results.

Then, around Memorial Day, heavy rains flooded an area near the Birch Hill Dam about fifteen miles from Gardner. A couple out canoeing in the flooded area noticed something had floated up and gotten tangled in some birch trees. Curious, they paddled closer.

It was Cote's nude body. Her arms had been tied together with a purple sock. The coroner determined she had been strangled.

The location of the body suggested a suspect: a construction worker named James "Jimmy" Randall, white, five-foot-nine, two-hundred pounds. That area near the dam was one of his favorite fishing holes, according to the victim's husband. Randall's wife Linda was Holly Cote's best friend. In fact, the night Randall met his future wife, he met Holly Cote too. Later, when Cote and her husband needed a babysitter, she sometimes called on Linda and her then-boyfriend, Randall. After the Randalls got married, they frequently socialized with Cote and her husband.

Most importantly, Randall had been part of the group who had gone with Holly Cote to Mr. D's Lounge.

"He was the last one seen with her alive," Cote's husband told reporters.

Yet police had a hard time connecting him to the crime. The body was too decomposed to provide any physical evidence. They had no real crime scene to analyze. The place where the body had been hidden was washed away by the flood that freed the corpse to float to the surface. The police questioned Randall, hoping to crack him, but he let nothing incriminating slip. They had to let him go.

Two years passed. Then Randall was arrested for assaulting a different woman—his wife. She said he had choked her, tied her up, and raped her.

The first time, she later testified, Randall arrived home at two in the morning, closed their bedroom window, demanded sex, and began choking her.

"I kept pushing him away," she said, "and he kept telling me, 'You better have sex with me 'cause no one's going to hear us.' "

The next morning, she gathered the children and moved into a women's shelter. Two months later, he came looking for her again, stopping her on a highway and kidnapping her, along with their children. She said Randall tied her up with her own shoelaces and choked her during two episodes of forced sex. He told the children, ages two and five, that if they got out of the car, he would kill their mother.

"I really thought he was going to kill me, I really did," she said.

During that second attack, she said, Randall brought up the murder of Holly Cote. She told investigators that he demanded to know if she wanted to divorce him because of what he called "the Holly thing."

"Did you give Holly a chance?" she asked.

"No," Randall replied, according to his then-wife.

A judge sentenced him to five to seven years in state prison for the assault. His comments did not lead to charges in the Cote case.

While behind bars, Randall talked to a psychologist. He said he remembered seeing his father pin his mother to a kitchen counter once. At aged ten or eleven, he said, he would play with his sister by choking her and letting her go. At fourteen, he experimented with choking a neighbor, but said he then blacked out. He said he later tried choking other women during intercourse, including his wife.

"He describes the experience as one of wanting to be in control and the choking of his sexual partner as asserting that control," the psychologist wrote in a report on Randall.

His wife divorced him while he was an inmate. He served five years, then was released in 1992. He was supposed to report to a probation officer to report where he was living and what he was doing.

Instead, he fled the state.

Hurricane Andrew had just flattened everything south of Miami, and he figured he could find work rebuilding South Florida.

•••

The first Florida victim turned up in July 1994—but on the opposite side of the state.

Ladonna Jean Steller was someone's child, someone's sister, someone's mother, someone's wife. She had three children, an estranged husband, and a persistent crack habit.

"She was a great, fun girl," her brother told reporters. "She loved dancing, going out to the discos…. She had a good heart. It's sad. Everybody in the family loved her."

A custody battle with her ex-boyfriend over her youngest child sent her spiraling downward, he said.

"It seemed like she didn't have anything to live for after her little girl was taken away," her mother said.

Steller had once been pretty and vivacious. She had worked at one of the Florida restaurants better known for its buxom servers than its food. She had also been a dancer at Pinellas County's many strip joints. Then she had turned to streetwalking to feed her addiction. The nationwide crack epidemic of the 1980s may have tapered off in some places, but it continued hooking new victims in the 1990s. She was one.

She'd been picked up by police repeatedly on prostitution and possession charges but always got out of jail after a day or so, her brother said.

At thirty-five, she had become a gaunt shadow of her former self. Someone found her nude body lying in the bushes in a vacant lot in downtown Clearwater, a former fishing port on the Gulf of Mexico a few miles north of St. Petersburg. The lot where she was found was near a popular hiking and biking path called the Pinellas Trail which had, more than once, doubled as an escape route for criminals.

Police identified her from her plentiful fingerprint records at the county jail. Initially, they couldn't tell how she had been killed, but the medical examiner ruled she had been choked to death.

Detectives concluded she had been killed elsewhere, then dumped in the vacant lot. They were able to trace her movements until two in the morning the day her body was discovered but came up empty on suspects or finding her clothes, purse, and jewelry. The investigation lost steam and detectives moved on to more pressing cases.

Then, another victim turned up.

•••

A year had passed. Then, on October 20, 1995, Wendy Evans's body was found in the brush along a roadside in the small town of Oldsmar, about a twenty-minute drive northeast of Clearwater.

She was forty-two, and she'd been beaten and choked to death—just like Steller.

There were other similarities. Both women's bodies were found nude. Both had been killed elsewhere and then dumped by a road or a trail. And both had been spotted working the dark end of a street called North Fort Harrison Avenue.

North Fort Harrison Avenue is the main drag through downtown Clearwater, a city of about ninety-thousand people at that time. The road runs north to south a couple of blocks from the waterfront. The most prominent business along the downtown part of that street is the old Fort Harrison Hotel, where in 1964 Keith Richards wrote the famous guitar riff that leads off the Rolling Stones hit "(I Can't Get No) Satisfaction." The building is now the world headquarters of the Church of Scientology, which gives rooms to the organization's followers.

Most of North Fort Harrison Avenue is lined with respectable businesses. You might see a doctor's office, a copy center, or a funeral home. The road skirts the harbor and leads to the Old Clearwater Bay neighborhood, where some of the city's grandest residences stand. But there were also stretches with the kind of businesses that don't work regular hours, and buildings with plywood over their windows where you could buy crack, or find a hooker—or where, most often, the hookers could find johns to pay for their services and then use the money to buy crack. The vacant lot where Steller was found was just two blocks from the North Fort Harrison strip where she'd worked.

But Evans's family at first insisted she didn't fit the pattern. They insisted the five-foot tall, curly-haired woman was not a prostitute. She had a criminal record, but it was for burglary and armed robbery. She had never been charged with prostitution. Her arrest records listed her occupation as "dancer."

She wasn't a dancer anymore, though. Just twelve hours before her body was found, two Clearwater police officers had run across her hitchhiking on North Fort Harrison Avenue. She was walking down the sidewalk, making eye contact with the drivers passing by, they said. She told them she was trying to get a ride to her daughter's house, but she couldn't tell them the address. Even more suspicious to them: they had spotted her doing the same thing in the same place just the night before.

What happened between that encounter and her body being found twelve miles away? The assumption was that she found a john to pick her up, and he killed her.

Evans's daughter said her mother didn't want to live on the fringe of society, but, like Steller, she was willing to sacrifice everything to feed her habit. She had tried to get straight just before she was killed.

"Two weeks before she died, my mom and I called every drug rehabilitation program in the area, and they all said they wouldn't take her without insurance," her daughter told a reporter. "They might as well have given her a gun and told her to go kill herself."

Evans's murder did differ from Steller's in one crucial way. It rained the night her body was dumped. In examining the area, a detective named Jeffrey Good spotted a muddy tire print about seven feet away from where the body lay. The significance of that clue was not fully apparent at first.

Meanwhile, Evans's family tried to get her ready for her funeral. She had a cherished dress she'd worn for Mother's Day. They thought of using it for her shroud. But the long and flowing garment was too low-cut, showing too many of her fatal injuries.

•••

Part of the problem police and sheriff's detectives faced was that they were dealing with more than just two dead prostitutes. Pinellas County had become something of a killing ground for sex workers. A number of black prostitutes had died violently in St. Petersburg, down in the southern part of the county. But Steller and Evans were both white.

And then a third white prostitute who had worked the North Fort Harrison beat turned up dead.

Her name was Peggy Darnell, and she was found in an industrial area well north of Clearwater, up near the county line that separates Pinellas and Pasco counties.

Unfortunately, her body had been lying in that same spot for about two weeks before anyone stumbled over it. As with Holly Cote, decomposition and the passage of time made forensic examination difficult. The medical examiner believed she had been beaten and choked to death but could not be certain. Darnell's body was so decomposed that determining when she died required consulting an entomologist from Indiana. Judging by the development of maggot larvae, the scientist said, she was killed between October 30 and November 4, 1995.

Then, three weeks after Darnell's body was found, Victim Number Four turned up. On January 18, 1996, a construction worker discovered the nude body of Cynthia Pugh, twenty-seven, near a trash bin outside a defunct Costco building on US 19 in Palm Harbor, several miles north of Clearwater. Pugh, too, had died from upper body trauma—beaten, and choked to death.

Pugh had moved back to Clearwater from North Carolina just the year before. She was separated from her husband, who had kept their four-year-old son. She had convinced her parents she had a plan for her life: she was going to get her high school equivalency degree, go to school to become a beautician, and then get custody of her son. She was staying at her parents' house while working on this plan. They didn't know she had a crack habit or that she'd been busted for turning tricks to earn the money for those rocks her body craved.

They went out to bowl, and, when they came back, she was gone. The next day, she was dead.

When word spread about Pugh, North Fort Harrison Avenue turned into a ghost town.

"After the Pugh death, we saw no females out at all for five days," a police sergeant told a reporter. "They weren't out walking, they weren't flagging cars." But, after no more bodies turned up, the sergeant said, "On the sixth day, we started seeing them return to the street."

At that point, though no one knew it yet, the killing was done.

•••

Just because a body has been dumped far from where the killing occurred and stripped of all clothing does not mean that it carries no forensic evidence.

From the bodies of the four white prostitutes, forensic technicians collected both hairs and fibers—just one or two of each, but it was better than nothing. The fibers, they determined, came from a pink carpet. The hair, they concluded, came from a dog.

They also found a very small shred of paper stuck to Pugh's left breast. At first, the techs didn't quite know what to make of it.

In the meantime, detectives started tracking down what sort of tire had made that muddy tire print Detective Good found near Evans's body. The pattern showed it was a Firestone Radial ATX for use on small trucks and SUVs. This type of tire had been on the market for only six months, which meant that only a few had been sold.

A check with the local Firestone franchise revealed that only one set of that type of tires had been sold in the three-county area during the six months it had been available. The vehicle driving on those tires was a 1985 Dodge pickup truck owned by a motel clerk named Terry Jo Howard.

A quick check showed that Terry Jo Howard had a criminal record. She had been a prostitute and had once worked the sidewalks of North Fort Harrison Avenue.

Howard lived in an apartment in the unincorporated Palm Harbor area north of Clearwater. Detectives watching the apartment noticed a man driving the truck. He also lived with Howard. He had a shaved head and a handlebar mustache.

Detectives wanted to be absolutely sure about the tires. They persuaded the Firestone dealership to call Howard and claim the tires had been recalled. Bring them in for a free set of replacements, they said. Sure enough, she brought the truck in. When the tires came off the vehicle, detectives grabbed them. Later, an engineer with Firestone testified he had examined the tires and that it was "a virtual certainty" the ridges in the mud near Evans's body were left by the right rear tire of the 1985 Dodge pickup truck Howard owned.

Detectives began following Howard and the man she lived with, tailing them as they traveled, sometimes fifty to sixty miles north or south. When the couple stopped at a fast-food restaurant, detectives catalogued their order. When they went to a video store, detectives noted what they checked out.

Investigators even mounted a camera on a pole outside the couple's Belcher Road apartment. It shot hours of images but captured nothing incriminating.

The man in Howard's life, they learned, was a forty-year-old ex-con named James "Jimmy" Randall. As the detectives pieced together his background—the choking of his ex-wife, his possible involvement with Holly Cote, what he told the psychiatrist—he became their prime suspect. When they showed his picture to the women of North Fort Harrison Avenue, several remembered seeing him cruising through

their area to pick up prostitutes. They also had heard that some said
he should be avoided. He had given a few "a bad ride," they said.

While Randall had fled Massachusetts for Miami in 1992, he
hadn't stayed there very long. In that post-hurricane disaster zone,
he quickly found work as a window installer, where he developed
a reputation as a hard worker. But then in 1993, his boss, Albert
Calcagni, had decided to move his business over to the state's Gulf
Coast, to the unincorporated Palm Harbor area near Clearwater.
Randall not only moved west to stay with the business, he also moved
into Calcagni's home, sharing space with his boss, his boss's wife, and
their six-year-old daughter. Calcagni later said he'd had no idea about
Randall's prison stint or what he'd done to earn it.

"He never told nobody about himself," Calcagni told a reporter
later. "He didn't talk about himself. Ever."

Randall stayed at his boss's place for six months, mostly keeping
to himself. After he moved out, getting an apartment in the small
town of Dunedin sometime in 1994, the two had a falling out, and
Randall quit. He met Howard when he picked her up on North Fort
Harrison on February 28, 1994. She soon quit hooking, and the couple
moved in together—and he began driving her truck.

•••

As the detectives watched Howard's apartment and followed the
truck, they learned a few things. One was the couple didn't go out
much, except to rent videos. The other was Howard and Randall had a
dog, a little pug.

This led them to the detectives' second ruse. Masquerading as dog
groomers, detectives Stephanie Campbell and Linda Hilliard showed
up at Howard's apartment offering to give her dog a free wash. They

said they had started a new door-to-door dog-grooming service and this was an introductory offer.

Of course, as they washed the pug, they also collected samples of its hair to compare with what had been stuck to the victims. They also spotted a pink rug in the apartment and passed that along to the team of investigators. Later, lab tests confirmed that the dog hair and carpet fibers were consistent with the hair and fibers found on the bodies of Pugh and Evans. You couldn't call it a match—the technology didn't exist to make such a match—but it wasn't different.

Detectives decided it was time to look their suspect in the eye. Corporal John Quinlan and a detective named Thomas Klein knocked on the apartment door, timing their visit to when Howard would be away. When Randall answered, they asked for Howard. They said they wanted to talk to her about whether, when she had been a prostitute, she might have encountered someone interested in choking prostitutes.

Randall played it cool, even when they showed him pictures of the victims. He denied having seen them. He said they'd never been in the apartment or in the truck. They could have slapped the cuffs on him right then, because there was a warrant for him out of Massachusetts. But the detectives weren't ready for that yet. They thanked him and left.

What they wanted was the truck. They wanted to seize it and search it. The next time Randall got behind the wheel, they planned to swoop in and nab him. That way they had probable cause to go through his vehicle without having to bother with a search warrant.

It didn't quite work out the way they planned.

•••

About fifteen minutes after the detectives left his front door, Randall was driving to work when he spotted blue lights behind him. He wasn't alone in the truck. He was giving a ride to a coworker named Maitland Nixon. He told Nixon he couldn't stop.

"I can't do that, man," he blurted out. "I can't do that. I got to go. I got to go. It's my life. I can't stop. They gonna—they want me. They're gonna ship me back." He kept repeating "It's my life." Nixon asked him what he meant, and Randall replied, "They want me for something up north."

He swung through a cul-de-sac and let Nixon out, then drove on. His pursuers stopped to check out Nixon, giving their suspect a chance to get farther ahead. Randall abandoned the truck, jumped a fence and ducked into the woods. Even after the detectives brought in dogs and a helicopter, they couldn't find him. They didn't know it, but he was lying in a ditch, covered in mud.

For the next four days, Randall eluded the largest manhunt in Pinellas County history. He slept during the day and moved only at night. He'd stolen a pair of window screens from the Chi Chi Rodriguez Golf Club and fashioned a way to wear them as camouflage. Finally, though, he went to his Dunedin apartment and rang the doorbell. When a waiting detective opened the door, he hit her with a stick and ran, but he didn't get far before a police dog grabbed him and brought him down.

"He told us he was hungry," a sheriff's official told reporters. "He'd been bitten by mosquitoes. He said he wished we'd caught him two days ago." That was all he'd say. Not a word about the victims.

Initially, he was charged with escape-related crimes along with the Massachusetts warrant. But then, the grand jury met and considered the four dead women.

Randall was listening to music on his Sony Walkman when
Good and Klein visited his cell to tell him he'd been indicted on two
counts of murder. Good told Randall he was being charged with
murdering Evans.

"Is that all?" Randall asked.

"No, not really," Klein said, and told Randall he had also been
indicted for murdering Pugh.

"Is that all?" Randall asked again, still listening to his music.

That was all. The grand jury had decided the evidence against
Randall wasn't strong enough to indict him for killing Steller
and Darnell.

When the case came to trial, though, prosecutors brought
those murders in anyway, along with what happened to his ex-wife.
They planned to prove their case by showing Randall had a pattern
of behavior.

The defense had a different view of the case, though.

•••

The Randall who showed up in court looked very different from the
limping, bug-bitten fugitive featured in his mug shot. He'd let his hair
start growing back. He wore a suit. He usually carried a paperback
book to read during the slow parts. One day, it was a thriller by
Ridley Pearson called *Chain of Evidence*, which concerned a detective
tracking a serial killer.

The attorneys facing off could not have been more different.
Leading the prosecution was Douglas Crow, short and slender with
a carefully groomed mustache. He was as smart as a tree full of owls
but with an intensity that could frighten. On the defense side, the
lead attorney was big, brassy Michael Schwartzberg. He had a thick
black beard, glasses, and a wisecracking manner he developed while

working as a roving insult comic at a renaissance fair. In addition to his legal career, he was president of the little local theater.

Crow's case against Randall featured two star witnesses: his ex-wife and Terri Jo Howard. Both testified that Randall derived sexual stimulation from choking them. Both said that Randall had injured them during the choking.

Howard's testimony was particularly dramatic. She entered the courtroom slowly, wearing a black dress that emphasized her pale, slender neck. She gave Randall a lingering look over her shoulder as she passed the defense table. At one point in her testimony, while the lawyers argued at the bench, the couple's eyes locked until she grimaced and he turned away.

Howard made it clear that Randall was special to her. She said he was the only man who had ever cared for her, the man who had helped free her from a life of drugs and prostitution. She said she had been arrested fifty-seven times before she changed her life with Randall's help.

When Crow asked why she allowed Randall to choke her during sex, her reply made courtroom spectators gasp: "I didn't want him to not get what he needed and then kill me two years down the road. I wanted him to have control over it."

She said when she stopped showing fear, Randall lost interest and stopped choking her. Schwartzberg reminded Howard she had once said she avoided showing any reaction to being choked, suggesting she was now changing her story.

"I tried not to show any fear, but I'm sure I did," she said. "You would too, if somebody had their hands around your neck."

Later, when Randall was arrested, she wondered why he hadn't killed her. Howard testified she visited him in jail and asked him, "Why not me?" Cautious about being overheard or observed, she said, he replied by writing in the air with his finger, "I hurt others so that I would not hurt you."

Schwartzberg challenged that story, noting she once told prosecutors she was confused about Randall's message.

"I was lying," she said.

"You were lying then, but you're not lying now?" Schwartzberg said, his voice thick with sarcasm.

Howard said that she had lied because she feared Randall would find out she was talking to the prosecution and hire someone to kill her.

•••

The judge in the case, a onetime gospel singer and former IRS agent named Susan Schaeffer, allowed prosecutors to introduce evidence about the other victims to show the behavior pattern at work. Each murder occurred when Howard happened to be out of town. Judge Schaeffer commented that the prosecution needed to show jurors the pattern because otherwise what they had was "a weak circumstantial case."

The prosecutors also linked Randall to the two murders through the forensic evidence: the dog hairs, the carpet fibers, and especially the tiny piece of paper found on Pugh's left breast.

That last item proved to be particularly important. Howard testified that she smoked cigarettes in the apartment, and, when she was done with them, she would drop the butts on the floor. Then, her dog would snatch them up and chew on them. The dog's nicotine habit left tiny shreds of paper all over the floor of the apartment Howard and Randall shared.

The paper fragment on Pugh's breast was definitely one of those slips of paper, said a forensic expert, because saliva in the paper contained DNA that matched Howard's. That bit of butt could not have landed on the murder victim in any way other than the victim being in the apartment at some point, something Randall told the police had not happened.

While Crow's team was doing its best to prove Randall was a serial killer, Schwartzberg's team focused on a different aspect of the case.

If Randall killed the two women, the defense contended, the poor man couldn't help himself. Randall could not resist his impulse to choke women because he suffers from a mental disorder, sexual sadism. He didn't intend to be a serial killer. It was an accident.

When he cross-examined the medical examiner who performed the autopsies, Schwartzberg asked if the force used to choke the victims "could be inadvertent pressure or unknowing pressure."

"I don't think so," the medical examiner said.

•••

In his closing argument, Crow pointed out how Randall took the women back to his apartment and tied their hands somehow before he killed them. Although detectives found no bindings, Crow said, the medical examiner found no signs the women had fought back, suggesting they were unable to move their hands.

Crow said Randall then dumped the women's bodies in areas where he knew he would not be seen by anyone, and the bodies would not be found until he was gone. This all showed planning and premeditation, Crow said, and so did his selection of victims "on the fringes of our society."

The jury of seven women and five men took six hours to find Randall guilty on both counts of first-degree murder. As the clerk read the verdict, the families and friends of the two murdered women

whispered, "Yes! Yes! Yes!" Several burst into tears, and some
scrambled across the courtroom benches to hug each other.

As Judge Schaeffer pronounced him guilty, Randall sucked on a
peppermint, looking bored. But when a bailiff took hold of Randall's
hands and inked his fingers to take his prints, Randall leaned over to
Schwartzberg and whispered, "Do I have to do this here in front of
everybody else?"

The next day, the jurors returned to court to consider what
sentence would be appropriate. After listening to testimony from a
pair of psychologists as well as Randall's mother, they quickly voted
12-0 to recommend that Randall be executed for his crimes. A month
later, Judge Schaeffer agreed with them, handing down a pair of
death sentences.

As Schaeffer read her eleven-page sentencing order listing the
reasons Randall deserved to go to death row, Randall seemed anxious.
He drummed his fingers on the defense table. He jiggled his leg and
squirmed in his seat. From time to time his gaze wandered toward an
empty corner of the courtroom.

Schaeffer said one reason for sentencing Randall to death
instead of life in prison was the cruelty of his method of murdering
Evans and Pugh.

"He took them to his home and bound at least one of them,"
Schaeffer said. "He tortured them and then he put his hands around
their necks and squeezed. He got sexually aroused as their eyes filled
with the terror and horror of knowing they were going to die."

Only Randall himself knew how long they suffered, Schaeffer said,
"until each slipped into blessed unconsciousness."

Schwartzberg's argument about Randall's lack of murderous
intent was not tenable, she said, because he'd killed more than once.

"Knowing he had killed Wendy Evans, this sexual sadist made
no effort to obtain any help so his homicidal violence would not

continue," she said. "Obviously the thrill and sexual gratification he received from humiliating and torturing Wendy Evans was more important to him. He went out and did the exact same thing to Cynthia Pugh, humiliating, torturing, and ultimately strangling her to death to satisfy his own perverse sexual needs."

As Randall was being led away by the bailiffs, he turned toward me and winked as if recalling a good joke. I just stared at him.

•••

Schaeffer's word usually would have been the final one. Before she became a judge, she had been a crackerjack defense attorney who frequently succeeded in keeping her clients off death row. She was personally opposed to Florida's death penalty law—but, when she became a judge, she swore to uphold the law. That meant she had to sentence some defendants to death. To make sure she didn't make any mistakes, Schaeffer made herself into one of Florida's top experts on the death penalty. She knew the law so well, she taught other judges how to handle death cases.

As a result, all the appeals courts usually went along with whatever she said.

But not this time.

Three years passed, and then the Florida Supreme Court issued its ruling in Randall's case. The highest court in the state approved of all of Schaeffer's rulings in the case—the admission of evidence of a pattern of choking, the testimony of the ex-wife, the girlfriend, and so on—except for one.

The sentence of death.

By bringing in the testimony of Randall's ex-wife and his girlfriend, the prosecution had inadvertently proved Schwartzberg's argument, the justices said. They "demonstrated a reasonable hypothesis that the homicides were other than by premeditated design…. In view of the fact that the other women that Randall choked during sexual activity did not die, it is reasonable to infer that Randall intended for his choking behavior to lead only to sexual gratification, not to the deaths of his sexual partners."

As a result, the justices wrote, "We agree in this wholly circumstantial case that the evidence does not support premeditated murder to the exclusion of a reasonable doubt. The evidence does support second-degree murder."

Therefore, they said, Randall's two death sentences would be converted into two life sentences. He would never leave prison again, but he wouldn't have to worry about the state sticking a needle in his veins and taking his life.

That was that. The prosecutors weren't happy (I heard someone in the state attorney's office fussing that you could argue that Randall screwed up once, but the second time should count as murder), but there was nothing they could do. They couldn't appeal.

So legally, Randall isn't a serial killer, except accidentally. He's more of a serial, accident-prone, sexual partner.

Years have gone by since this case ended. Schwartzberg died in 2005, Judge Schaeffer in 2016. Doug Crow retired. Randall, meanwhile, remains in prison, serving out his two life sentences at the Taylor Correctional Institution in the lumber-mill town of Perry, about an hour south of the state capital. He's in his sixties now. According to the photo on the state Department of Corrections website, he still looks about the same, just a little grayer.

I still think about his case from time to time. Randall was no criminal genius, no Professor Moriarty, but he might have gotten away with at least two murders and maybe five. The hair and fiber evidence wasn't conclusive—it was just similar to what was found on the bodies, not identical. The tire print could be explained away—he could have driven near the spot where Evans was found and not stopped to dump a body.

When you get right down to it, the only thing that conclusively tied him to the murders was that one little scrap of paper, the little bit of a cigarette that had his girlfriend's DNA.

And the only reason why that tiny scrap of paper was there was because her little pug dog had the weird habit of chewing up her discarded cigarette butts. If not for that dog, Randall might have gotten away with everything and possibly kept on killing women every time his girlfriend popped out of town for some reason.

The name of that dog that nailed Randall is one I will never forget. It was Princess Penny Pickles.

The Rat Man

JOE TURNER

On July 23, 1989, police entered the home of twenty-six-year-old print technician Tsutomu Miyazaki in the Saitama Prefecture of Japan. Following a bizarre incident that saw Miyazaki running naked along a Tokyo riverbank, police believed the same man might be linked to the murder, mutilation, and defilement of four young girls throughout the Greater Tokyo area that had all occurred within the past eleven months.

After authorities gained access to the man's unkempt, two-room bungalow, they discovered a mountain of evidence confirming that the mild-mannered, introverted Miyazaki was undoubtedly the suspect dubbed "The Little Girl Murderer" by press and terrified citizens alike. Inside the home, authorities uncovered a collection of almost six thousand videotapes including horror, exploitation, and slasher films, cartoon and anime movies, and thousands of extreme and illegal pornography tapes.

And among them were amateur footage and photographs of the same four girls who had been kidnapped and ultimately murdered during the past year.

As the facts of Miyazaki's crimes emerged, they painted a picture of a lonely and desperate young man, trapped in a detached fantasy world of which murder and pedophilic acts were the ultimate extension of his warped aspirations. He had committed acts of cannibalism and necrophilia to appease his twisted desires, and he had taunted the families of his victims with phone calls and left on their parents' doorsteps charred remains of children.

He was a man not fit for the society he inhabited, partly due to Japan's emphasis on success and academia, at which Miyazaki failed in every sense, but also due to his lack of decent upbringing and his willingness to isolate himself from the rest of the world.

As a substitute for meaningful relationships with friends, family, or partners, Miyazaki found solace in media. He was an obsessive collector of comic books, manga, and hentai. This later progressed to a love of film, particularly violent horror films and extreme pornography—something which would echo in the horrific deeds he later committed. When Miyazaki's obsession with such materials became known after his arrest, his label of "The Little Girl Murderer" evolved into "The Otaku Murderer," "otaku" being the Japanese term often used in a derogatory sense for someone obsessed with a subject—often anime, manga, or similar subjects—to the point of detachment from reality.

Like most beginning serial killers, Tsutomu Miyazaki was a product of his environment. While a man responsible for such brutal and incomprehensible acts usually possesses a degree of mental illness, Miyazaki's disturbed nature was undoubtedly magnified by the events of his childhood. In order to paint a full picture of this human monster and perhaps begin to understand the nature of his violent compulsions and his lust for savagery, we must study his life from chapter one.

A bleak shadow was cast over Tsutomu Miyazaki's life while he was still in the womb. Born in Itsukaichi, Tokyo, on August 21, 1962, Miyazaki was premature and weighed only 2.2 kilograms. However, perhaps more concerning was that Miyazaki clearly suffered a severe deformity. The joints between his wrists and hands hadn't developed correctly during gestation, causing his hands to adopt an abnormal shape and greatly inhibit his movement. Miyazaki couldn't bend his wrists upward without lifting his entire hand in tandem, which, although a significant restriction for everyday tasks, was little in comparison to the taunts and embarrassment he endured due to the limbs' unusual appearance.

His parents, Katsumi and Rieko Miyazaki, had high hopes for the young boy, but, despite their efforts, they soon realized their hopes were in vain. While Miyazaki showed signs of being gifted during his time at Itsukaichi Elementary School, he found it impossible to emotionally connect with any of the other children. When later questioned on how Miyazaki behaved during his school years, his elementary teachers and classmates barely recalled him at all. He was lonely and quiet, seemingly invisible to everyone he interacted with. Naturally, Miyazaki blamed his inability to make friends on his deformed hands, which continued to be a source of amusement to his classmates until his late teenage years. He would often hide them beneath his clothing or cover them with gloves to avoid further embarrassment, but it was to little avail.

Miyazaki's father was a prominent figure in the Itsukaichi and surrounding areas, wielding a decent amount of political sway as well as being the owner of the *Akikawa Shimbun*, a local and well-regarded Japanese newspaper. Katsumi Miyazaki had aspirations of his son inheriting his business once his studies were complete, but, despite a brief glimpse into Miyazaki's giftedness, he saw his son's interest in academic pursuits rapidly decline.

Instead, the young Miyazaki would stay up long into the night devouring comic books cover to cover. Much to the dismay of his parents, he would forego homework in favor of consuming whatever media he could lay his hands on. It was around age eleven when Miyazaki's interest in studying hit its lowest. Though he eventually passed his high school entrance exams, his grades gradually diminished while he suffered from bullying and taunts about his deformities and "creepiness." This only served to isolate Miyazaki further. Instead of spending his spare time socializing, he retreated to the safety of his parents' home, where he found comfort in comic books, movies, and anime. When he consumed all avenues of escapism he could find, he created his own. He invented his own fictional character: a bizarre, eyeless humanoid with a rat's head whom Miyazaki dubbed "the Rat Man," who appeared in his home-drawn comic books and cartoon strips and would later return to Miyazaki's story.

His short-lived ambition to enroll at Meiji University and major in English never came to fruition. Miyazaki finished in the bottom quarter of his class and even failed to receive the customary recommendation to the university affiliated with his high school. Instead, Miyazaki enrolled in a photo-technician course at a local college. It was a major disappointment to Miyazaki's parents, who prayed that perhaps their son would find his ambition once he settled into adulthood.

During college, Miyazaki's behavior evolved from introverted timidity to something else entirely. While his social skills were severely underdeveloped, his sexual urges were far beyond those of his peers. He began to collect and consume adult magazines and videos in favor of comic books. While this was not completely irregular for a sexually aware teenager, Miyazaki's lack of social interaction combined with his grim perversions led him down a sinister path to achieve his sexual thrills. As a substitute for interacting with girls his own age, Miyazaki would secretly film women from his college, regularly taking his video camera to the sports fields to capture crotch pictures of his classmates. But aside from these secret operations, Miyazaki avoided the opposite sex entirely.

Throughout college, his isolation only increased while his behavior worsened. When his amateur films weren't enough to gratify his sexual thirst, he turned to more extreme forms of pornography. Later claiming that adult magazines "blacked out the most important parts" (as is customary in certain adult Asian materials), Miyazaki turned to the most taboo form of media there was: child pornography.

After his graduation in 1983, Miyazaki took a job in a printing plant owned by an associate of his father's and moved back in with his parents in their Itsukaichi home. Now with two younger siblings, Miyazaki was forced to share the home's two-room annex with his eldest sister.

While there was hope that graduating and attaining his own source of income might stabilize Miyazaki, his same patterns continued to repeat. He would work by day, then return to his beloved collection of videos and comic books by night. Nothing changed. It was clear to many that Miyazaki, now in his early-to-mid-twenties, suffered from a handful of mental health issues. He later claimed that around this point in his life he began to contemplate suicide and that he desired nothing more than to be "listened to about his problems." However, Miyazaki knew that his parents would simply disregard his feelings.

Like many Japanese fathers, Katsumi was largely absent from his son's life during his formative years. The bulk of the work was left up to Reiko, who would regularly purchase lavish gifts for Miyazaki in a hollow attempt to repair the dwindling relationship between the parents and their child. She supplied him with everything from comic books to clothes to a Nissan Langley, but Miyazaki recognized her efforts as empty gestures.

On many occasions, Miyazaki did indeed try to discuss his mental health troubles with his parents, but he was each time impassively cast aside. Although Japanese culture emphasizes respect and courtesy, it also emphasizes favoring the collective over the individual. Issues in the vein of mental health are notoriously overlooked, something which is often referenced when discussing the phenomenally high rate of suicide in Japan. Katsumi and Reiko, like the majority of Japanese parents, were highly traditional in their cultural values. They saw their son's issues as mere weaknesses that they believed could be brushed over with acts of affection.

Alas, they could not. However, there was one person in Miyazaki's life whom the troubled boy felt he could confide in—his grandfather, Shokichi Miyazaki. His father focused all of his efforts into his work, his mother merely kept up appearances, his two sisters regarded him as "repulsive," and he had no friends or acquaintances to talk to. Therefore, Shokichi was the only person with whom Miyazaki felt even a minor bond.

In only a few short years, Miyazaki would begin his descent into madness, culminating in the brutal slayings of four little girls. While his psychosis had developed throughout his troubled life, his suffering was by no means unique. Thousands of people daily endure the same misery as Miyazaki and don't resort to serial murder. So what pushed Miyazaki over the threshold?

The trigger, it seems, may have been the death of his grandfather. In May 1988, Shokichi Miyazaki passed away, leaving his grandson alone in a world that shunned him. In an act of bizarre desperation, Miyazaki attempted to "preserve" his grandfather in the only way his disturbed mind allowed: by eating his ashes.

Miyazaki's only attachment to humanity was severed. He was the black sheep of the revered Miyazaki family, with only his ever-expanding fantasies for company. At age twenty-five, he was now more alone than ever.

The cracks quickly began to show. After his youngest sister caught him spying on her in the bathroom, she scolded him, only for

Miyazaki to frantically assault her. His mother caught wind of the
incident, exclaiming that Miyazaki should spend less time obsessing
over his media and focus more on his work, to which Miyazaki
responded in the same manner. He physically attacked his mother,
undoubtedly shedding the last of what little bond they had left.

On August 21, 1988, Tsutomu Miyazaki celebrated his twenty-
sixth birthday. The following day, he prowled the streets of Saitama,
eventually coming across a little girl named Mari Konno.

"I felt all alone. Whenever I saw a little girl playing on her own, it
was almost like seeing myself."

The four-year-old girl walked the short distance between her
and her friend's apartment complex in Iruma Village in Saitama.
However, before she made it to her destination, a Nissan Langley
pulled up beside her. A young man with a stubby face and bushy,
overgrown hair climbed out of the driver's seat and asked the girl,
"Wouldn't you like to go somewhere where it's cool?"

The naïve child immediately agreed, believing that the stranger
might help her find relief from the blistering summer heat. Mari
Konno leaped into the man's car, and the two sped off far away from
Mari's home into an area of barren woodland on the outskirts of
Tokyo. They drove for ninety minutes, ending up over fifty kilometers
away from Saitama.

The man didn't know the little girl's name, nor she his. However,
each would be the catalyst to the other's demise.

The man exited his car with Mari in tow. Sunlight filtered through
the treetops above as the pair trekked through dense forestry toward
an unknown destination. After thirty minutes of walking, the man
stopped and sat down several meters off a path near Old Komine
Tunnel (then known as Komine Pass). Mari sat next to him, now in
the throes of distress. Although she remained silent, he could see the

tears welling up in her eyes. At any moment, she might begin to sob, thus drawing attention from passing hikers.

The man panicked. Impulsively, he clasped his hands around the girl's tiny neck. He placed his thumbs over her larynx and throttled until all the color drained from her face.

Mari Konno took her last breath, then her body fell limp in the man's arms.

Tsutomu Miyazaki had claimed his first victim.

However, his desires were not fulfilled by simple murder. Miyazaki undressed Mari, caressed her naked body, then pulled out his camera and committed his cruelty to film. Finally, he posed Mari on the ground, collected her clothes, and stumbled quietly back to his vehicle. He left her in the same place she died: outspread like an angel in the forest dirt.

The following day, fifty thousand posters of Mari Konno's face were plastered across Tokyo. Below her pale features and her short, bobbed hair was the word MISSING.

Shigeo Konno, Mari's father, had frantically called the police at around six the previous evening, unaware that even by this point, his four-year-old daughter was lying dead fifty kilometers away.

A city-wide police search ensued but yielded very little clues. Two young boys and a housewife claimed to have seen Mari walking with a stranger near Iruma River, although it remains unconfirmed whether it was indeed Miyazaki and Mari Konno.

In days following Mari's disappearance, her mother, Yukie Konno, appealed on television for help finding her missing daughter. The next day, she received a mysterious postcard through her door. It simply read: "There are devils about."

Although it was dismissed as a hoax, the postcard had been sent by the same man who had taken her child. However, this wouldn't be realized until much later.

The search for Mari went cold, despite the case's nationwide coverage. Japan's status as a peaceful and harmonious paradise was under threat. Parents throughout the city walked their children to nursery each day, and most streets were uncommonly devoid of children's laughter from dusk until evening. Such serious crimes were so rare that it was difficult for authorities to label the Konno case as a murder investigation. Therefore, she was labeled only as a missing person. However, the grim truth would soon surface.

Miyazaki's cooling-off period lasted only six weeks before the urge to escalate his fantasies struck again. In an almost step-by-step reenactment of his first murder, Miyazaki prowled the streets of Hanno, Saitama Prefecture on the afternoon of October 3, 1988. There, he noticed seven-year-old Masami Yoshizawa walking along the roadside, only a few kilometers from Miyazaki's home. He lured the young girl into his Nissan Langley, then sped off toward the same destination where Mari Konno had met her fate only forty-two days earlier.

In the hills above Komine Pass, Masami Yoshizawa looked confusedly toward the silent Miyazaki as they sat on a rocky path beneath a darkening sky. Less than a hundred meters away, the decomposing body of Mari Konno lay hidden between a sea of trees.

Once again, Miyazaki swiftly fastened his hands around his victim's neck, choking the girl until her struggling came to an end. He stripped her, sexually violated her corpse, then photographed Masami's dead body like an artist savoring his masterpiece. A post-mortem muscle spasm jolted Masami's dead body while she lay on the ground, causing the startled Miyazaki to flee in terror.

Masami Yoshizawa was reported missing the same evening. As with Mari Konno, thousands of missing person posters were spread throughout the city, along with countless house-to-house visits conducted by Japanese police. They discovered no leads during their investigation, but they were quick to connect the two missing girls as potentially the work of the same perpetrator. As no bodies were discovered, Masami Yoshizawa was also officially labeled as a missing person.

Miyazaki returned to his life of seclusion, now with a hoard of photographs of two dead corpses in his possession. This appeased his disturbed fantasies for a total of ten weeks, but his bloodlust returned in the early weeks of December 1988.

Miyazaki spotted Erika Namba walking through the streets of Kawagoe, Saitama, when he pulled over and offered her a lift. This time, Miyazaki would not be content with a blitz-attack murder of the four-year-old girl. As found so often in sexually motivated killers, Miyazaki needed to chase a greater thrill in order to achieve the same high he felt with Mari and Masami. His fantasies were intensifying, meaning he had to escalate his crimes to appease his growing desires.

With Erika Namba in the back seat of his sedan, Miyazaki pulled into an empty parking lot at the Youth Nature House in Naguri, Saitama. Ignoring the little girl's cries, Miyazaki demanded that she strip naked. Erika followed Miyazaki's orders while he furiously snapped photographs of the now-terrified girl from the front seat. Suddenly, a beam of light from outside the vehicle illuminated Miyazaki's face, pulling him from his hypnotic-like trance. Another car had pulled into the parking lot, but, luckily for Miyazaki, the car quickly left.

This brief interruption caused Miyazaki to panic. Without hesitation, he seized the young girl by the neck and clambered on top of her in the back seat. He easily overpowered her, despite her furious struggling. Within one minute, Erika Namba became Tsutomu Miyazaki's third victim.

It was just after seven in the evening on December 12, 1988. By this point, Erika Namba's distressed parents had informed the police of her disappearance, numb with terror that their innocent daughter may have fallen prey to a potential kidnapper or worse. Meanwhile, Miyazaki was transporting Erika's corpse into a wooded area behind the parking lot where she had been strangled. It was here that Miyazaki's reign of terror almost came to an end. However, for the second time that night, blind luck was in his favor.

On his journey into the woods, Miyazaki momentarily lost control of his vehicle. One of his wheels fell into a deep gutter on the roadside, causing the car to suddenly halt. He became stuck.

Miyazaki turned on his hazard lights, but he knew he'd be a fool to flag down assistance with a dead body in his car. Therefore, he wrapped Erika Namba's corpse in a sheet and took her deep into the woods. He disposed of her, then returned to his car with the empty sheet folded in his hands. But it was here that Miyazaki saw an alarming sight. There were two men standing beside his car.

Miyazaki quickly explained to the men that he had veered into the gutter and gotten his wheels wedged in the dirt. He returned the white sheet to his trunk as casually as possible, and luckily, the two men didn't inquire as to what he'd been doing alone in the woods. They then helped Miyazaki lift his car from the gutter, and Miyazaki sped off into the night without offering them a word of thanks.

The following day, Miyazaki's veil of anonymity began to slip when an employee at the Naguri Nature House stumbled upon a pile of Erika's clothes in the woods. Her disappearance had already been reported by her parents, and it was quickly linked to the cases of Mari Konno and Masami Yoshizawa. However, this was the first time a physical piece of evidence of "The Little Girl Murderer" had been discovered.

Five hundred police officers arrived and scoured the woods in full, eventually discovering the corpse of Erika Namba in a different area than where her clothes were found. Her hands and feet had been bound with a cord, and her corpse showed strangulation marks and signs of severe sexual assault. Although it likely occurred post-mortem, exactly when Miyazaki raped Erika is unknown. Similarly, it is unknown when or why Miyazaki restrained Erika's hands and feet, although it may also have occurred post-death as a means to appease a specific fantasy of his.

While discovering the body was a significant breakthrough for the police, it cemented the case as a murder investigation rather than a missing persons case. The hopes of discovering Mari Konno and Masami Yoshizawa alive were now almost zero, bringing a new wave of despair to the parents and a new wave of terror to Saitama and the surrounding regions.

When details of Erika Namba's death were made public, the two men who helped Miyazaki uplift his vehicle several nights before came forward. It would have been the police's biggest lead—and perhaps saved another life—had the men not incorrectly identified Miyazaki's vehicle as a Toyota Corolla instead of a Nissan Langley.

In light of Erika's murder and the lack of police leads, a bleak cloud was cast over Saitama Prefecture. The term *serial killer* hung loosely on the lips of residents, despite it being an alien phrase within the mostly crime-free haven of Japan. However, it was undeniable. The police then began to treat the case as a serial murder investigation.

Tsutomu Miyazaki retreated to the shadows, but he didn't stop playing his games. A week after Erika Namba's murder, her father received a strange postcard, as the Konno family had after Mari's murder.

In the Japanese writing system of Kanji, each character cut from different magazines, were the words: "Erika. Cold. Cough. Throat. Rest. Death." A hoax was immediately suspected, but Shin'ichi Namba instinctively knew that he was being taunted by his daughter's killer.

But more sickening insults were still to come. On February 6, 1989, the father of Mari Konno left his home to find a box waiting on his doorstep. He opened it up to find a note with the strange message: "Mari. Bones. Cremated. Investigate. Prove," staring back at him. In the box were charred bones, baby teeth, ashes, and multiple photos of clothing—the same clothing Mari had worn on the day of her disappearance. Shigeo Konno was holding what remained of his little girl.

He immediately handed the box to authorities, who passed it on to Tokyo Dental University to examine what lay inside. Initially, it was stated that the ten baby teeth in the box did not belong to Mari Konno. However, the overseeing doctor quickly reversed his statement, eventually declaring that the teeth matched Mari's dental x-rays in full. Additionally, forensic officers confirmed that the 220 grams of crushed-up bones did indeed belong to Mari Konno.

It was a torturous revelation for the Konno family. They now had proof that they'd never see their daughter again. But, still not content with putting Shigeo and Yukie Konno through unimaginable pain, Miyazaki made contact twice more.

After seeing the televised conference in which Dr. Kazuo Suzuki made the claim that the box did not contain the remains of Mari Konno, Miyazaki felt the need to right this wrong. In the same conference, Yukie Konno spoke of her brief hope that Mari might still be alive, and so Miyazaki attempted to end what he deemed to be unnecessary suffering. He wrote the Konno family a letter, unaware they had already received confirmation that their daughter was dead.

Both the Konno family and the *Asahi Shimbun* (one of Japan's national newspapers) received a letter on February 11, 1989. It read:

"I put the cardboard box with Mari's remains in it in front of her home," it began. "I did everything. From the start of the Mari incident to the finish. I saw the police press conference where they said the

remains were not Mari's. On camera, her mother said the report gave
her new hope that Mari might still be alive. I knew then that I had to
write this confession so Mari's mother would not continue to hope in
vain. I say again: the remains are Mari's."

A photo of Mari was attached, along with a signed declaration
from a "Yuko Imada," which translates to "Now I will tell" or "Now I
have courage."

This time, police believed the letter to be from the genuine killer.
Handwriting experts were brought in, as were forensic specialists to
examine the letter, the photo of Mari, and the box of her remains.
Indeed, few leads were discovered but were not followed up with
the necessary weight. The photograph was discovered to be taken by
a Mamiya camera, often used by professionals within the printing
industry. The box was made of corrugated cardboard, also used
to transport delicate electrical goods such as cameras and lenses.
Additionally, the postcards sent to the Konno family had been written
with a phototypesetter and copied with an industrial copier, neither
of which were readily available to the general public at the time. But,
despite these clues and for reasons unknown, police didn't conduct
a search of print shops throughout Saitama Prefecture. If they had,
they may have soon found their perpetrator and potentially saved one
more innocent life.

On March 11, 1989, the charred remains of Mari Konno were
laid to rest, but "Yuko Imada" had one more taunt for her grieving
parents. On returning from their daughter's funeral, they discovered
another note waiting for them. Gone was the artificial compassion,
and in its place was pure malice.

"Before I knew it, the child's corpse had gone rigid. I wanted to
cross her hands over her breast but they wouldn't budge…Pretty
soon, the body gets red spots all over it…Big red spots. Like the
Hinomaru flag. Or like you'd covered her whole body with red Hanko

seals…After a while, the body is covered with stretch marks. It was so rigid before, but now it feels like it's full of water. And it smells. How it smells. Like nothing you've ever smelled in this whole wide world."

It was clear that Miyazaki's genuine reasons for contacting his victim's family were for his own gratification. Such contact allowed him to relive his crimes in a more thrilling manner than sitting alone in his bedroom staring at photos and videos.

More taunts came over time, not all of them directed at the Konno family. All of the victim's families received regular nuisance phone calls. Miyazaki would call until someone answered, sometimes ringing out for more than twenty minutes. When someone picked up, Miyazaki would say nothing, then hang up.

Months passed by, and Miyazaki grew impatient. His beloved photographs, videotapes, and comic books could only take him so far. His fantasies were too extreme to be fulfilled by media alone. He knew he had to kill again.

On June 1, 1989, Miyazaki struck up a conversation with a young girl outside Akishima Elementary School in western Tokyo. Although he managed to convince her to undress for him, locals spotted the incident and hurried toward Miyazaki, who was perched with his camera on the rolled-down window of the driver's seat. Miyazaki saw he had been discovered and sped off before anyone could come close to him.

The young girl got a lucky escape, but, only five days later, Miyazaki would take the life of his final victim.

Her name was Ayako Nomoto. She was five years old, and Miyazaki found her playing alone in a park in Ariake, Tokyo Bay. He approached her and politely asked if he'd be okay to take some photographs of her. Ayako agreed, and, after she became comfortable in his presence, Miyazaki asked if he could continue taking photos of her inside his vehicle.

Within seconds, Ayako Nomoto was sitting in the back of his Nissan Langley. Miyazaki drove the pair a kilometer away and parked. Ayako, full of youthful vibrancy and entirely unaware of her captor's true intentions, commented on Miyazaki's deformities as he faced her with his camera in hand. In a surge of rage, Miyazaki threw down his camera, pulled on a pair of gloves, and leapt on top of Ayako in the back of his car. He grabbed her by the throat, fought off her panicked kicks, and choked until she fell limp. He bound her hands and feet with rope, as he had done with Erika Namba, then wrapped duct tape over her mouth. He draped her body in a sheet, then placed her in the trunk of his car.

Not content with disposing of Ayako's corpse in the woods as he had done with the others, Miyazaki headed back to his two-room bungalow with the dead body in tow. Once suitably isolated, Miyazaki took the dead girl to his room and laid her out on a table. He washed the body down before using industrial tape to spread open her vagina. With his camera perched on the edge of his bed, he then recorded himself sexually violating Ayako Nomoto's corpse.

Miyazaki kept the body in his possession for two days, but the overbearing stench of death was too much to handle. He also feared that a family member might inquire about the smell, should the odor seep into other areas of the house. Therefore, he decided to dispose of her remains elsewhere.

The feat was messy, but he took sadistic pleasure in it. Miyazaki sawed off Ayako's hands, feet, and head with a knife to hinder identification should she be discovered. He discarded the torso near a public toilet in Hanno's Miyazawa-ko cemetery before returning home to cook what remained of Ayako in his back garden. He ate some of her hands—perhaps a highly symbolic gesture—then dumped the leftovers into the hills of Mitakeyama.

Tsutomu Miyazaki's bloodlust was now at a ravenous high. Spending considerable time with Ayako Nomoto's dead body behind closed doors without having to worry about interruption had given him a satisfaction his other victims hadn't. If he were to kill again, he would likely have been compelled to repeat this same scenario.

Miyazaki found his next potential victim on July 23, 1989. Driving through Hachioji, western Tokyo, he exited his car and made his way toward two young girls he'd spotted playing in the street. This was the first time he'd approached multiple girls at once, and, fortunately, would also be the last. Miyazaki told one of the girls, a nine-year-old, to "stay here," while he lured the younger into a more secluded area. However, the older girl ran back home and alerted her father to the strange man's interest in her sister.

Minutes later, the girl's father hurried to the scene, discovering Miyazaki completely naked and holding a camera between his daughter's legs in the back of his car. The father pulled open the door and hurled his fist into Miyazaki's head, sending him sprawling from the back seat out onto the road. As the father reached in and grabbed his terrified daughter, a naked Miyazaki fled, his silhouette gradually fading from view along a muddy riverbank.

Police invaded the scene. It wouldn't be long before they traced the vehicle's owner, but they didn't need to. It was perhaps the last thing they expected, but Tsutomu Miyazaki shamelessly returned to the vehicle of his own free will. One of the largest serial killer investigations in Japanese history came to an end when the culprit literally walked into the arms of police.

He was a far sight from the demonic fiend that his crimes alluded to. The Saitama serial killer was neither imposing nor visually remarkable. He was a short, pudgy young man with shaggy black hair reaching his eyes and round glasses too large for his face. He was arrested on the spot.

Police suspected the loner Miyazaki was responsible for "The Little Girl Murders," but he remained silent for more than two weeks during police interrogation. By this point, the press had already found their way into Miyazaki's home and plastered images of his towering collection of videos and comic books on their front pages, officially cementing Miyazaki's new moniker as "The Otaku Murderer."

Police were soon granted access to Miyazaki's cluttered residence, and it didn't take them long to discover amateur footage of Mari Konno among the 5,763 videotapes piled high in his bedroom.

They had little doubt that the disheveled young man sitting in their holding cell was the Saitama child killer, and, after informing Miyazaki of their findings at his home, a full confession followed. He first claimed responsibility for murdering Ayako Nomoto, which lead the police to her remains in the Okutama hills. He then one by one confessed to killing Erika Namba, Mari Konno, and Masami Yoshizawa. After intense searching, police discovered Masami's decayed body in the same spot Miyazaki had left her eleven months before. Nearby, they also found the severed hands and feet of Mari Konno, which Miyazaki had dismembered on one of his visits to her corpse.

Following Miyazaki's arrest, his crimes became international front-page news. The case sparked a moral outrage against otaku culture in Japan, although a direct link between the media Miyazaki consumed and his crimes was never truly established. The majority of his comic books, manga, and videotapes were neither sexual nor violent in nature. However, it was believed that they propagated the fantasy world he inhabited.

"His absorption in a video world removed his consciousness from reality," said Dr. Susumu Oda, a psychologist who examined Miyazaki after his capture. "The little girls he killed were no more than characters from his comic-book life."

Despite his wealth and prominence, Katsumi Miyazaki refused to hire a defense lawyer for his son, claiming it would be unfair to the victims. The revelation that Tsutomu was responsible for such gruesome deeds took its toll on the Miyazaki family, who all went into hiding when the details of his crimes became public knowledge.

Miyazaki was appointed a state lawyer by default, his defense resting mostly on the fact that Miyazaki was not of sound mind. If he was found to be legally insane, Miyazaki could skirt the death penalty and settle for life imprisonment. Many psychologists examined Miyazaki, most coming to the conclusion that he suffered from a myriad of mental illnesses. When the trial began on March 30, 1990, Miyazaki spent his time in the courtroom doodling cartoons on his notepad and falling asleep. When questioned on what drove him to kill, he strangely blamed his actions on the "Rat Man," an alter ego of Miyazaki's who had appeared in his home-drawn comic books as a teenager.

While this bizarre claim aided Miyazaki's insanity defense, it wasn't enough to persuade judges. And so, on April 14, 1997, after an extensive trial, Tsutomu Miyazaki was sentenced to death by hanging.

Incarceration was familiar territory for Miyazaki. He'd spent most of his life sitting alone in a small room. Only now, it was his own death that was forthcoming.

His mother visited him to replenish his supply of comic books, as she had done for most of his life. However, his father was nowhere to be found. After making a public apology regarding his son's actions and closing down the *Akikawa Shimbun* in the early nineties, Katsumi Miyazaki took his own life in 1994 by throwing himself into a river.

While awaiting his execution, Miyazaki showed no remorse. The only person whom he showed compassion for was his mother, writing her a letter stating: "Mother, I've caused you so much heartache." He signed off with: "Don't forget to change the oil in my car, or it'll get so you can't drive it."

Like all Japanese death row prisoners, Miyazaki was unaware exactly when his last day alive would be. But on the morning of June 17, 2008, Miyazaki's tragic story finally came to an end. He was escorted from his cell in Tokyo Detention House to the prison's execution chamber, where he was greeted by a hanging rope swaying beside a bronze Buddhist statue. Authorities blindfolded Miyazaki with a white cloth, attached the noose around his neck, and positioned him above the trap door that would drop him to his death.

Fifteen minutes later, a prison doctor announced Tsutomu Miyazaki dead.

The case of "The Otaku Murderer" continues to be one of the most morbid and fascinating in true crime history, with Miyazaki's legacy still plaguing the locations he dwelled. Old Komine Tunnel—the site where Miyazaki killed two of his victims—remains a particularly haunted area of Saitama. It was here that Miyazaki returned to dismember Mari Konno's body, and, to this day, many people claim that a handless ghost can be seen wandering the tunnel by night.

In the decades since the case, many devout otaku followers have attempted to undo the damning effects Tsutomu Miyazaki's actions had on their subculture. While societal acceptance of otaku culture—both in Japan and the western world—is at an all-time high, it still comes with an air of negativity its followers are desperate to shed. However, victims' families will likely feel Tsutomu Miyazaki's destructive presence for years to come.

Fred and Rose West:
The Cultural Legacy of Serial Murder

FRANCESCA ROE

Cromwell Street is an unremarkable residential road in the British cathedral city of Gloucester, with one curious feature. Halfway down the street is a landscaped walkway that punctures the row of townhouses and emerges a stone's throw away at St. Michael's Square. This is not a typical feature of British terraced housing. The broad walkway feels like a luxury that Cromwell Street, with its townhouses and tiny front gardens, can ill afford.

At first glance, the walkway might seem insignificant, an innocuous attempt to inject some green space into one of Gloucester's more rundown areas. This is not the case. Twenty-five years ago, a building stood here—25 Cromwell Street. It was home to a married couple, Fred and Rose West, and their various lodgers and children. In 1994 the bodies of nine young women were discovered buried on the property, among them one of the Wests' own daughters. Some of the women's bodies had been buried for more than twenty years.

Gloucester, a city with a population of just under thirty thousand, found itself at the center of one of the worst serial murder cases Britain had ever seen. The killings still resonate today. Canon Adrian Slade, an Anglican priest who works in the city and has strong memories of the killings, describes the city as having been "deeply traumatized," noting how residents still define Gloucester first and foremost as the home of Fred and Rose West. It's not just locals. When I think of Gloucester, I think of three things: a cathedral, the well-known children's rhyme "Doctor Foster went to Gloucester," and the West murders.

Nor was the impact of the killings restricted to Gloucester. On a national level, the murder cast serious doubt upon the effectiveness of the UK's protective agencies after it emerged that the Wests' children were known to social services, having arrived at the hospital with injuries on thirty-one separate occasions. Rose West's lawyer, Leo Goatley, believes the killings drove a subtle shift in public morals, with the shock of seeing a "proper nuclear family, properly married couple" outed as sadistic murderers taking the sheen off traditional notions of marriage. The case also challenged beliefs about the role of women in violent crime, with Rose's active role in the killings putting an end to the notion that female murderers were directed by their husbands rather than their own impulses. Underlying all this was the fundamental question of nature versus nurture, of how far the Wests' crimes could be attributed to their own upbringings—both of which had been traumatic and bear closer scrutiny.

THE MURDERS

There was never any debate in court regarding whether Fred and Rose were legally sane and therefore fit to stand trial. Both were deemed to be aware of the seriousness of their crimes and fully cognizant of the suffering they had inflicted. And yet, it is difficult to believe that childhood trauma did not to some extent impact their behavior as adults. Fred and Rose may have been found criminally responsible, but their childhoods and early adult experiences were undoubtedly brutal and dysfunctional.

Rosemary Letts was born in Devon in 1953. Her mother, Daisy, experienced severe depression and underwent electroconvulsive therapy throughout her pregnancy, leading to speculation that Rose experienced prenatal brain damage that could account for her crimes (there is, however, no medical evidence to support this theory). What is certain is that Rose's father, Bill, was prone to violence, likely as a result of untreated paranoid schizophrenia. He was also sexually abusive, raping Rose from the age of ten. When Rose was thirteen, she began abusing her younger brother, Graham, while continuing to be abused in turn by her father. Rose's parents separated when she was in her teens, and her father moved to the small town of Bishop's Cleeve near Cheltenham.

It was here that the fifteen-year-old Rose first met Fred, age twenty-seven and living in a caravan along with his daughter and stepdaughter from a previous marriage. The following year, Rose moved permanently into her father's home. Despite his own abuse of Rose, Bill was furious about his underage daughter's relationship with an older man and threatened to call social services. The rift resulted in Rose leaving her father's house and moving into Fred's caravan to care for his two children. Rose quickly became pregnant, and the couple moved to nearby Gloucester, first setting up their home at 25 Midland Road. In 1970, aged sixteen, Rose gave birth to the couple's first daughter, Heather. Rose may have left her father's house, but she did not escape his influence. Bill was a frequent visitor to their next home on Cromwell Street and continued to have sex with his daughter well into adulthood. When Rose's children would later tell her that Fred had raped them, Rose would respond that it was a normal part of growing up.

Fred's childhood initially seems less troubling. He was born in 1941 to Walter and Daisy West in Much Marcle, a village in rural Herefordshire. The Wests were a farming family, poor but well-regarded in the village. After his arrest, however, Fred alleged that his parents had been sexually abusive and that he was introduced to bestiality and incest by his father—claims disputed by other family members. As a teenager, Fred attended a social club in nearby Ledbury, where he quickly became notorious for sexually harassing girls. In 1958 Fred was involved in a motorcycle accident and suffered a fractured skull. Two years later, he fell down a fire escape and was knocked unconscious for twenty-four hours. His family later claimed that Fred began to display uncharacteristic fits of rage after the accidents, leading to speculation that Fred, like Rose, may have suffered brain damage. As a young man, Fred is known to have raped and molested young women in the village; in 1961 he was accused of molesting and impregnating his thirteen-year-old sister, Kitty, who could not be named at the time. When Fred was questioned by police, he freely admitted to molesting young girls, saying, "Well, doesn't everybody do it?" The case collapsed after Kitty refused to testify against her brother.

In 1962 Fred was reacquainted with a young Scottish woman, Catherine "Rena" Costello, whom he had met two years previously at a dance in Much Marcle. Costello came from Glasgow but had fled to England after becoming pregnant during a relationship with a Pakistani bus driver (it is likely that Rena left Glasgow due to the stigma of being an unmarried woman with a mixed-race child). Fred married Rena in 1962. In 1963, Rena gave birth to her daughter, Charmaine, and the couple moved back to Glasgow, where Rena gave birth to another daughter, Anne Marie, before returning to Bishop's Cleeve in 1965. They were accompanied by two female friends from Glasgow: Isa McNeill, a neighbor and sometimes nanny

to Charmaine, and sixteen-year-old Anne McFall, a friend of Isa
and Rena. Both women were living on the breadline in Glasgow and
hoped to find a better life in England. It didn't turn out that way.
In 1966, Rena left Fred and the children, claiming he had become
controlling and abusive toward her. Over the next five years, Rena
would return to England sporadically to visit her daughters, engaging
in an on-off relationship with Fred during her visits. Fred, however,
had taken up with the younger Anne McFall, who quickly became
pregnant. Anne vanished in 1967. She was never reported missing.

Even before meeting Rose, Fred West had an extensive history
of sexual and domestic violence. Unbeknown to the authorities, he
had also committed his first murder. The remains of Anne McFall
and her unborn child were found buried in a field in Much Marcle
in 1994, twenty-seven years after her death. She was the first in a
series of young women who were not always missed. It is not clear
whether Rose knew about Anne's murder, but she quickly showed
her own propensity to violence. In 1971, Fred was sentenced to six
and a half months in prison for stealing car tires and a vehicle tax
disc. Rose, aged just seventeen, was left to care for the couple's young
daughter, Heather, along with Charmaine and Anne Marie. On or
around June 15, 1971, Rose murdered eight-year-old Charmaine.
Rose never confessed to the murder, but it seems most likely that
Charmaine was beaten or stabbed to death. Fred's second daughter,
Anne Marie, would later state that Rose had been viciously abusive to
the children and that she had a particular disliking for Charmaine's
"defiant" nature. When Fred was released from prison, just days after
the murder, he helped to move Charmaine's body from the coal shed
to the yard. The couple explained Charmaine's sudden disappearance
to her school and concerned neighbors by claiming that her biological
mother, Rena, had taken her back to Glasgow. Their account was
never questioned.

Over the next fifteen years, Fred and Rose went on to kill another eight women. In 1971, Rena, who had growing concerns regarding her daughter's whereabouts, returned to England to locate Charmaine and bring her back to Glasgow. Rena was last seen getting into a car with Fred. Her remains were uncovered more than two decades later in a field near Much Marcle. Again, it is unclear whether Rose was aware of the murder. Like Anne McFall, Rena was never reported missing to the police.

Up to this point, the murders committed by Fred and Rose West might be classed as crimes driven primarily by expediency, the desire to get rid of an unwanted wife, partner, or child. In 1973, though, a new pattern emerged—one of sexually motivated murders, committed jointly by Fred and Rose. Lynda Gough was a nineteen-year-old woman from Gloucester who was in a relationship with one of the Wests' lodgers, Benjamin Stanniland. She was a frequent visitor to Cromwell Street and became one of the Wests' regular babysitters. Lynda vanished in 1973. Unlike Anne and Rena, she was missed: Lynda's mother visited the West house during her efforts to track down her daughter, only to be told by Rose—wearing Lynda's slippers and with Lynda's clothes hanging on the washing line in the garden— that her daughter had gone to Weston-super-Mare, leaving her belongings behind. Lynda's mother had no reason to suspect Rose and went to Weston-super-Mare to continue the search for her daughter. Lynda's body was discovered in 1994. She had been sexually abused and strangled in the cellar of 25 Cromwell Street.

In November 1973, the couple began to abduct young women at random. Carol Ann Cooper lived in a children's home in Worcester and was fifteen years old when she was taken from a bus stop and murdered by the Wests. In December, the Wests offered a lift to Lucy Partington, a final-year student at Exeter University who, unlike the previous victims, came from a middle-class family (Lucy, in fact, was a cousin of the famous novelist Martin Amis, who would later write about her death and its effect on the family in his memoirs). Her disappearance was reported, but the investigation quickly petered out. The following year, a twenty-one-year-old Swiss student named Therese Siegenthaler vanished while hitchhiking. She had planned to travel to Ireland but failed to return to her student accommodation after the Easter holidays. Her disappearance was reported to police, but the investigation again went cold. Later that year, fifteen-year-old Shirley Hubbard vanished during a work experience placement in Worcester. Like Carol Cooper, Shirley had lived in children's homes as a child.

In 1975, seventeen-year-old Juanita Mott disappeared. She was a rebellious young woman who had been in trouble with the police and had recently left home to move in with friends. Her family did not report her disappearance to police, presuming that Juanita had simply decided to cut contact. In 1978, the Wests murdered their lodger, eighteen-year-old Shirley Ann Robinson. Shirley had been introduced to prostitution by Fred and Rose and was pregnant with Fred's child when she died. In 1979, sixteen-year-old Alison Chambers vanished. Like so many of the women murdered by the Wests, she was living in a children's home at the time of her disappearance and had drifted toward Cromwell Street in the months before her death.

In 1986, seven years later, the Wests killed their last known victim—their sixteen-year-old daughter, Heather, who had confided in a school friend that she was being abused at home. The Wests told various stories to explain Heather's absence: she had gone to work in Torquay; she was in a lesbian relationship and had gone to live with her girlfriend; she was involved in credit-card fraud and was on the run from the police. In fact, she was buried at Cromwell Street along with the bodies of seven other women, her grave marked by a pine table in the back garden where Fred would host family barbecues.

There are several conspicuous gaps in the timeline of the murders, and it seems likely that the Wests committed other murders. Fred West in particular is likely to have been responsible for more killings, having confessed to murdering more than thirty women. Although we cannot take these confessions at face value, several additional victims have been suggested; in 1967 a fifteen-year-old boy named Robin Holt was found hanging from a noose in a barn on the outskirts of Gloucester, surrounded by pornographic magazines. Someone had drawn nooses around the necks of the models. Robin was known to be friendly with Fred West, but police were never able to establish a definite connection. Fred's son Stephen also claimed his father confessed to the 1968 murder of Mary Bastholm, a fifteen-year-old from Gloucester who waitressed at a café Fred was known to frequent. Mary's remains were never found. There has been speculation that Fred murdered up to four women while living in Glasgow with his first wife, Rena; he is said to have been fond of digging up his allotment in the early hours of the morning, but neighbors noticed that only a small portion of the ground had actually been cultivated. The allotment is now buried under the M8 motorway.

One possible reason for the gaps between the murders are the distractions posed by the Wests' involvement in prostitution—Rose worked as a prostitute from her home in Cromwell Street, encouraged by Fred, who would frequently watch her having sex with clients—and sexual abuse. In 1972, the Wests raped and sexually assaulted a young woman, Caroline Owens, who had moved into Cromwell Street to work as a nanny. Owens reported the Wests to the police but was too traumatized to testify in court. The sexual charges against the Wests were dropped, although they pled guilty to the lesser crimes of indecent assault and causing bodily harm.

The Wests were also serial abusers of their own children. In 1992, Fred was charged with raping his daughter, Louise, after she told a school friend about the sexual abuse she had endured; Rose was charged as an accomplice. As part of the investigation, lead Detective Constable Hazel Savage interviewed Anne Marie, the daughter of Fred and Rena Costello, who confirmed she too had been sexually abused by her father. Yet again, the case fell apart when Louise and Anne Marie refused to testify against their parents. But the Wests' luck was running thin. As part of her inquiries, Savage questioned Fred and Rose about the disappearance of their daughter, Heather. She was not satisfied with their answers. Twenty-seven years after Fred's first known murder and six years after Heather's death, 25 Cromwell Street was finally about to fall under police scrutiny.

ARREST AND AFTERMATH

The 1992 rape investigation was not Savage's first encounter with Fred West. She had known Fred's first wife, Rena, whom she had interviewed some twenty years previously after Rena had been caught stealing while visiting Fred and the children. Fred had appeared as a character witness for Rena, and he had stuck in Savage's mind due to the stories Rena had told about his unusual sexual tastes. Something did not sit right for Savage, and her sense of unease was confirmed when Fred's name came up years later in connection with the alleged rape of his daughter. It was this lingering sense of something being not quite right that led Savage to pursue discrepancies that welfare agencies and police had missed. First among those discrepancies was Heather.

After the rape case against Fred collapsed, it would have been easy for police to wind down their investigation—after all, the court case had failed to secure a conviction. During the course of her interviews with Fred's children, however, Savage had heard about a darkly humorous family joke that Fred told his children: if they didn't behave, they'd end up under the patio just like their sister Heather. Savage was not convinced the joke was innocent. Her superiors were initially reluctant to authorize a full search of 25 Cromwell Street, fearing another failed case against the Wests would begin to look like harassment. Their fears proved unfounded. On February 25, 1994, after being confronted with a search warrant, Fred confessed to the murder of his daughter. Heather's remains were removed from the garden the following day. Buried alongside them was a third thigh bone that was later identified as belonging to Shirley Robinson. When a third set of bones was discovered, officials widened the scope of the search.

When police began investigating Heather's disappearance, there was no suspicion that Fred might be implicated in other murders. And yet, as the dig at Cromwell Street continued, Fred signed a written statement confessing to a further nine murders—"approx." Rose, meanwhile, had been escorted to a police safe house. Although Fred insisted she had no knowledge of the murders, police were not convinced. After all, Rose had been implicated in the assault of Caroline Owens along with her husband, with both being found guilty of indecent assault and actual bodily harm. The brutal sexual assault to which Owens had been subjected bore parallels with the increasingly disturbing evidence uncovered at Cromwell Street: several of the women's skulls had been found encased in masking tape, belts, and other restraining devices, and Owens had been beaten with a belt as she was raped. On April 25, Rose was charged with the murder of Lynda Gough. By May 6, Fred and Rose had been charged jointly with five murders. They would be sentenced to a whole life order, meaning that both would die in prison. Fred West had other ideas, taking his own life in prison in January 1995. Rose West has fought unsuccessfully against her conviction and is still incarcerated. She maintains her innocence.

Serial killings, by their very nature, are exceptional events. But the West case is exceptional even among serial murders, generating immediate notoriety and a lasting cultural legacy. This reputation can be attributed in great part to the sheer brutality of the murders. It may seem pointless to rank serial killings by order of violence, but the details of the West case are relentlessly awful. The women were subjected to increasingly severe torture, immobilized, and silenced with homemade masks found still attached to their skulls. In some cases, it is not clear whether injuries were pre- or post-mortem. When Heather was found, her fingernails were discovered neatly stacked in a pile. We can assume they were removed after death, but it is difficult to know for sure. It is these details, and the sense of uncertainty that surrounds them, that make the West murders particularly difficult to stomach.

There is also a lingering sense of disbelief at the moral vacuum in which the Wests operated. Quite apart from the murders themselves, the litany of incest, rape, and abuse that took place at Cromwell Street could have been lifted directly from a Victorian penny dreadful. It was this complete absence of all social rules and constraints that led the crime writer Gordon Burn to describe his work about the West killings, *Happy Like Murderers*, as the hardest he ever had to write— how can you begin to make sense of a "moral abyss"?

The facts of the case quickly become confusing: multiple wives, murders committed individually as well as together, murders of expediency as well as sexual gratification, uncertainty about exact numbers and dates, possible additional victims. It is difficult to impose order on a chronology that is not always linear. Writing about the West murders is like trying to disentangle a ball of knotted thread. Do you begin with the murders committed jointly, Fred's early crimes, or the murder of their daughter Heather that finally saw their luck run out? Whichever starting point you choose, you end up jumping backward and forward in time.

Time also helps to explain how the manner in which the crimes were discovered has contributed to the power of the West murders. In other well-known serial murder cases—the Yorkshire Ripper killings, for example, or the Moors murders—police were aware from the outset that a crime had been committed, with the difficulty being how to identify and apprehend the perpetrator. This was not the case with the West murders. Human remains dating back two decades were found within the space of a few days, a brutal and swift shock to the system. The realization that Fred and Rose West had operated undetected by police and social services for so long was difficult to bear—particularly given the fact that several of the West children, as well as the numerous young women who had had the misfortune of coming into contact with the couple, made allegations of sexual assault that had floundered in court (although both had been convicted of grievous bodily harm after their attack on Caroline Owens), which should have placed Fred and Rose West firmly on the radar of the authorities.

A further reason for the notoriety of the murders is the active role taken by Rose in the killings—the type of violent sexual crime that is usually considered the domain of men. Even today, women are often held to be the nurturing, caring sex, and this belief can produce a curious double-bind whereby female perpetrators face a double judgment: they are condemned once for the crime itself and again for being a woman committing a crime that is held to go against the "feminine nature." Feminist academics have highlighted the ways that Rose's crimes were presented during trial as horrific not only on account of their brutality but also because they were carried out by a woman rather than a man. Rightly or wrongly, the idea of a young woman raping, torturing, and murdering other women has lent the murders an added layer of fascination.

Even today, the Wests' crimes exert a powerful psychological hold. In 2004, the reporter Euan Ferguson, who had covered the case when it first broke, returned to Gloucester on the tenth anniversary of the murderers' arrest. Ferguson's interview with a German-born pastor named Stefan who lived in Gloucester at the time of the murders described the city's desire to forget the crimes as akin to the reluctance of Germans to confront the crimes of the Holocaust. The comparison may seem exaggerated, perhaps even flippant, but there is little doubt that the murders exerted a lasting trauma for those closest to them. Indeed, the trauma of the Holocaust appears elsewhere in reporting on the West case. Marian Partington, sister of Lucy Partington, has spoken about finding solace in a work by Eva Hoffman, *After Such Knowledge*, which explores the possibility of coming to terms with the Holocaust. On an infinitely smaller scale, it seems that the West murders evoke some of those same feelings of loss and confusion, and similar questions as to why and how—why the killings happened, how they were allowed to continue, and how nobody could have known.

Why did the killings happen? The coldly logical explanation is that both Fred and Rose West experienced profoundly traumatic events during childhood and young adulthood—incest, rape and domestic violence—which collided with pre-existing psychological characteristics to devastating effect. There is an element of chance, too; although Fred and Rose had both killed separately, the majority of the murders were a joint enterprise. It seems unlikely that Fred or Rose would have been responsible for so many deaths had they never met; psychologically, having a partner in crime legitimized their actions, and it would have been logistically difficult for Fred or Rose to commit so many murders and abductions without an accomplice.

And yet, the horror of the West murders seems greater than the sum of their parts. Logically, we might understand that the most brutal crimes can be driven by an unhappy combination of childhood trauma, individual psychological traits, and opportunity. When Rose West dismissed her children's accounts of incest and rape by telling them it was a normal part of growing up, we can even feel sympathy for a woman whose sense of normality and decency had been so warped by the abuse she herself had suffered as a child. And yet, when we are confronted with the prolonged suffering inflicted on the Wests' victims, no rational explanation seems adequate. We can understand on a logical level, but the emotional jolt of the crimes cannot be rationalized.

All of which leads to a further question—could something like this happen again? Initially, it appears unlikely. The West case, after all, has been cited as a wake-up call for social services, ensuring that services shared information and worked more closely together. But there are increasing concerns for the state of the UK's safety net. In March 2019, the *Guardian* ran an investigation into care homes in the UK, finding that record numbers of vulnerable children had gone missing from the group homes where they lived. The news comes only a few years after the UK was shaken by a series of child sex-grooming scandals, in which gangs of men operating out of takeout joints and taxi firms were found to have systematically abused and exploited vulnerable young girls—many of whom, like the Wests' victims, came from impoverished and dysfunctional backgrounds. After years of austerity, senior government officials have warned that a lack of cash is driving child-protective services to the breaking point. One of the most shocking dimensions of the West case is the length of time for which the perpetrators were able to evade the authorities, exploiting women who in many instances were neglected and easily forgotten about. As protective services in the UK increasingly struggle for funding, it is far from clear that such crimes could not happen again.

Buxom Belle:
Her Own Story

VICKI HENDRICKS

*B*rynhild Paulsdatter Størseth was born into poverty in Norway in
1859 and traveled to the US in 1881 to eventually become Belle
*Gunness, a wealthy landowner and notorious serial killer, with a body
count up to forty men. In looking superficially at facts, pure greed seems
to have been her motivation, but of course, human personality is never
that simple. The following account is a fusion of known fact, theory,
and imagination, narrated from Belle's point of view.*

APRIL 16, 1908

I claw at my cheeks and growl in frustration. I must give up the
search for a woman six feet tall, near two-hundred pounds. For this
I am likely to go to prison for the rest of my days—or soon to hell.
My "Lonely Hearts" letters in the *Skandinaven* and *DecorahPosten*
bring the men flocking, all sizes, many from Chicago and Iowa. The
simple mention of potato dumplings and pork with cream pudding
for dessert rekindles childhood memories and replaces every caution.
They expect to marry me and recreate their family life and Norwegian
Christmases in the lonely new country. They rarely question my

request to come immediately and bring cash. But finding a woman
of my size, the right body to replace mine, has proven impossible.
Asle Hegelien will arrive in two weeks, frantic as a boar after his first
sow, to find his missing brother, Andrew. My plan must be complete
before the La Porte authorities can knock on my door. I hate what I
do. I wish no harm. They make me do it. These men.

The most recent response to my letter is neatly printed without
embellishment. Esther Carlson is lacking the means to survive,
desperate for a home, since hers will soon be forfeited to the bank due
to the death of her husband. No children, no relatives—a requirement
for me. In answer to my queries, she admits being only five-foot-two
and 130 pounds, but claims fitness and strength beyond her size,
which she does not realize is no asset for my purposes. It is possible
that the fire can be blamed for burning away flesh and bone if enough
evidence of my identity counters the discrepancy in our sizes. I invite
her to come to La Porte, to "visit my lovely Indiana farmhouse,"
having run out of time to find anyone more suitable.

APRIL 26, 1908

On the day before I will set the fire, I await Mrs. Carlson's arrival at
the train station. Perchance a shopkeeper or neighbor might see me,
so I have disguised myself as a man by covering my hair with a low-
brimmed hat and strapping my bosom down inside a heavy fur coat
that belonged to one of my largest suitors. It would be impossible to
fool anyone as a woman since I am the largest female person this town
can claim. I approach a short, buxom lady, who stands near the wall
timidly looking around.

"Good day, Mrs. Carlson? I am here to take you to the Gunness
farm. Mrs. Gunness is preparing for your arrival." I motion to the

buggy and offer my arm to help her up. Her neck has shrunk down so that the brim of her hat nearly rests on her shoulders. I sense that she is distressed with the unexpected company of a man and has taken punishment in the past from one such demon. It is unfortunate that she will never have the opportunity to thrive in an atmosphere apart from male authority, as I have led her to expect—a matriarchal family, like that of my dear, highly intelligent piggies. Perhaps, Esther has even dared to hope for intimacy of a physical nature with me.

I sigh and pick up her small, worn valise. She follows sheepishly, as women are meant to do. She will succumb swiftly to the poison, never needing to learn the terrifying capabilities necessary to become a "free" woman in our world, never needing to counter men's self-righteous entitlement and the rage that often accompanies their privileges.

At the farm, I lead her to the closest guest room, asking her to stow her bag in the closet and to meet Mrs. Gunness momentarily down the hall in the parlor. It is the closest room to the basement. I go to my bedroom to remove the disguise. I have sent the farmhand, Ray Lamphere, on an errand for the day, but everything must be tidy before the children get home from school. The older girls have become curious as to the sudden disappearance of my last few suitors, and forbidding the children's entry into the basement seems to make them more determined to get in. I cannot let their innocent minds grasp the horrors I have been forced to commit in order to keep them comfortable and well-fed and to avoid detection. I must remind myself that it will be better for them to die with innocent minds and perfect bodies than to live long lives as victims, gathering scars. They will experience unusual, but not severe, symptoms and slip into unconsciousness feeling secure with me holding them in my arms. Fear, the worst part of death, will be absent, and they will fly as angels straight to heaven. If I had any hope that I could follow in that direction, I would.

Esther is admiring the pieces on the mantle when I appear as myself. I offer her a cup of coffee over which to get acquainted. The fact that I tower over her seems no longer a threat now that I wear feminine attire.

She has removed her gloves and hat and tidied her pompadour. "Pleased to make your acquaintance," she says. I give her an accepting nod. She smiles and follows me to the parlor, where I leave her to inspect the luxury of my rugs and velvet loveseat, the comfort of which she expects will be afforded to her for sharing the farm work. In the kitchen, I measure out the strychnine, in the amount I have learned for controlling the men, and boil up strong coffee. I might not need as much powder for her, but I have always done it this way to avoid long suffering.

When she has finished her coffee, complimented my delicious apple cake, and discussed her new responsibilities with me, she seems altogether pleased with herself. This is as I wish, to end her life with the contentment of having made the right choice—a rare state of mind to be cherished. I feel an emotional twinge that our lives will not proceed in the manner I have described to her, with camaraderie to dispel the pain of work, cold, and loneliness. I rub a tear from my cheek, an unusual overflow of emotion that I have learned well to hide. "We are kindred spirits," I tell her, squeezing her small fingers.

Soon after, her head begins to twitch so slightly that one without my experience would not notice. She is starting to feel nervous, a condition that comes from the strychnine. I invite her to start a tour of the house in the basement, where I claim to have many jars of tomatoes, peaches, and blackberry jam. She ignores her minor symptoms and rises. There is no reason to wait until her legs spasm and she goes into convulsions; I would be forced to drag her down the stairs. I have already grown fond of her and want to condense the pain into an instant. I light a candle and walk ahead. At the bottom of the stairs, I hand her the taper, and she squints into the blackness, perhaps smelling the remains of blood or spotting some chunk of bone I have missed. I swing my practiced blow to her pompadour. One hard tap and she goes down without fear or pain. With the candle flame held close, I cannot perceive any breath. I kiss her forehead and stand before her. I have done this forty times, or more, without feeling such regret.

I rush to lock the basement door and get down to the work of it. The rest is crude and messy. I must remove the head so that the gold teeth I am known for are not seen as missing. Perhaps, the police will suspect that someone has stolen my head in order to sell the gold. The fire will consume much, and the police will be left to theorize.

NORWAY, 1870s

As a girl, I was fragile. I had not yet learned to handle men by their needs. I had dreams like every girl—marriage, babies, and cuddling and eating cream pudding by the fire while the snow swirled outside. Of course, I expected days filled with household drudgery—the only life for a woman of poor birth. I had grown from childhood on meager food and constant work, from collecting firewood to caring for farm animals, including much milking. Our family included seven children and often partook from the welfare system. Yet, I thought I would be content with love that was returned by a husband and children in the future.

At seventeen, a wealthy young landowner looked my way, an impossible wish come true. He was handsome and took a liking to me. I thought it was because I was smart. We spent afternoons in the meadow kissing and dreaming. He touched me most gentle and respectful, firing me inward, a feeling new to me that took away hunger and cold, even just in the remembering of it.

Against his upbringing, he dared to dance with me in the public hall, to show he cared for me more than his wealthy status. A bold promise, I thought it was. We found time that night, tucked into a nest of our making, amid the roots of a giant sugar maple in the woods not far from the hall. His hand went into my corset, releasing my flesh to the cool night air, my pink nipples near glowing by moonlight as he nuzzled them with his cheeks. His strong hands pulled me close by the hips, and I felt the hardness of a man for the first time. "Special girl. You deserve the nicest things."

I believed that I deserved nice things, and my happiness soared. His emotions were strong, and he hiked my skirt and put his fingers into the moist, soft skin and slid that solid part into the hollow place that I had never seen, but was on my mind always thereafter. I had not expected such easy pleasure or how much it would rule the rest of me. For weeks, I stole out every night to meet him under our tree and give him "some maple sugar" when he would ask.

I was still innocent in mind, if not in body. When I began to swell, my mother looked at me, horrified and helpless, but it was with utter happiness that I approached my lover, as I then knew him to be. He was quick to get between my legs that night, even as the words came from my mouth, but his eyes soon burned red with anger, not tears of joy. He pumped me hard, banging my hips on the gnarled roots and frozen earth, growling, as a beast I had never seen in him. "Whore, whore!" he whispered into my ear. "I should have known your tricks."

When he finished, I lay crying. I had no tricks. He rose and stood over me, his flesh dangling, his face in a sneer as he tucked himself into his pants and closed his belt. A boot struck my ribs like a hammer, and I heard the sound of bone breaking for the first time.

One toe he shoved inside of me, while he stomped on my belly with the other boot, and I felt myself burst inside; the little one, I imagined, fine-boned like a small herring, crushed. I knew at that moment, if I lived, there were more beatings to come, because men could do what they wanted.

For weeks, I suffered and prayed to die. Looking back, I believe Brynhild did pass away. I recovered with a soul that was no longer hers. My older sister Nellie often stated that I was a different person, and I know she did not mean an improved version. Living in this world so cruel or going to hell—it was all the same, except for the vengeance lodged in my soul. My lover was never charged with the beating he administered to end the life he had begun. I learned the best use of poison and sent that man to hell. It was so easy, so perfect, diagnosed as stomach cancer. I fooled them all, the men.

1881

Life in Norway would never change for us, poor and female. My older sister Nellie managed to save enough money to sail to the New World and settle in Chicago, where she married. Her letters glowed with promise. A photograph showed her in lavish Sunday clothes, a velvet hat with a tall pink plume taken from some exotic bird and a ribboned bustle that would have suited my figure well. To me, the ownership of such attire was testament to the opportunity of wealth for a woman of ambition.

Nellie generously paid my way to come and live with them. Once there, I found that she was reliant on her husband for finery. Unperturbed, I began taking in laundry, sewing, and cleaning houses, much as I had done throughout my girlhood, managing only enough to contribute to our maintenance. I resolved to reach beyond my

station. I was hard of muscle and head, and I could not abide this
life or any of the lives I saw women leading all around me. Taking a
husband seemed the first necessary step in acquiring what I wanted.

1884

Mads Sorenson was my first husband. I married wearing a black dress
that suited me well, tightly bustled and ruffled. Mads presented a
charming smile that soon lost its shine. His job as a night watchman
at the department store did not cover more than our basic needs,
especially after I took in the infant Jennie Olsen. Many women could
not afford to feed their yearly births, and overwrought mothers would
be relieved to accept my offers of care for a small sum of money. I
wanted to feed and cuddle them, all those cold, hungry children such
as I had been, but due to Mads' small salary, I could only adopt eight-
month-old Jennie when her mother died.

Mads tried his best to stand beside me as a husband, but he
was lacking in gumption. I was forced to take the lead. I saved
up and, with Mads's contribution, bought us a little candy store
in 1885, joyous and hopeful we'd build a successful business to
feed our children. It was such a pleasure to stock the shelves with
cigars, magazines, newspapers, groceries, and especially Whitman's
chocolates, candy corn, and, my favorite, Cracker Jack. I brought
in the newest confections, and we worked ourselves to the bone but
gained no advantage. Or, I worked myself to the bone. Mads was
mostly a talker. I never knew why, but after several months customers
became sparse, and we were in financial trouble.

One day, I was alone in the shop, and a kerosene lamp exploded.
The breeze flared the curtains at just the right moment, and they burst
into a plume of fire. It spread to the wallpaper in seconds, and I barely

escaped with my life and my toddler, Jennie. It was terrible luck. Nobody could have moved more quickly than I did, running into the street, shouting, "Fire, fire!" I could smell the tobacco and lovely licorice candies being consumed on the shelves, but there was nothing I could do. Our little shop was a total loss, and all of our savings had gone into it.

We did have insurance to cover our investment, and they disputed my story for a short time, not finding any evidence of exploded glass. But the company was reliable and eventually paid out our deserved sum. When the money came, both of us realized we would not miss putting in all the effort to please people who could never be pleased, and that was most of our clientele. With the settlement money and some income from adoption, we were able to live and care for four more children. Between our own and adopted, I never made any difference. Nevertheless, Caroline died at five months of bowel inflammation and tiny Axel at three months of hydrocephalus. I had wondered for a time how we would continue to feed ourselves and four children with Mads now working for the railroad and bringing home twelve dollars a week. But even with two children, times were hard.

Soon, there came a chance for him to join a prospecting company, seeking gold in Alaska—a grand adventure, the answer to many prayers. We had to put up our remaining money and the deed to our home as collateral and Mads would be gone for months, but the company would pay his wages, plus thirty-five dollars for the household each month, banking interest on the mines he located, and a huge amount of stock in the corporation. He was excited about exploring that wild territory, not so different in climate from his beloved Norway. I would miss his warmth in my bed, but I felt relieved that I wouldn't have to churn over every idea and household decision with a person of lesser understanding and backbone. We were both excited about his trip, and, although the job required all our recovered money, nothing as lucrative was likely to come along with Mads's limited skills.

We waited for two months. His bag was packed when Mads discovered that there would be no gold-mining expedition. The deal was a swindle. He had no other prospects, and we needed to hire lawyers to keep from losing our home. Mads was forlorn, and his health began to deteriorate. He returned to his job as a night watchman, forever broken. I thought he might die of humiliation or kill himself rather than live in that desolate state.

Again, fire broke out, a common occurrence, this time from a defective heater, and although our house was saved, the contents were ruined. We received a settlement of 650 dollars, enough to keep us going for a while. At that time, Mads also owned a life insurance policy that would soon expire, and he decided to let it lapse and get a new one for more money. I agreed it was a good idea. When the paperwork came in for the new policy, we saw that there was an overlap of one day.

"Is that a mistake?" Mads said, pointing it out to me. "If I should happen to die on July 30th, they will pay out two-thousand dollars from the first policy and three-thousand dollars from the new one."

I took the sheet from his hand and confirmed the amounts, in ink on legal documents.

"That is more money than I could ever afford to leave for you and the children," he said.

His pale blue eyes shone with strong intention. It was a gift from God. He loved us deeply, and this was his only chance to be a good provider, the cure for his unhappiness, the money needed for his family to thrive.

JULY 30, 1900

When the day came, he awoke with a powerful headache. He could talk of nothing beyond the pain and seemed to have forgotten the significance of the date. I worried that the hours might slip by, and our gift from God would not be claimed. It began to feel like a sin to ignore God's benefaction. Mads begged for me to get him something for the headache. He was nearly out of his mind. It was not the time to remind him of insurance policies. I found the strychnine that I kept for rodents and put it into a small folded paper, such as headache remedies are sold in. He watched as I mixed it into a glass of water and drank it down fully, hoping for fast relief, not knowing that what I gave him was the cure for all pain forever. His suffering was hard to watch but brief.

After his death, the doctor concluded, from the symptoms I described, that Mads had died of a brain hemorrhage. He was buried next to our two infant children. There was a short inquiry due to the coincidence of the two policies, but my grief was not questioned. The insurance companies held their reputations and paid our just benefits.

NOVEMBER, 1901

With that sum of money, it did not take long for me to locate a suitable property for our new home. Chicago had become crowded, and I desired to move where the children could enjoy the outdoors and we could have animals, fruit trees, and crops, feed ourselves, and not be bothered by close neighbors. The farmstead in La Porte fulfilled all my dreams with its thirteen rooms and forty-eight acres of rich soil. The insurance money was ample enough to replace the flooring and brighten the interior. It was impressive, what a woman could do with money and hard labor. I raised pigs, chickens, and cows, planted apple and pear trees, and grew vegetables. I could afford to hire men but was as capable as any to do the heaviest work. Soon, the neighbors were marveling at my ability and strength.

APRIL 1, 1902

Peter Gunness, my next husband, was a Viking of a man, as certain people of La Porte liked to say, for his muscled stature, blond hair, and chiseled jaw, a fringe of beard that seemed to glow at sunset. They had only an inkling of his Viking ways, playful as a pup and randy in bed, a man who could handle my two-hundred and more pounds— when I let him—and look into my eyes from above my six-foot height. He had been an acquaintance of Mads and me a few years before. I captured his belly through my Norwegian cooking first, his heart with memories of Norway, then his eyes with my motherly bosom. Men would always fasten on that area. As a strong farm woman, I was also valued for my ability to work.

Peter was, of course, also attracted by my extensive property and the lovely two-story, red-brick farmhouse procured through good business sense, tastefully refined with polished wood and soft leather.

I had learned young how to keep a gentleman happy. "You purr like a kitten," they said. As time went on, I learned that men easily developed obsessive love for me, though they sometimes feared my physical and mental strength. Not only letting a man grunt himself to pleasure but to praise the miracles he works on a female body, delight in his ideas, and enlarge his pride—that was my secret.

Peter came to me a widower with a seven-month-old daughter, but she was frail and died of edema of the lungs only a week after our marriage.

DECEMBER 16, 1902

Peter's fateful day started as every other. I was up before the first bird, my fingers barely warmed by cows' teats, my ankles frozen in mud and pig slop. I still lacked enough time to finish the chores before sunset. I boiled up a pot of brine late in the day and left it on the stove for pickling pigs' feet the next morning.

Peter must have been half asleep when he stooped to fetch his shoes from behind the oven where he warmed them, and, while straightening, he hit the pot hard enough to splash and scald his face. I was already in bed and heard his scream. He called "Mama!" as he always referred to me. I rushed to help, and he was whimpering on the floor. He whined that his cheeks would scar and his hair fall out, vanity that I found hard to abide in a man, a "Viking." The injury did not seem severe enough to cause permanent damage; the red skin was already subsiding to pink. I had suffered far worse in my lifetime.

Peter dragged himself into the parlor and—I cannot say how— the ax was in my hand. In horror, I had watched him use it on my hogs to finish their lives quickly. I must have given him a tap, just enough to stop the flow of self-pity. He was less hard-headed than I had believed. I returned to the kitchen, knowing it was now time to plan, and saw the auger part of the heavy iron meat grinder that Peter had not pushed back on its high shelf after last use. With a slight shove, it toppled. I would name it as the culprit, imagining just how it might have bounced off his head, had the head been as hard as I once thought.

Oh, dear. Could I have imagined he fetched his shoes? I cannot be sure. Perhaps I had not gone to bed at all and tipped the cask of brine myself onto Peter's face in frustration at the sort that men are apt to cause most every day. Sometimes, it is most difficult to parse out the real from the desired, and by then I knew well that love was easier to find than money.

I set about dragging him to the kitchen near the auger and cleaning up the blood before it would become a stain on the highly polished wood for which I had paid dearly. Then I did leave him and ran to the stairs, hollering to wake Jennie, my foster daughter, now sixteen, so she could be a witness to her stepfather's demise. I sent her to the Nicholsons' farm for help and took my place beside him on the floor, caressing his cooling brow and dappling his pinkish cheek with my tears. There would be questions, and I was wary of questions but confident in my ability to answer with innocence. I would flesh out the details of the terrible scene as I had done before, with a shaking voice and the feeble manner of women often struck by the hand from which they have learned to beg. Peter had never hurt me, and, as an adult, I never begged, but my eyes were good enough to know the world and how it worked.

The inquest dragged on for most of a day, but Jennie told her story similar to mine, and the neighbor, Swan Nicholson, testified that Peter and me were "like children together." There was no evidence to support anything but an accident, though rumors persisted in town. The final judgment, it seemed, was based on the belief that women did not have the emotional control or stamina to commit such a crime.

After Peter, I learned to work the farm alone. Even in the icy winter, I cared for the animals as lovingly as for the children. They grew from plump pink and black piglets to hearty stoats and sows and recognized me as their mother. I adored the feel of their stiff bristled snouts as they nuzzled food from my hands. Since hogs were an important part of our income and food, the knowledge of what I would have to do grew more horrible and the task more daunting as their size increased. At last, when we needed meat for our table, I had no choice. The first butchering of one of my dear animals put me into bed for the rest of the day, distraught and in tears, but there was no one to lift the burden of my responsibilities and allow me to coddle myself. Nor did I want someone else in charge. I remembered the lessons of my childhood on a farm. I felt grateful there was meat to be had. Through muscle and willpower I learned the least painful method of putting down a hog with one blow. The carving afterward came more easily.

Over five years, there were many Norwegian suitors who came in response to my letters in the newspapers, but none I had any intention to marry. They arrived on the train but never left, sometimes gone from this world in a day or two. It took only a measure of strychnine and, when the clenching became intense, a dose of chloroform, all available in town. Or simply the swift blow I had learned so well. My solution was perfect on both sides: my need for money was satisfied for the time being and the men were relieved of their suffering forever.

Sometimes, I enjoyed their company, especially in the cold season when the warmth of lively flesh could end the day most pleasurably. I erred in letting time slip by sometimes. It was dangerous to let them stay long enough to become known. I recall telling the neighbor, nosy Chris Christofferson, that Olaf Limbo found a free ride to the World's Fair, in St. Louis, and he planned to buy some land around there.

Sometimes, townsfolk saw a man arrive at the station but never the means by which he left. I easily manufactured details, and, by choosing my suitors well, there were rarely close relatives to become curious. In the cases where I heard of someone who might make an inquiry, I wrote letters to the deceased suitor. I had the knack of being convincing, choosing my words as if I were dismayed and concerned with the man's absence and hoped to reunite. I told Henry Gurholt's father that Henry had gone with some horse traders to Chicago, and that the idea had been worrisome to me. I often wore the fur coat

Henry arrived in, but his father could know nothing of that, though Christofferson often brought it up to me. A gift, I told him. I did take some pleasure in my cleverness. Forty men or more enjoyed my company and went to their afterlife.

Andrew Helgelien was the man who gave me the most trouble, both living and dead. He stole my heart with his wonderful letters, but in person did not live up to his portrait, and eventually his heartiness in bed could not compete with my need for cash. His presence set Ray Lamphere into jealous outrage, which kindled more trouble. It took two blows to send Andrew on his way, and he looked me in the eye after the first swing of the ax. That I had been too taken by his lively correspondence and neglected to find out about his brother was the mistake that brought about the end of the farm.

APRIL 27, 1908

Asle Helgelien was on his way, in search of his brother Andrew, and I could put off the horror no longer. I took the children to town, and we bought supplies for a party—colorful ribbons and ingredients for pudding. I surprised them with lollipops, the newest confection. So sad that I would give way to tears, I tried not to think about the night to come. I purchased two gallons of kerosene, and Ray Lamphere carried it out to the cart for me, as was his job. Mrs. Shultz, who owns the shop with her husband, engaged me in conversation, and I mentioned Ray's most recent harassment.

"I'm afraid he's going to burn down the house with us in it," I told her.

Her face lit with fright for me.

Ray was a good enough farmhand and sweet on the mattress, but he was known as a shiftless drunk in town. It was no secret that he had been percolating with jealousy ever since the arrival of Andrew Helgelien. Ray predicted that Andrew would usurp his rightful place as my future husband and half-owner of the pig farm. He never suspected that Andrew's place would be in the ground, eventually buried by Ray himself inside a burlap sack. Pig remains, I always told him when I had him dig a new pit. That time, I had come to feel it was the truth. But Ray hinted that he knew something, and that was another reason life on the farm had to end. I felt sorry that my other hired hand, Joe Maxson, would be part of the conflagration. He was a good worker, had done no harm, and suspected nothing.

That evening, Maxson and I enjoyed some games of Snap with the children, and I did the dishes before serving dessert. I kept putting their bedtimes later. Maxson retired to his room, and the children waited for me to bring their cream pudding into the parlor. They were laughing, the two girls playing Jacob's Ladder, the boy building a house with blocks, his pink tongue showing between his lips as he concentrated. I had doctored the pudding with half a dose of what I give the men. I almost let the tray drop to the floor so that the glass and mess would be the only catastrophe that night. But the fear was too great. If I went to prison, the children would be taken somewhere as miserable.

Time passed too quickly. "Mama, tummy hurts," Phillip said. I picked him up and squeezed my face into his belly for a kiss. I took Myrtle into my arms next to him.

"Me too. I hurt all over," she said.

"Me too, my little dears," I told them. It was no lie. Mine was the pain of despair.

The oldest girl said nothing as was her way, never a complaint. I ruffled the boy's blond locks and kissed them each on the forehead. Not one was mine by birth, though I let people think so. I had given them a short but pleasant life.

"We have all eaten far too much. If we go to sleep, the pain will go away." I told them I would help them fall asleep. Sleep has always worked for gas pains, so they held their tummies and snuggled close. I hurried to put cotton pads bathed in chloroform under each one's nose in turn. When they were peaceful, I carried each to the basement. No one was fearful, which is the worst part of pain. They soon flew to heaven. I knew that I had done the best I was able by sparing them this world of unending work, cold, and punishment.

I arranged them with Esther's headless body, her arms around them, as if I were comforting them when we were trapped by the fire. I had a bed situated underneath my bedroom so when everything burned and the floor collapsed, it would seem that we had died above and our remains fallen into the heap. It was my hope that the sheriff would assume that my head was entirely burned off, at least long enough for me to disappear. There was no way to leave the gold molars that I am known for, since the bridgework is attached to my permanent teeth. Perhaps the value of gold would invite suspicion that someone had sifted through the ashes ahead of the police.

I detested the idea of my children going to heaven near the body of a stranger, but I could not do otherwise to make my death seem genuine. My dear Lucy and Myrtle. They were not hardy souls capable of inventing themselves outside of the strictures of society. They had no inner strength nor outer girth to construct a life for themselves. Likely, had they lived, they would own nothing, live as servants or slaves, the more descriptive names for wives. Nor could I kill the girls and allow Phillip to live, an orphan for a second time in his meager two years. Had I any hope at all that I could join them in heaven, I would have taken my own life.

"Asle Helgelien, bastard," I said aloud, the cause of all this death and waste. I spat, as a man might do at any moment without loss of dignity.

The two gallons of kerosene waited in the kitchen where Ray had put them that afternoon, ready for filling the lamps for the morrow that would never come. I gathered a few necessities while I waited for the wee hours so the Nicholsons would be asleep, and the fire could not be put out too quickly. It would be the time of night when Ray would return from town, drunk and in a temper to take vengeance. He was likely to be blamed for arson and murder. Although he might have loved me even more than some others, he was not as discerning in life as most of my hogs. "Belle would marry me if I had money," he had boasted, unaware of the true meaning of his statement.

APRIL 28, 4:00 A.M.

I have packed a few belongings into Esther's valise, and I carry a gunny sack containing her head to bury at a distant site. It is a tiny bag, a quick job. I set both bags and a lighted lamp outside the door while I slosh kerosene around the edges of the room and in the next room. The fumes burn my nostrils, and the taste of hell settles on my tongue. I step outside and toss the lamp. It crashes, and fire sprays across my lovely hardwood floor. All means of exit from the front go up in a whoosh.

From the edge of forest darkness, I watch the flames and choke on the smoke of my labors. The sight is hypnotic and horrendous. The back wall of my rich Indiana farmhouse falls inward, the comfy home where I spent almost seven years and buried four children ripples in front of my eyes. It is agony, yet a part of me comes alive. I will outsmart the boorish police once again and will perhaps replace the winter days of bread-baking, mending, milking, and butchering with adventure.

I check my bag for Esther Carlson's birth certificate. I allow myself one long look to be sure the area between the house and the pig pen is not going to catch. Axel and Nellie, my breeding pair and favored companions, squeal and push at the six-foot fence, nearly breaking my heart. But they are smarter than most people and will find the unlatched gate as they edge away from the heat. It has been a good year for acorns, and I have cached enough corn in the woods to help them stay fat and happy till they learn to feed themselves. A tear trails cold down my cheek. The end of many good things. I am sorry for much, now and forever, and hope this will be the end of the slaughter. I scuffle some dead leaves with my feet to obscure the spot, turn on my boot heel, and pick up my bags. The world awaits.

•••

Harold Schechter's definitive text, Hell's Princess: The Mystery of Belle Gunness, Butcher of Men, *is a lively and deeply documented history of the life and times of Gunness including the court proceedings and the profusion of interest that surrounded "Murder Farm" for many years. According to Schechter, it was never clear whether Belle escaped or burned. Neighbors claimed to have seen Belle after the fire from as close as twenty feet and recognized her face as well as her unusual figure and lumbering male gait. For many years, reported sightings persisted of Belle, real or phantom, wearing veils on trains and on the street in nearly every state, plus Canada and Mexico. That Belle had taken the identity of Esther Carlson remained a plausible theory for eighty years when finally, a search of public records in Sweden revealed that Carlson was in fact the Swedish woman she claimed to be, seemingly another far less productive black widow.*

The "Coroner's Inquisition" used in the court proceedings states that the body of sixteen-year-old Jennie Olsen, Belle's foster daughter, was discovered in a grave on the farm. Other graves held mingled remains of many unidentified men and a woman, including John Moe, Henry Gurholt, Olaf Limbo, and Ole Budsberg, all of whom had family members or neighbors who testified as to particulars of the bodies or the men's last known whereabouts and correspondence with Belle. The burned ruins of the house produced bodies identified as three-year-old Phillip, seven-year-old Lucy, and another unidentified female child, which seems to have been Myrtle. Joe Maxson was awakened by smoke at 4:15 a.m., chopped a hole in the front door, and escaped the fire. He testified as to the layout of the house and the location of the five bodies found inside.

Schechter notes that very little of the mystery was resolved. The jury believed it was Belle's body in the ruins, and Belle's head was theorized as completely burned to ash. Her body would have had to be reduced from nearly three-hundred pounds to seventy-three. The children, however, were found with their skulls attached, and a much smaller percentage of weight loss. Bridgework containing gold was sluiced out of the cinders of the house by a miner several days after the fire, but some expert testimony indicated that the bridgework could not have survived so perfectly intact if Belle's skull was incinerated. Eyewitness testimony stated that the miner pulled the bridge from his pocket instead of the sluice. The abundance of contradictory evidence and testimony leaves much open to conjecture.

Ray Lamphere was tried for murder and arson, but there was not enough evidence to convict him of murder. He was fined five-thousand dollars and sentenced to prison for arson but died of tuberculosis within a year.

"Ye Should Nae Kill":
Glasgow's Bible Bashing Serial Strangler

LEE MELLOR

The recently deceased "Moors Murderer" Ian Brady proposed that certain crimes linger in the public conscience due to "atmosphere. The mystical and sometimes almost romantic evocation of a memorable era or ethos. Plus a theatrical, dramatic setting in keeping with murder or, better still, enhancing its spine-chilling qualities." Brady observed that upon hearing the moniker "Jack the Ripper" our minds immediately populate with a foggy landscape of cobblestones, gas lanterns, clip-clopping hooves, and shadowy figures gliding through alleys filled with gin-addled whores. Though we may cringe at the notion of agreeing with a sexually sadistic child murderer, posterity reveals the cold truth of Brady's observation: when it comes to murder, place and tone often determine whether a crime is forgotten or enters the dark pantheon of cases that become the subject of popular obsession. Such features may explain why the three known sex slayings attributed to Glasgow's infamous "Bible John" linger in the popular imagination as the foremost unsolved homicides in Scottish history.

Glasgow is a bleak, industrial port in the northwest United Kingdom—a hard city that breeds hard people accustomed to drowning their despair in whiskey and lager only to have it resurface in hair-trigger acts of violence. Despite ongoing attempts at pacification through gentrification, a 2012 study by the United Nations Office on Drugs and Crime determined that the city had the highest murder rate per capita in Western Europe. This is to say nothing of broken pint glasses thrust into ruddy faces, vicious and rageful head stompings, and the abundance of non-fatal stabbings. If these were taken into account, Glasgow would likely emerge as the most historically violent European city west of the former Soviet bloc.

Following World War II, competition from the rising industrial powers of West Germany and Japan along with a series of misguided economic policy decisions in both the public and private sectors saw a devastating decline in Glasgow's manufacturing. The eminent French sociologist Émile Durkheim once wrote that when a community experiences a drastic change in economic fortune—whether a sudden influx of wealth or, in the case of Glasgow, financial downturn—there is a period of time in which members of its population come to feel alienated and without purpose, as the standards and values of the "way things were" fail to apply to their current situation. This loss of identity and guidelines leads individuals to commit suicide or, sometimes, extremely deviant forms of murder.

When the Swinging Sixties arrived in grimy Glasgow, it was like a blast of pure oxygen to a city choking on the stench of its own decay. Of course, not everyone would view sex, drugs, and rock-and-roll as a social panacea. In fact, for one young man, the "Second City of the Empire" had now become Sodom to London's Gomorrah.

...

On Thursday, February 22, 1968, twenty-five-year-old Patricia Rose Docker, a pretty brunette nurse, donned her yellow wool minidress and gray duffle coat and headed out for a night of dancing. Her husband of five years, Alex, was a Royal Air Force (RAF) corporal recently stationed in England. When Alex was assigned to RAF base Lincolnshire, Patricia and the couple's four-year-old son moved southeast to live with him, but, before long, their marriage collapsed. Patricia returned to Glasgow to live with little Alex at her parents' home at 29 Langside Place in the Battlefield district, south of the River Clyde.

Before exiting into the frigid night, she told her parents she was going to the Majestic Ballroom in Glasgow city center. Whether Patricia lied or had simply been swept along by circumstance, she ultimately ended up at the Barrowland Ballroom's "Over-twenty-fives night" on the opposite bank of the Clyde. The evening was a notorious magnet for adulterers, with casual sex occurring in the downstairs toilets, and the prospect of violence hanging over the bar like a brooding storm cloud. Nobody truly knows what happened to Patricia Rose Docker that night, only what was discovered the next morning.

Sometime before eight o'clock, Maurice Goodman, a joiner by trade, was driving to his workshop on what was then Carmichael Lane when he saw a body lying supine in his garage doorway and called for the police. Arriving on the scene, detectives from Glasgow CID (Criminal Investigation Department) noted the corpse was that of a nude white female, head turned slightly to the right. Her personal items were missing save for the wedding band still clinging to her cold stiff finger and red, high-heeled shoes scattered nearby. Without clothing to analyze for cuts or tears, there was no way for investigators to determine whether or not the victim had undressed willingly, under duress, or been forcibly stripped of her garments before or after death. Furthermore, they had no means of identifying her. Pathologist Dr. James Imrie confirmed the presence of ligature marks around her neck—most likely she was fatally strangled with a belt—along with accompanying injuries to her head and face consistent with having been kicked and punched. Glasgow CID were dealing with a homicide.

Rigor mortis had set in, but a night of heavy frost made the time of death difficult to determine, forcing Dr. Imrie to the rather conservative conclusion that the victim had been dead for a number of hours. Door-to-door inquiries revealed that, at some point in the night, a woman in the neighborhood had heard a female voice cry, "Let me go" or, "Leave me alone." A thorough search of the area yielded an important discovery: a used sanitary pad soiled with dry blood. During the autopsy, it was determined the victim was menstruating at the time of her demise. She had been raped, too, though there was an absence of semen.

Eventually, she was identified as Patricia Rose Docker—strangled to death a mere four blocks from her home. One by one, her friends, family, and acquaintances were alibied and ruled out as suspects. Patricia's grief-stricken parents informed the detectives she had gone dancing at the Majestic, inadvertently throwing the CID a red herring. After weeks of chasing this false lead, the investigators finally learned she had left the Majestic at ten thirty and headed to the Barrowland, which was open until midnight and was roughly an hour's walk or fifteen-minute drive from the crime scene. By this time, none of the staff or customers recalled having seen her. Though Patricia's bracelet, watchcase, and purse were eventually retrieved from the River Cart, a tributary of the River Clyde in Renfrew located nine miles northwest of the crime scene, the investigation soon stalled.

Eighteen months later, the killer struck again. On the evening of Saturday, August 16, 1969, thirty-two-year-old Jemima "Mima" McDonald, a single mother and resident of 15 MacKeith Street in Bridgeton—a crime-ridden wasteland of abandoned buildings east of the city center and north of the River Clyde—left her three children in the care of her sister, Margaret, and headed to the Barrowland. With her thin build and dyed brown hair, she bore a superficial resemblance to Patricia Rose Docker. When Mima didn't return home or collect her children the following day, Margaret began to feel uneasy. By Monday, she was at her wits' end. Then, rumors began circulating that some local children had stumbled across a corpse in an abandoned tenement block at 23 MacKeith Street.

Margaret went to see for herself. To her horror, Mima's semi-nude body was lying facedown in an alcove—her nylon stockings cinched around her neck. Arriving on the scene, detectives quickly concluded they had been ripped from her legs during a struggle. In an eerily familiar pattern, Mima had been repeatedly kicked and punched in the face, raped without ejaculation, then slowly murdered with an improvised ligature. Moreover, her handbag was missing, and a used sanitary pad placed beside her body. She, too, had been on her period when she unexpectedly met her end.

Fortunately, *unlike* the Docker case, the police located multiple eyewitnesses. Several patrons of the Barrowland remembered seeing Mima dancing the night away with a handsome man between the ages of twenty-five and thirty-five. Her suitor stood out from the rest of the regulars because he wore his reddish hair unfashionably short. The two had left the club together and were seen strolling along London Road toward MacKeith Street about forty minutes after midnight.

The investigators asked Lennox Patterson, a lecturer in graphic design at the Glasgow School of Art, to interview two eyewitnesses and put together a sketch of the suspect. In the late sixties, publishing images of suspects before their arrest was prohibited by Scottish law, which forced the police to file a special request with the Crown Office and Procurator Fiscal Service. To their delight and surprise, it was granted, marking the first time Edinburgh had consented to such extraordinary measures. It wasn't long before the suspect's face was plastered on newspapers and television screens all over the United Kingdom.

The hunt for the killer stepped up to a new level, including a televised police reconstruction of Mima's half-mile walk home from the Barrowland to MacKeith Street to help jog the memories of potential witnesses. While her family offered a one-hundred-pound reward for information leading to the killer's arrest, the constant police presence at the Barrowland resulted in a marked decline in business. Blue uniforms and vice, apparently, do not make good bedfellows. Yet, despite the CID's substantial efforts, the man who had murdered Patricia Docker and Jemima McDonald continued to elude them. He would reappear to claim his last known victim on Halloween in 1969.

•••

Like Patricia Docker, twenty-nine-year-old Helen Puttock was an attractive brunette married to a military man and enjoyed dancing at the Barrowland on Thursday nights. On October 30, 1969, Helen and her sister, Jeannie, left their homes in West Glasgow and went to the ballroom to let their hair down. Soon after arriving, a well-dressed man introducing himself as "John" asked Helen to dance, though he proved a rather clumsy partner.

With his short hair, suede boots, and brown suit and tie, he seemed distinctly outmoded in appearance compared to the working-class regulars who did their best to emulate the latest style with what little money they had. Though they openly snickered and mocked him, he seemed unfazed, as if he was above their plebeian opinions. And, unlike the rough and tumble crowd of 1960s Glasgow, John never drank or swore and was surprisingly chivalrous, standing whenever Helen returned to the table. Yet, despite his well-rehearsed manners, he was haughty and dismissive of Jeannie's dancing partner, a regular bloke claiming to be from the southern Glaswegian district of Castlemilk. In fact, the two couldn't be more different. Where Jeannie's partner was friendly but uncultivated with the rough hands of a laborer, Helen's John had well-manicured fingers and a silent, ornery arrogance. Several times over the course of the night, the man from Castlemilk whispered to Jeannie that he didn't trust John and suspected he was an undercover policeman. Indeed, John seemed slightly nervous, fingering a pin on his lapel to cover it up or as an unconscious tick to reassure himself.

At eleven o'clock, the foursome decided to call it a night. While they were exiting the Barrowland, Helen slotted some coins into a cigarette machine, only to discover it was broken. Determined to dislodge the packet, John grabbed the machine and shook it back and forth. When his efforts proved unsuccessful, he called over to the manager, who approached him accompanied by a bouncer. Helen and Jeannie looked on in shock as "John" sternly reprimanded the manager for the malfunction in a cavalier manner that should have resulted in a brutal beating from the Barrowland's notoriously pugnacious staff. To their surprise, the manager responded with deference, promising John he would return Helen's money if she came by to collect it the following morning.

But John's mood had taken a turn for the worse. As they stood in the crowded queue to leave the establishment, he scowled and said, "My father says these places are dens of iniquity. *They*, the management, set fire to this place to get the insurance money and done it up with the money they got." Among the commotion, Jeannie heard Helen playfully ask John where his courage came from. John offered a response and Helen appeared to shake her head in disbelief. Reaching into his coat, he quickly flashed a piece of identification, which seemed to change Helen's attitude from one of skepticism to satisfaction. Curious, Jeannie asked him if she could see it too, prompting John to tap the side of his nose and say, without a trace of humor, "You know what happens to nosy people." Now convinced that John was a policeman, Jeannie's partner bid them farewell, climbed into a taxi, and rode off into the night, never to emerge again. The remaining three decided to share a cab to the West End where Helen and Jeannie had residences in Scotstoun and Knightswood.

Riding through the Glasgow night, John's demeanor darkened further. He became visibly cold, devoid of any chivalric charm he may have shown at the Barrowland. Jeannie sensed her presence annoyed him because he thought she was coming between him and her sister. Anxious to lift the palpable tension, Jeannie began to make light conversation, offering flattering remarks and asking John about his job and where he lived. But John remained silent and cagey. Even when Jeannie raised the topic of which soccer team he supported—the rivalry between the Rangers and Celtics, reflecting Protestant versus Catholic sectarian animosity and necessitating a near-mandatory stance in Glasgow—John was dismissive, responding that he didn't care for soccer and preferred golf instead. He offered that no matter how hard he tried, he could never get a hole-in-one, though a cousin had recently managed to pull it off. At one point, he mentioned having a sister, but then seemed to wish he hadn't, trying to pass himself off as a foster child. When Jeannie asked him if he liked dancing, his disposition changed from icy to Old Testament fire and brimstone. Where he had previously declared himself agnostic and denounced religion as "claptrap," he suddenly began ranting about licentious adulteresses at the Barrowland and recounted Biblical tales of cheating wives being stoned to death. He gave references to Moses, followed by a story about a woman standing at a well. Flustered, Jeannie switched the topic.

"What do you like to do for New Year's, John?"

"I don't drink on Hogmanay." His eyes burned like twin coals. "I pray."

The taxi, which had been meandering all over the city, passed a high-rise apartment building on Kingsway as it drew nearer to Helen's home on Earl Street. Glancing at the building, once the site of a foster home, John mumbled about a family member who had worked there long ago. Seeing an opportunity to get more personal information, Jeannie again asked him about his job and residence. This time, John replied that he worked in a laboratory in Yoker, northwest of where Jeannie lived in Knightswood. Reaching into his pocket, he produced a packet of Embassy tipped cigarettes and offered one to Helen, who took it, but ignored Jeannie altogether. Jeannie pointed out his rudeness, and, when he failed to acknowledge her, made a grab for the packet. However, John was too quick and returned them to his coat without taking one for himself. *Back at the Barrowland, I thought he said he didn't smoke?* Jeannie remembered.

When the cab pulled onto Earl Street where Helen lived, John suddenly ordered the driver to drop Jeannie off at her home on Kelso Street first. Jeannie, who couldn't wait to get out of his company quickly enough, remained silent. Minutes later, the taxi arrived at the roundabout at the bottom of Kelso, and Jeannie told the cabbie she would get out there. She reasoned she would rather walk the rest of the way than let John know where she lived. Opening the car door, she wished them all a goodnight and said to Helen, "I'll maybe see you next week," before stepping onto the pavement. *That John's one of the most horrible men I've ever met in my life*, she thought as she walked home, huddled against the autumn chill. She had no idea.

•••

Helen Puttock's nude and battered body was found early the next morning near a wall in the back garden of 95 Earl Street—less than a block away from where her worried husband George sat waiting at their home on the corner of Balmoral. Leaving through the rear door at seven thirty to walk his beloved dog Smokey, resident Archibald McIntyre had been immediately led to what he initially thought was a pile of rags by the black Labrador. As he drew closer, he was shocked to realize it was a discolored female form.

"I didn't know at the time if she was dead or not, but she didn't look well," he would later tell police. "She was wearing her coat, but it had been pulled roughly up over her head. I asked her if she was okay, but she didn't reply." Filled with dread, Archie hammered on his neighbors' doors to no avail before running across the street to ring emergency services on a payphone.

An ambulance arrived on the scene with two EMTs, who quickly ascertained through rigor mortis that the woman had been dead for some hours. A stocking, later determined to be the victim's, was bound around her neck, and her torn dress and coat were discarded nearby along with a gold necklace that had been broken in the struggle. Her nose and mouth were stained with drying blood. By the time constables from the CID arrived, the crime scene had been severely compromised by curious neighbors who wanted to see what the big fuss was about. It is estimated that at least one hundred people observed the scene either by walking past or from tenement windows. The fact that none of them could identify the victim, who lived less than twenty doors down, is a testament to how brutally she had been beaten. Substantial bruising to her face made it obvious she had been viciously and repeatedly kicked and punched, with bite marks from crossed teeth embedded in her wrist. A single, inexpensive cuff link lay nearby. Most chilling was the sanitary pad tucked into her armpit. Once again, her purse was conspicuously missing, only this time a semen stain would be found on her stocking.

From examining the forensic evidence at the scene, investigators concluded the assailant and his victim had traveled to the back garden from Earl Street, though it was difficult to determine whether this had been attained consensually or through some kind of coercion. Torn tufts of grass on a railway embankment behind the area indicated the victim had fled in that direction before her attacker had caught up with her, dragging her back into the garden where the murder took place. A subsequent medical examination confirmed she, too, had been raped. The killing had occurred at least seven hours earlier. By late morning, George Puttock appeared at the scene and explained to the constables that his wife, Helen, had not returned from dancing the previous night. At last, police had a name for their victim. Following basic procedure, George Puttock was examined and cleared as a possible suspect in his wife's murder.

At least fifty members of the Glasgow police began canvassing the neighborhood for information, while the CID appealed to the general public for knowledge. The taxi driver who had driven the trio that night recalled that after he had dropped Jeannie off, he had doubled back to Earl Street and let Helen out at number 95: a curious choice, as she actually lived at 129, which was closer to Jeannie. Furthermore, this address was conveniently located at the corner of Balmoral, while 95 was farther from the intersection. The man who the cabbie had presumed was her partner, "John," had paid the fare and exited after her. He had seemed irritated with Helen for immediately walking off the moment the vehicle parked. Thinking it was simply a bickering couple, the cabbie had driven away without giving it a second thought. In the following days, other witnesses came forward with accounts from the night of the slaying. One claimed to have observed

a man with a grass-stained coat walking briskly down Dumbarton
Road. Others reported seeing a figure who fit that description step
onto the Number 6 night bus heading east on Dumbarton between
Gardner and Fortrose at two in the morning—a forty-minute walk
from 95 Earl. The man had a mark or scratch under his eye and was
visibly self-conscious about his scruffy appearance, attempting to
tuck the open cuff of his shirt sleeve into that of his jacket. He had
stepped off the bus at the corner of Dumbarton and Derby about ten
minutes later.

The patrons of the Barrowland, estimated to be three hundred in
total on the night in question, were a priceless source of information.
Though it was difficult to know for certain, the police believe
they interviewed about 95 percent of them. One notable omission
was the man claiming to be from Castlemilk who had suspected
"John" of being a policeman. Whether he had been cheating on his
wife or feared some other repercussion from coming forward, he
never volunteered himself to the police, placing them at a major
disadvantage. Not only had he observed John in great detail, but he
had also conversed with him. The only witness better positioned to
provide useful information was Helen's sister, Jeannie. Having spent
much of the night with John, including the long, foreboding taxi ride
home, the account she gave to the investigators was revelatory. To
quote Detective Joe Beattie, with whom she spoke extensively and
repeatedly: "Jeannie's recollection of events was incredible, from the
overlapping teeth the man had, to the way he acted and dressed. It was
clear that the man we wanted was someone who held some authority,
but in what form? That could be a doctor, minister, a fireman, a
soldier, or a sailor. It may even be a cop. We had no clue what we
were looking for. It was going to be a matter of elimination." Drawing
upon Jeannie's description, the investigators rendered an improved
drawing of the killer.

Glasgow Police held a press conference and on November 4, 1969—four days after Helen's murder—the *Glasgow Herald* soon published an article with the headline " 'Bible Quoting' Man Sought by Murder Hunt Police." It described the suspect as "between 25–30, 5 ft. 10 ins. to 6 ft. tall, of medium build with slight auburn reddish hair, styled short and brushed to the right. He has blue-gray eyes, nice straight teeth with one tooth on the upper right jaw overlapping the next tooth, fine features, and is generally of smart modern appearance. He is dressed in brownish, flecked single-breasted suit, the jacket of which has three or four buttons and high lapels. There are no turn ups on the trousers and the suit is in a modern style. He has a knee-length brownish coat of tweed or gabardine, a light-blue shirt and a dark tie with red diagonal stripes. He was wearing a wristwatch with a broad leather strap of military style. He may smoke Embassy tipped cigarettes. He is known to go to Barrowland on occasions and is thought to go alone. The man is thought to be called by the Christian name John. He may speak of being one of a family of two, his sister and himself, and of having had a strict upbringing and make references to the Bible. He is quite well spoken, probably with a Glasgow accent and does not appear to be engaged in heavy manual work. He may have marks on his face and hands of recent origin."

As months of investigation passed without any substantial leads, the media became increasingly involved in the hunt for the killer, at one point even turning to famed psychic Gerard Croiset, who predictably proved to be totally useless. In another attempt, after airing a half-hour special on the killings, reputable BBC journalist Hugh Cochrane appealed directly to the perpetrator to come forward and quoted Jeremiah 23:24 in a vain attempt to use his religiosity against him. In 2019, the fifty-year anniversary of the final killing, the only name we have to put to the man who raped and strangled Patricia Rose Docker, Jemima McDonald, and Helen Puttock was coined by a local newsman, John Quinn, in the weeks following the third slaying: "Bible John."

Interview with a Serial Killer

JAMES YOUNG

Today, Tiago Henrique Gomes da Rocha, the *"Maníaco de Goiânia,"* is in the Aparecida de Goiânia Complex in the metropolitan area of the hot and dusty city of Goiânia of Midwestern Brazil. I have never been to the jail, so I do not know what it looks like. But I can imagine. I have seen other penitentiaries in Brazil and watched news reports of the chronic overcrowding, degrading, unsafe conditions, and riots and murder that are rife in the country's prison system. In 2018, a disturbance in the Aparecida de Goiânia Complex left nine dead and fourteen wounded, while fifty-six prisoners died in a prison riot in the city of Manaus, in the heart of the Amazon, in 2017. In 2013, inmates cut off the heads of a number of murdered rivals at the Pedrinhas prison in the state of Maranhão, in the north of Brazil.

Thirty-one-year-old Gomes will have plenty of time to get used to the conditions. To date, he has been sentenced to more than six-hundred years in prison for the murder of twenty-nine people. His usual *modus operandi* was to pull up alongside his victims on his motorbike, take out his gun, and shoot them, normally at point-blank range. Most were women, and sometimes he would shout "Robbery!" and show his gun to make them come closer. After pulling the trigger he would ride off, blending quickly into the traffic—anonymous among the thousands of other motorbikes that swarm the streets of Goiânia, invisible behind his helmet and visor.

I met him in October 2014, a few days after he was caught by police.

●●●

It is hard to know when it begins. And so it is hard to know how to tell this story.

When he was arrested, Gomes, a hospital security guard, confessed to thirty-nine murders. The first was sixteen-year-old Diego Martins Mendes in 2011. According to Gomes, the two met at a Goiânia bus terminal and went into the woods to have sex before he was overcome with rage and strangled the boy. But Diego's body has never been found, and, in 2018, a judge cleared Gomes of the murder. It is a little like Schrödinger's cat—Diego may or may not be dead, and Gomes may or may not have killed him.

Between 2011 and 2014, Gomes says he killed a number of homeless people and prostitutes. One was twenty-two-year-old Thiago Fernandes de Carvalho who, on December 11, 2012, was shot twice in the head while sleeping rough on the corner of Avenida Independência and Rua 44 in downtown Goiânia. Another was Marcos Aurélio Nunes da Cruz, aged thirty-four, who was sleeping near a supermarket in the Setor Coimbra district of the city when he was murdered. In March 2014, twenty-year-old *garota de programa* (or prostitute) Taís Pereira de Almeida was shot and killed in Aparecida de Goiânia. Gomes has been convicted of all three murders. No Schrödinger's cat here.

Or perhaps a whisker. Because, at the time, no one paid much attention to the murders of Thiago, Marcos, or Taís apart from their friends and families, if they had any. There are more than fifty-thousand murders in Brazil every year, and, at the end of 2018, there were over eighty-thousand registered missing person cases. Less than 10 percent of murders are ever solved by police, while most homicides barely warrant more than a paragraph or two in the back pages of the newspapers or a few seconds on the local TV news. Or perhaps they'll flash up on the gory teatime crime shows, often accompanied by footage of a blood-spattered corpse or two, as the presenter bellows "*Que país é esse?*" ("What kind of a country is this?"). Then they'll disappear from view, the files left to gather dust in a forgotten storeroom, almost as if the murders had never happened at all. In a town like Goiânia, who was going to care about or even notice a few homeless people or prostitutes getting killed? Other than those close to them, no one was going to remember the victims or how they died for very long.

Not many paid much attention either when seventeen-year-old student Ana Rita de Lima was killed on December 13, 2013, a block from her home in the neighborhood of Vila Santa Tereza. According to witnesses, the killer approached on a black motorbike, grabbed her by the arm, told her she was being robbed, then shot her and fled. Police worked on the hypotheses that the murder was connected to the girl's boyfriend, who a witness claimed had a reputation for violence, or a dispute between local soccer hooligan gangs, or *torcidas organizadas*, with whom Ana Rita was rumored to be involved. Neither they nor the public would have held out much hope that the case would ever be solved.

Even when fifteen-year-old schoolgirl Ana Karla Lemes da Silva was shot and killed by a man on a black motorbike in the Setor Jardim Planalto region of the city a few days later, residents of Goiânia would likely have read about the killing on their phones, computers or in their newspapers, given a collective shrug, and flicked back to Facebook, the soccer scores, or the latest political corruption scandal.

And who can blame them? Most murders in Brazil involve poor young black men from the *favelas* or the shabby *periferias* of the country's big cities, who are often involved with or victims of violent drug trafficking gangs. But femicide is rife too—a report in 2019 by the Inter-American Commission on Human Rights said that four women are killed in Brazil every day. In a place like this, who would even notice a serial killer?

It is hard to connect the dots when there are so many of them.

•••

That black motorbike, though. Was it a clue? Did it make Gomes more or less identifiable?

Motorbikes—most of them black—are everywhere in Brazilian cities. Dozens rev their engines like furious insects at every red light or buzz between lanes of stationary traffic, enraging drivers trapped in their cars. Motorbikes are cheap. Motorbikes can negotiate the winding lanes of the *favelas* and the narrow alleys of the ramshackle working-class suburbs. Motorbikes deliver takeaway meals, documents, pet food. *Motoboy* is a job for hundreds of thousands of Brazilians, while moto-taxis proliferate in many smaller towns.

But motorbikes are something else too. Motorbikes are dangerous. Not just for the riders, though they're that too. *Assaltos* are carried out by boys with guns on motorbikes. Motorbikes allow fast getaways. To the untrained eye, most motorbikes look the same, especially the black ones. On a motorbike, you can wear a helmet and visor, making you invisible. Motorbikes are suspicious. A friend of mine in the chaotic, often violent city of Recife in the northeast of Brazil was once an hour late to meet me. After he apologized, he told me that he hadn't been able to find the bar and that people had edged nervously away when he stopped to ask for directions—because it was night, he was black, and he was on a motorbike.

My ex-girlfriend was shot from a motorbike. She was hit in the wrist and chest but survived. The friend she was with didn't. The bike pulled up beside them, and the boy riding pillion pulled out a gun and opened fire. Then the bike sped off. The riders would never be caught. It was a drugs-gang thing, though my ex-girlfriend wasn't involved. Still, because she was a witness to the murder of her friend and of her boyfriend, who was shot and killed a few weeks later, both of whom *were* involved, she had to get out of town fast. So she came to stay with me for a few months. For a while, she would flinch every time she heard the whine of a motorbike engine behind her. But, after a while, she got over it. People usually do in Brazil. There isn't much else you can do. Eventually, she started dating a guy. He rode a motorbike.

•••

The killing in Goiânia continued. On a Saturday afternoon in January 2014, fourteen-year-old Bárbara Luíza Ribeiro was waiting for her grandmother on a bench in a square in the lower middle-class neighborhood of Lorena Park on a Saturday afternoon when a black motorbike stopped alongside her. She may have thought the rider was lost and looking for directions. Or, as in the case of Ana Rita de Lima, perhaps he pretended it was a mugging. She may have prepared herself, with a resigned mental sigh, to give up her few possessions— an inexpensive cell phone, a few *reais.* But she would not escape so cheaply. The killer shot her in the chest and rode off.

In 2016, Gomes was convicted of Bárbara's murder and sentenced to twenty years. By then he'd been found guilty of killing Ana Rita and Ana Karla too.

•••

In October 2014, I am living in the Brazilian city of Belo Horizonte, around nine-hundred miles from Goiânia. I have been in Brazil for nine years—teaching English, translating, writing, doing a little journalism. In July, I write an article for an American news site about a series of unsolved killings by a man on a motorbike in Goiânia, where I once lived for a year. At this stage, there have been more than a dozen seemingly similar murders of young women in around seven months. But the police remain skeptical about the existence of a serial killer, citing discrepancies in witness descriptions of the killer's motorbike, clothes, and physique. Plus, well, this is Brazil. You don't get serial killers here. Not many, anyway. Fifty thousand murders a year, sure. But serial killers? Not so much.

But the murders keep coming. There is twenty-three-year-old Beatriz Cristina Oliveria Moura, who is shot and killed the day after Bárbara Luíza Ribeiro as she walks to the *panadaria* to buy bread.

There is Lílian Sissi Mesquita e Silva, a twenty-eight-year-old housewife murdered as she goes to collect her young children from school on February 3, 2014.

There is parliamentary assistant Ana Maria Victor Duarte, gunned down in front of her fiancée and a friend at a snack bar in March. And Wanessa Oliveira Felipe, shot in the back in a drugstore on a warm night in April.

All by a man on a motorbike.

There are others too.

By now, people have begun to notice that a lot of young women are being killed in Goiânia. In August, angry street demonstrations are held to protest against the lack of progress the police are making.

"We don't believe there's a policy to beat the violence in Goiás [the state of which Goiânia is capital]. On the contrary, there's a culture of murder gangs…[killing] homeless people, teenagers, women involved with drugs, young black men, and now these young women…with no explanation given by the Public Security Department," announces Kelly Gonçalves, the leader of a Goiás women's organization.

Understandably, the frustration is greatest among the friends and families of the victims. "We go to the police station, and it's always the same answer—we have no leads, we have no suspect. The investigation is ongoing. But he's already killed fifteen. What kind of an investigation is that?" a distraught Carlos Eduardo Valczak, Lílian Sissi's husband, rages in the Brazilian media.

Eventually the police announce that a special task force will be formed to investigate seventeen potentially related crimes that occurred that year—the murders of fifteen young women, plus one attempted murder, and the killing of a male store owner.

All by a man on a motorbike.

•••

On Friday, October 17, I am at home in Belo Horizonte when I get an email from an editor at a British tabloid newspaper. She says the paper's regular correspondent is out of the country, and they need someone to cover a story in Goiânia, where a hospital security guard called Tiago Henrique Gomes da Rocha has been arrested and has confessed to killing thirty-nine people, mostly women. It is not a newspaper known for its in-depth foreign coverage. But everybody loves a good serial killer story.

I fly to Goiânia and meet up with Micheli, a Brazilian freelance photographer hired by the paper. We visit some of the spots where the women were killed, and I interview relatives of the victims and the detectives involved in the investigation. We spend a day at the squat, bunker-style holding center where Gomes is kept following his arrest. Not long after he is caught, he tries to commit suicide in his cell by cutting his wrists with a broken light bulb. But the cops on duty stop him before he can bleed out, and medical assistance is called to help him. The desk sergeant shows us the photos of Gomes' slashed bloody wrists on his iPad and lets Micheli take pictures of them.

Just as we are preparing to leave the station, Gomes's lawyer, Thiago Huascar, struts past us in the reception area with the swagger of a subtropical Saul Goodman. One of the cops tells him who we are and mentions the paper we are working for. Huascar suggests an interview.

"He [Gomes] wants to be famous," he chirrups from behind large sunglasses. "He's done his research. He thinks he's fourth on the list of Brazilian serial killers."

"Okay," I say.

"He's crazy," Huascar mutters under his breath, before disappearing into the secure area beyond the reception desk. Behind his sunglasses I imagine him winking.

I look at Micheli. She shrugs.

We hear Huascar greeting his client in the cells.

"How's it going, Big Tiago?" he shouts.

Soon after this Huascar will remove himself from the case, allegedly because of a dispute over legal fees.

•••

Not far from Lorena Park, where Bárbara Luíza Ribeiro was killed, lies Rua Potengi, a quiet, slightly scruffy street in the Goiânia suburb of Goiá. It is a neighborhood like many in the Brazilian *periferia*, as such lower-class urban areas are known—small, shabby houses hidden behind graffiti-splattered walls, cracked pavements, the whiff of an ancient urban drainage system. On the main drag, there are grimy bars, auto repair shops and building supply stores. Somewhere the musical staple of the Brazilian Midwest, *sertaneja*, a sickly sweet variant of country music, booms from a car stereo.

On January 28, 2014, ten days after Bárbara's death, Arlete dos Anjos Carvalho, a fourteen-year-old schoolgirl, is gunned down by a passing motorcyclist as she walks home.

"They [the police] asked us if she was involved in prostitution. They never once came to our house to ask us what we thought," Rita Carvalho, Arlete's stepmother, tells me when I visit the family in a sprawling, unfinished lot of government-built houses in the small town of Goianira, just within the limits of the Goiânia metropolitan area. The tiny white houses float like islands amid a sea of rust-colored earth. The family moved here shortly after Arlete was murdered.

Who was going to care about a few homeless people or prostitutes getting killed?

"She loved dancing. She had music playing in her room night and day," Rita says in the living room of the boxy family home, under a glaring fluorescent light. The room is dominated by an enormous portrait of her stepdaughter and a giant TV.

"She was so beautiful," says Raimunda, Arlete's grandmother. "Now she'll be beautiful forever, up there with God."

"I just want to speak to him once," says Francisco, the girl's father, in a resigned, quiet voice. "So I can ask him why he did it. Just like any father would do."

And then, it is time to go. As we drive away toward Goiânia, bumping across the unpaved roads of the lot, I look back and see Arlete's family silhouetted in the doorway, silently watching our taillights fade into the sweltering night. And I think of Gomes on his black motorbike, disappearing among all the other black motorbikes in Goiânia. Just as his victims would disappear among all the other murder victims in Brazil. Remembered, like Arlete, only by their friends and families.

•••

Ana Lídia Gomes is the last of Gomes's victims before he is caught. She is fourteen years old. She is killed on August 2, 2014, in the Goiânia suburb of Morada Nova as she waits for a bus to take her to an arts and crafts fair where she is planning to help her mother with the family stall. Police security cameras film her walking down a street toward the bus stop, followed shortly afterward by a black motorbike. In the video, the sun is so bright that the street appears to have been bleached white. A few moments later, the same bike is seen traveling at speed in the opposite direction. Ana Lídia is already dead.

But before Ana Lídia, there is twenty-four-year-old Janaína Nicácio de Souza, killed in a bar in the Jardim America neighborhood on May 8. And on the same day, Bruna Gleycielle de Sousa Gonçalves, murdered as she waits at a bus stop on her way home from work.

There is fifteen-year-old Carla Barbosa Araujo, who is shot and killed on May 23, 2014, as she sits on a park bench with her sister. A few weeks after that, there is Isadora Aparecida Candida dos Reis, also fifteen and a keen practitioner of the Brazilian martial art of *capoeira*, who is murdered as she walks home with her boyfriend.

There are others too. There always are in Brazil.

•••

It is not easy to get permission to interview a serial killer in a police jail cell. For days now, Brazilian TV crews have been camped outside the station, trying to get access to Gomes.

"The prosecutor's office has banned any more media appearances," says Eduardo Prado, the police chief on the task force that eventually caught Gomes. It is the day after I speak to Huascar, and we are sitting in Prado's office. A large, leather-bound Bible dominates the detective's desk.

But it is also a lot easier than it possibly should be.

"Just let me call my boss and see if we can make an exception," the jowly, jocular Prado says, winking. And after a lengthy phone call, his boss says yes. Goiânia, which is a long way from Brazil's media hotbeds of Rio de Janeiro and São Paulo, appears a little starstruck by all the attention it is getting.

Then, we wait for Gomes to make himself presentable. It is mid-morning, and the temperature outside is rising. The heat in Goiânia is stifling, suffocating, and energy-sapping. It makes everything—including talking and sometimes even thinking—slow and difficult, and gives things a soporific, even dreamlike quality.

"He's very vain," explains Prado. "He asked for a comb to fix his hair, and a nice shirt. He said he wants to look good for the photos. He wanted to have a shave too, but we drew the line there, ha-ha!"

"Ha-ha," I say.

Prado says Gomes becomes tense and angry around women and demands that they leave the room before he speaks. So Micheli ties back her hair and puts on a baseball cap. We wait for a few minutes more, and then—suddenly and without any kind of a fanfare—Gomes is led slowly into the room by four beefy, heavily armed cops in flak jackets. He sits on a chair in front of Prado's desk and stares into the middle distance. The "Maníaco de Goiânia," local journalists will eventually christen him. But Gomes doesn't seem much like a maniac. Rather, he looks like a doughier, less-chiseled version of Ben Affleck, although Ben Affleck isn't usually surrounded by four gun-toting Brazilian cops when he gives interviews.

He looks around the room, his eyes flickering from face to face, object to object, never resting on one thing for long.

"No filming," he says.

"Tiago! I told you, didn't I? No film cameras," Prado chirrups. "Don't you trust me? You have to trust the police!" As he speaks, he thrusts his hands forward, palms outward, in a gesture of mock innocence.

Eventually, Gomes is satisfied there are no cameras in the room. But he is still not happy.

"Too many people in here," he says.

"Do you mean women?" says Prado.

"It's got nothing to do with that," mumbles Gomes.

Nonetheless, there is a shuffling among the group of police officers clustered near the door, and a number of people leave the room.

Finally, Tiago Henrique Gomes da Rocha, the Goiânia serial killer, is ready to talk. And the first thing we talk about is films.

"What movies do you like, Tiago? I like *Gone with the Wind*. What about cop movies? *Die Hard*? *Rambo*?" asks Prado, presumably to break the ice. Like you might do at a party, or to start a sales pitch.

Everyone in the room laughs.

"That one. *Die Hard*," says Gomes. He is softly spoken and polite. When he speaks, he makes eye contact for a brief second before his gaze slides away to the floor or the walls, as though he is shy or nervous.

"What about *Halloween*?" Prado suggests. "What's that other one...*Saw*? You like crazy movies, don't you, Tiago?"

His tone is humorous, almost goading.

"No," Gomes says, looking down at the floor. "I've got pretty eclectic tastes."

It could be a conversation in a bar or café anywhere in the world. If it wasn't so awkward and stilted. And if it wasn't for the armed cops.

•••

By the time of Ana Lídia's death, rumors of a serial killer roaming the streets have begun to sweep across Goiânia. Suddenly, even a city as inured to violence as this becomes paralyzed by fear. There are stories of women taking taxis, rather than walking, from the gates of their workplace or university to their cars parked just a few hundred yards away or arranging their hair into ponytails to avoid attracting the attention of the killer (most of Gomes's victims had long hair).

The city's usually bustling bars and restaurants fall silent as people, terrified at the prospect of becoming the motorcycle murderer's next victim, elect to stay indoors.

"Sales are down," saleswoman Cristina Ribeiro tells Brazilian TV. "I used to meet clients in the evening, but now no one wants to go out at night. It's too dangerous."

"I say a prayer every time I walk to the gym. It's terrifying, especially as the last murder was nearby," says journalist Kamila Borges Fabino, who lives just three streets away from where Ana Lídia was murdered.

The buzz of a motorbike, once a familiar part of Goiânia's aural backdrop, becomes a sinister, even terrifying sound. "For me, any one of them could be a suspect," says civil servant Luciene Ferreira, forty-four, adding that she no longer allows her thirteen-year-old daughter to go out at night.

"People's behavior has changed," says bus conductor Gean Carlos dos Santos, owner of a black motorbike like the one used in the murders. "When I pull up alongside a car, I notice people close their windows and lock their doors."

That black motorbike again.

•••

In Prado's office, the air-conditioning wheezes manfully, but it can do little against the oppressive afternoon heat. Gomes talks in a soft, flat monotone, adding to the sleepy mood. I feel that if I close my eyes, I could drift away, perhaps to dream, though of what I do not know.

"I had a normal childhood," Gomes is saying. "Like any kid. But then I was [sexually] abused by a neighbor, twice, when I was eleven. He threatened to kill me if I told anyone. I was living with my grandparents at the time. There was no one I could tell."

No one says anything for a while. It is as though no one wants to consider that Gomes, too, might have suffered in some way. That he might deserve our sympathy.

"What happened after that? What changed inside you?" I ask. Or at least I think I do. I can hear my voice saying the words. But it feels like someone else is speaking.

"I felt...like nothing," Gomes says. "Empty. That was when everything started."

I nod as though I understand. As though "everything" means losing your temper every now and again, rather than shooting dozens of people.

Gomes says he was bullied at school, perhaps because of his quietness and his air of isolation. Predictably he says he didn't have many friends, even when he left school and started working.

Someone in the room (I am not sure who) asks him what he used to do in his free time—presumably meaning before his hobby became killing people.

"I drank," says Gomes. "I started slowly, but then it got worse."

"Where did you drink?" I ask him. "At home or in bars?" Again—it may be the heat, or the fact that I am interviewing a serial killer—I experience a slight out-of-body sensation, as though I am watching myself from above or listening to a recording of myself. But I feel it is important to picture Gomes when he went from law-abiding citizen to killer. Was he pacing back and forth in the rooms of the small, modest house where he lived, muttering to himself, clenching and unclenching his fists? Would he throw beer cans at the wall? Or was he sitting in bars, staring balefully at the smooching couples and the boisterous groups of friends or gazing sullenly at the glistening, cheesy, deadening world of the *sertaneja* singers on the TV? I want to find some kind of connection with something I know. And if you have lived in Brazil for nine years, the chances are you know Brazilian bars pretty well.

"Mostly in bars," says Gomes. "Sometimes at the gas station."

This I can picture—the yellow plastic chairs and tables, the ice-cold, 600 ml beer bottle, its brown glass frosted from the fridge. The small *copo americano* glasses. Or glass, in Gomes's case, for he was always alone.

"Were you drinking the first time you killed someone?" I ask.

"Yes," says Gomes. He sits with his legs wide apart and his arms folded in what, in a different setting, might be a relaxed pose. But even here, with the hands of the cops around us never straying far from their guns, he gives little sense of threat or danger. He looks not so much like a crazed killer as a minor guest caught uncomfortably in the background of a family wedding snap.

•••

Gomes grew up in a quiet street in Vera Cruz, another working-class neighborhood of Goiânia where, like much of the city, the cracked and pitted streets and sidewalks are stained with the rust-colored earth of the Brazilian Midwest. He was raised by his mother and, when she was out working as a cleaner, by his grandmother. It is a common enough arrangement in Brazil, where fathers are often absent and mothers are forced to work long hours to make ends meet.

"He didn't talk much, but he was polite," says Carmen Costa, a neighbor, as she sits outside her house, hoping for a cool breeze to relieve the suffocating afternoon heat. "He went to work early and came home late. I almost died of fright when I found out it was him."

Another neighbor, forty-two-year-old Maria Rosa, agrees. "There was one day when we both left for work at the same time," she remembers, as the dusty fronds of tired-looking palm trees rattle above our heads. " 'Somebody has to work, I suppose,' I said as a joke. But then he followed me to the street corner. I felt pretty nervous," she adds, staring at the bars of the intimidating gray gate in front of Gomes's home.

•••

Eventually, the conversation in Prado's office turns to the murders themselves. Gomes says he experienced feelings of tremendous anger since he was abused at the age of eleven. But what changed between then and his first murder in 2011, apart from the heavy drinking? Why did he go so long without killing anyone and then embark on his murder spree?

"I had this anger inside me," he says. "And I was very alone…I started thinking crazy things…eventually you reach a point…

you're scared…but you have no choice, you have to do it…you have to risk it."

All of his answers are given in the same flat monotone, as though he is paying for bread at the local *padaria.* As though he is thinking about something else, something more important. The questions come thick and fast from everyone in the room—Prado, Micheli the photographer, occasionally one of the policemen standing guard. It is the Brazilian way, to all talk at once, to keep things moving, to avoid the dread of silence—even if the conversation is about serial killers and dead girls and women. I worry that Gomes, intimidated, will clam up under the barrage of questions, but he keeps talking, even if his answers are short.

"But there are other ways to control that type of frustration, aren't there? Like doctors and psychologists?" I ask him.

"I never tried them," mutters Gomes.

"There are people who smash things up, break a plate, that kind of thing. When I'm stressed, I shoot at the ceiling. I don't like my neighbors much. Ha ha," jokes Prado. "Why did you have to kill people?"

"The way things are in society today…people just think about themselves, no one helps anyone," says Gomes, his eyes flicking from one side of the room to the other.

"Were you disgusted by society?" asks Prado.

"Yes," says Gomes.

"And did you feel rejected by society?" asks Prado.

"Maybe," says Gomes.

Throughout the interview, Prado's large black Bible squats on his desk. Gomes is on record as having said that he sometimes went to church. I ask him if he believes in God.

"Yes, I believe in God. But the force inside me was bigger than my faith," he says.

Did he ever think about the consequences of his actions in religious terms?

"Of course. But only God can judge me. Only he knows what was going on inside me," he mutters.

It is a recurring theme in Gomes's discourse—I was abused; there was a force within me, an anger I could not control; only God knows what went on inside me. In other words, it's not really my fault—I am ill, or driven by forces greater than myself. I ask him if he feels he is a victim in any way.

He nods his head. "Yes," he says.

A rare silence settles over the room. People do not like it, it seems, when a mass murderer describes himself as a victim.

•••

According to Prado, God played a big part in Gomes's capture too.

Though before we get to that, he explains that denying the existence of a serial killer was always part of the police's plan.

"We told the public that we didn't think there was a serial killer at work, because we didn't want to create panic or drive him underground," he says. "But we knew the same man was responsible for all the murders. And we knew we had to catch him."

I am not sure I believe him, though of course I have no reason not to.

According to the detective, the killer's eventual capture was down to herculean efforts on the part of the task force. "The same man was described as robbing six drugstores," he explains. "Witnesses said he was very cool and collected, had a penetrating stare, and didn't shout. There was video footage for three of the robberies, and, each time, the thief was dressed in black, with a black rucksack and helmet."

That description fit with security camera footage and eyewitness descriptions of a number of the murders as well as that of a man filmed stealing a motorbike number plate in a supermarket car park— it later transpired that Gomes would replace the license plate of his motorcycle with those stolen from other bikes to avoid detection by security cameras.

The police say they spoke to more than two hundred witnesses of the murders and robberies, and analyzed 576 license plates, fifty-thousand photographs of traffic infractions, and more than three-hundred hours of security-camera footage. Eventually, they believed they knew what the killer looked like and even carried out posture analysis exams to ensure the man caught on camera was the same each time. But, as he was using stolen license plates, there seemed little chance of finding him in a city that is home to over 1.4 million people and thousands of motorbikes.

That was where God came in, according to Prado.

"Eventually, we got all the 120 officers involved in the investigation together and decided to pray together, to ask for God's help," he says softly. "We finished our meeting at 19:40 on October 14. Ten minutes later, the first car to leave the station on patrol called in and said they'd seen a man who looked like our suspect."

When he was pulled over, Gomes immediately confessed to the murders of the young women. But he didn't stop there. By the time he had finished talking, he had admitted to a total of thirty-nine murders, making him one of Brazil's most prolific ever serial killers.

•••

It was the murders of the young women in 2014, rather than the homeless people, which attracted media and public attention and eventually forced the police to act. As a result, much has been made of his attitude toward the opposite sex.

"People say you have problems with women, that you don't like them," I say to him.

"I think I have a kind of mental block," he says. "I find it difficult to talk to them."

A former lover of Gomes, who had lived with her husband in the house in front of the killer's home, spoke to Brazil's *Folha de São Paulo* newspaper about their relationship. "He was quiet and shy in bed," she said. "He would ask me to go more slowly." Obviously, then, Gomes is not a virgin and has had girlfriends in the past. Yet the police and the newspapers say he acts in an uncomfortable, even hostile, manner around women.

"No, that's not true," says Gomes.

"Still, you always killed women. In one of the murders, in a bar, there were both men and women there. And you killed the woman. Why always women?" asks Prado.

"Maybe it's because of the mental block I have with them," says Gomes.

"Were you rejected by women when you were younger? It happens a lot, and it can piss you off, especially when you see your friends picking up girls," asks Prado.

Gomes doesn't answer.

"Were you ever violent with women in the past?" questions Prado, pursuing the issue.

"I'm not that kind of person," snaps Gomes, anger flashing in his eyes. It is the first time he has shown any kind of emotion.

"Of course, of course," soothes Prado. "Only when you're angry, right. You're a good guy, Tiago."

"I'm not a violent person," says Gomes, insistently, almost pleadingly.

It is Micheli the photographer who comes up with perhaps the most pertinent question of this long, hot afternoon.

"How do you feel about everything that's happened?" she asks Gomes.

There is a long pause.

"I regret everything," Gomes says eventually, staring impassively at the wall behind Prado. "I want to ask forgiveness."

"And if you were somehow forgiven," says Prado, "and were released, do you think you could control yourself?"

"With help, maybe I could," says Gomes.

"Many serial killers don't feel regret and are described by the media as monsters," I say. "Are you like that? Or do you think you're a normal person who ended up on the wrong path?"

"I don't know," says Gomes. "When I committed the crimes, I went blank…it was like I'd already left the place I was in."

"Like someone else was in your body?" asks Prado.

"Yes," says Gomes, so quietly that he is almost whispering.

"Did you ever cry?" asks Micheli.

"Yes," says Gomes, staring down at the floor. "When I got home, afterwards."

I decide to ask him about his suicide attempt following his arrest.

"You tried to kill yourself in your cell a few days ago," I say. "How did you get to that point?"

"By thinking about what I'd done," comes the answer, in the same dull, flat monotone.

"People say you're a serial killer, Tiago. Do you consider yourself to be a serial killer?" asks Prado.

"I don't know. I was just being myself, doing what felt natural," says Gomes.

"And the future, Tiago?" I ask him. Our time is almost up, and I experience a growing sense of relief. "Would you do it again? What lies ahead for you?"

"I just want to know what's wrong with me," he mutters, before he is led back to the darkness of his cell, his head bowed, making eye contact with no one.

•••

It is something he will have plenty of time to ponder. In the years following his arrest, Gomes has been found guilty in twenty-nine of the trials he has faced. In most of the cases, he was given twenty or more years in jail, making his total sentence over six hundred years.

God came up again at one of the first trials, for the murder of Janaína Nicácio de Souza, the young woman murdered in a bar in May 2014. In a letter to the presiding judge, Gomes wrote, "Knowing thyself is perhaps our greatest challenge," before going on to describe state of mind when committing some of the murders. "At times I would go out drunk, and really hyped-up. After I saw the victim, it was as though I had gone blind, and I only regained consciousness when I was making my escape."

The main point of the letter, however, seemed to be to ask forgiveness from his victims' loved ones. "Today I ask for the pardon of the families I have hurt, if it is what God wants," wrote Gomes.

On the day of his transfer from the holding center to prison, he lashed out and kicked a newspaper photographer, despite being surrounded by heavily armed guards. And upon arrival at the jail, according to police, he shouted out that he was going to kill his fellow prisoners. Unsurprisingly, this was met with reciprocal threats from the inmates. Since then, however, he has shown no further signs of aggression. "He follows a normal routine. He eats and he goes out in the yard for some sun for a while. He is being monitored by psychologists and hasn't displayed any aggressive behavior," prison manager Leandro Ezequiel told the Brazilian media around the time Gomes was incarcerated.

In September 2018, the Brazilian media reported that Gomes planned to marry twenty-one-year-old Jéssica Alves dos Santos, an inmate in the women's wing of the Aparecida de Goiânia prison. At the time the story broke, the two had not met in person—Jéssica, jailed for the 2016 armed robbery of Uber driver Lindimar Ferreira Santos, during which Santos was stabbed and died, is one of dozens of women who have sent Gomes love letters during his time in prison.

Everybody loves a good serial killer story.

The wedding has yet to take place, with prison authorities citing administrative issues.

•••

A few things happen after the interview with Gomes. Spotting the Bible on Prado's desk, Micheli asks him if he is a man of faith. Prado confirms that he is. Micheli asks him if he would like to join her in a prayer to give thanks to God for giving them their health, their safety, and allowing them to do their work. Prado says that he would. They stand together in the middle of the room, not far from where Gomes has been sitting, surrounded by records of murder. Then, clutching each other's hands, they pray fervently and loudly while I sit with my head bowed, thinking about how much I would like to get out of the station.

I go back to the hotel and file my story. The copy editor at the British tabloid seems to like it, though she is not so happy with Micheli's photos of the police station and Gomes.

"What's wrong with them?" I ask.

"Well, normally we like our reporters to get in the photo with the people in the story. You know, to show they were really there," she replies.

"Right," I say. "So you mean I should have got in the photo with Gomes?"

"Yes," says the editor. "Was that not possible?"

"I should have got in a photo with a serial killer surrounded by heavily armed police guards?" I say.

"Yes," says the editor. "Could you not?"

"Not really," I say. For a moment I imagine standing next to Gomes for a photo. Would I have put my arm around him? Would we all have given Micheli a thumbs-up sign?

"Oh well," says the editor. "Never mind. Maybe next time."

Maybe next time.

I leave Brazil for good a few years later. Now, I live in London, where, unlike in Goiânia, it is often cold. There are not as many motorbikes (or at least they are less visible) and a lot fewer murders. Tiago Henrique Gomes da Rocha and the memories and stories of Arlete Carvalho, Bárbara Luíza Ribeiro, Ana Lídia Gomes, and all the other young women he killed seem a lifetime or a world away.

So far away, it is as though none of it ever happened at all.

The Stranger in the Square

DANUTA KOT

This is a story about something that happened to me in Sheffield, a city in the north of England, in the mid-1970s. It was the end of May 1975 when I met a stranger in Havelock Square, in an area of Sheffield known as Broomhall, named after a fifteenth-century hall that still stands in the center of the district. Broomhall, once a wealthy enclave where the homes of the steel magnates stood, had fallen on hard times and was an area known for high levels of crime, violence, and prostitution.

It was a cold February night, and I was walking home. It must have been closing time, as people were pouring out of the pubs. I was walking from the city center up West Street, a street that was popular with the local students. It was cold, but I wasn't wearing a coat. I never bothered with coats in those days. I didn't feel the cold much and, anyway, I was too broke to waste my money on what at the time seemed like an inessential garment.

Cars were moving up and down the street, police cars along with the cars of people who'd been out for the night. Men rolled down their windows and whistled and called at women. Groups of men, drunkenly owning the pavements, shouted sexual remarks at any women who walked past. There was an edginess in the air that said this entitlement could tip very easily into violence.

I was walking fast, and I was probably visibly upset—not by the behavior of the men, that was part and parcel of life. I walked past the hospital and looked across at one of the ground-floor windows that was protected from the outside gaze by opaque glass. That was where I had spent most of my evening until, not able to stand it anymore, I'd left and wandered the streets for a while.

Now, I was walking home against the flow of pedestrians who were heading into town to continue their Saturday night. Men made their usual comments as I went past. I paid no attention—what did I expect in those days, walking the streets on my own? One man knelt down on the pavement in front of me and tried to look up my skirt. Why didn't I kick him in the face? Because I'd probably break my foot with all the kicking I'd have to do to walk from one end of the street to the other.

Anyway, I had other things to think about.

Behind that hospital window was the intensive care unit where my boyfriend, "my partner," I would say today, was struggling to survive. A misdiagnosed perforated ulcer had almost killed him. After two days of increasingly severe illness, Brian collapsed completely, and, by the time the surgeons got to him, he was suffering from peritonitis and septicemia. He survived the operation, but his life hung in the balance.

I can remember on that first night I tried to take in what the doctor had just told me. He'd called me into his office and said a lot of stuff about Brian's operation, the state he was in when he arrived, the state he was in now. But he wasn't telling me what I wanted to know. I kept saying, "But he'll be alright, won't he?" and the doctor just wasn't taking his cue. He wouldn't give me the answer I was expecting to hear, even though I gave him several chances. "He'll be alright, though, won't he?"

Until it dawned on me that Brian wasn't going to be alright. The doctor was telling me there was a good chance he would die. I sat by his bed. He wasn't conscious enough to talk, but he squeezed my hand once or twice, so he knew I was there. It was the last time we were able to communicate clearly for a long time.

For loved ones of patients, severe catastrophic illness consists of moments of sheer terror, ongoing stress, worry, and, conversely, times of deep boredom. I can remember sitting by Brian's bed, holding his hand, not knowing if, through the coma he had been in since that first night, he even knew I was there. I talked to him, played the music he enjoyed, The Dubliners in particular, the wheeze of the ventilator making a suitable backing for the edginess beneath the jaunty tunes, the scraping fiddle and the harsh voices.

And sometimes, like that night, I ran away.

It wasn't like my life was stable anyway. It wasn't. It was a mess. A few years earlier, I'd met, married, and left an abusive man. I was struggling to bring up our very young son with no money, no proper home, and little expectation of either. My life was chaotic, and so was I, with no real direction or plan.

That winter's night, it felt like the nadir. I didn't want to cope with it anymore, but there wasn't any alternative I could accept.

So there I was, walking in the winter night, hassled by drunken louts, heading for a temporary home where my son and I were crammed into one small bedroom with no privacy or life of our own. And, at the hospital, the doctors didn't hold out much hope. We were all waiting and sometimes—can I be honest here?—I almost wanted the end to come, to bring it all to the expected conclusion with no more waiting.

And did I feel sorry for myself? You bet I did.

Fast forward to several weeks later: things were looking up. Brian was still in the hospital, but he was making progress. I moved on from spending nights at his bedside waiting for what looked like an inevitable end, from sleeping lightly, expecting the phone to ring at four in the morning, until, gradually, the threat of his dying receded, and he began the long, long process of convalescence, still in the hospital's intensive care unit because, though he was recovering, he had an open wound in his stomach that would not heal.

Brian was a small, wiry man, not much taller than me, very Irish in his looks with pale skin and dark and curly hair; he had a wicked and irreverent sense of humor. Like me, he was a drifter with no real goals in life; like me, he moved with the currents; like me, his life was chaotic. We were drawn to each other and disastrous for each other, Brian with his endless rejection of authority and conformity, me with a Groucho Marx complex the size of the Eiffel Tower. (This man says he cares about me and is sweet to me? There must be something very, very wrong with him.)

His illness, for all the sudden shock of his collapse, the rush into the hospital, and the surgery, had one compensation. It gave us a chance for stability and a compulsion for truth, something a close encounter with the Grim Reaper tends to promote. We stopped playing those dangerous and destructive games with our relationship that troubled people are prone to, and we began to be honest.

During this quiet time of his recovery in the small unit, where they had moved Brian to a private room, we just enjoyed being together with all our agendas put to one side. We lay on the bed together (strictly forbidden in the hospital, but the staff were very understanding toward us), talked, watched television, listened to music, or were just quiet. Brian still slept a lot. We didn't, to be honest, think too much about the future. We just enjoyed that time for what it was: a sort of golden time away from the harder realities we would have to deal with when he left the safety of the hospital. In a way, we were living in a cocoon.

Or maybe a bubble.

Because in the world outside the hospital, something very dark was growing. There were no signs of it, no metaphorical clouds in the sky, no sand trickling from a dam wall that was about to burst. What came, came out of a clear sky.

In a world where rape victims were photographed and their ordeals described in detail in newspapers for the titillation of the public, where student magazines published graphic cartoon depictions of rape to entertain their readers, where the murder of certain classes of women was so commonplace we barely noticed it, where young men thought nothing of hassling women going about their business, the strange thing is that a series of bloody murders of women took us so much by surprise.

For me and for Brian, the golden time was enough. It was made of good days, high days and holidays, and right then, that was all we needed.

Until I met the stranger.

•••

It is late May, almost the start of summer. It must be well after nine, because I'm on my way home from the hospital after visiting a pub for a drink with friends, and the light is starting to fade. I've taken care with my appearance—I always dress up for Brian to compensate for the institutional bleakness of the ward, and to compete with the glamorous and scantily clad dance group Pan's People, who were then appearing on a music program, *Top of the Pops*. I'm wearing my favorite skirt, mid-calf with a swirl of frill around the hem. Around my waist, I have a broad, shiny, red belt, and I'm wearing a cream-colored blouse. My hair is hanging down around my shoulders, and my earrings are jangly. I have on brown knee-high boots.

I'm feeling happy. Earlier in the day, one of the senior surgeons, Miss Platts, came to see Brian, accompanied by her posse. Miss Platts demands respect both for her skills and for rising to the top of her male-dominated profession. She hasn't married, and I wonder, as I walk, if she has had to make a sacrifice of family life or if this is not something she wants or needs. I can't imagine how tough it must have been for her, and she scares me a bit, because I don't think I could have done it.

Though she seems intimidating, she's also kind. In the earlier days of Brian's illness, when he was hanging by a thread, she touched his shoulder and smiled at me. "He's a fighter," she said.

This afternoon, she came into Brian's room followed by the long trail of medics and therapists, all in white coats. They assembled around Brian's bed and stood there staring at him, their faces solemn. Brian looked up from his book and studied the group over his glasses. "I expect," he said, "you're wondering why I called this meeting."

There was a moment of silence, and then the ice broke, and everyone laughed. I tell our friends about it in the pub later to reassure them that the Brian they knew is back, and, as I walk toward home, the memory of it makes me laugh out loud again.

So it's been a good day, and, even better, they are talking about moving Brian to a general ward, where he will be just another patient on the road to recovery. That step up from intensive care to ordinary nursing will take us further away from what almost happened and toward safety. The next step will be something that seemed impossible on that winter's night so many weeks ago—his discharge from the hospital.

We are in the final stretch. Thinking about it lifts my step as I head briskly for home.

My way back takes me through Broomhall, that once prosperous area with big, old, stone houses hidden behind mature and tree-filled gardens, four-story spacious terraces, but also partly demolished slums that used to house the people who serviced the mansions.

Broomhall may have become an area of crime with its quiet corners, dark shadows, multiple-occupancy houses, and the place where the street prostitutes ply their trade, but it's also an exciting place of good pubs and parties: a place Brian and I know well.

I walk the streets of Broomhall confidently. I'm not afraid, not yet.

I come through a narrow alley that runs past an old convent, then up the hill and along a residential road that takes me into the heart of Broomhall toward Havelock Square.

It's quiet enough tonight. On weekends, Broomhall is a party place, but, on weekdays, the streets can be empty. This early in the week, even the street prostitutes are few and far between.

I'm thinking about tomorrow as I walk along the road, and I'm making plans, but cautiously, because hubris is a dangerous thing. I'm thinking about the day Brian will leave the hospital—where we will live and how we will manage.

Absorbed in these thoughts, I'm miles away.

And then, a man speaks behind me. "Nice night," he says. It makes me jump. I didn't hear anyone following me. As far as I am aware, there was no one else around. He must have stepped out from one of the gateways.

People don't usually exchange casual chat with strangers at night here, but the voice is pleasant and its owner unalarming, young, and good-looking, with a dark beard and dark hair.

"Yes," I agree. I don't want to get into a conversation. I'm not looking for an encounter, but I don't want to be rude to him. A pleasant comment on a warm evening in late spring is nothing to take offense at.

"Are you walking this way?" he says.

Now, I'm a bit more wary. If he's looking to buy—and around here, that is very likely—I don't want any misunderstandings to arise. "Yes," I say. "I'm going home."

He's looking at me very intently. "I'm looking for the girl who lives in Havelock Square," he says. "And charges five pounds a time."

"It's not me," I say sharply and turn away to walk up the hill.

"I'll walk with you," he says. "It isn't a good place for a woman to be alone."

Because of people like you, is what I think, not what I say. I don't want to make him angry. I'm suddenly aware of how alone I am. The light has almost gone—the streetlights are still pale, and the roads and pavements are empty. The gateways are deep pools of shadow.

There may be people in the houses, but, around here, they tend to keep away from trouble. My lovely evening is turning into night, and he is spoiling it, walking beside me, apparently oblivious to my reluctance, chatting about the weather, the area, how much he likes the city. His voice is northern, but not local. He's not a Sheffield man.

And suddenly, it all spills out. Suddenly, I'm angry. I tell him about Brian and how ill he was and how ill he still is and how I spend my evenings, each evening, week after week, sitting by his bed, terrified he was going to die and how now, things are looking better, and the last thing I need, really the *last* thing I need is someone who thinks I'm a prostitute walking with me when I asked him to go away.

He doesn't say anything. He just keeps walking, whistling faintly between his teeth. We're coming to the edge of Broomhall, to the road that will take me up the hill and home. I turn onto it, and he walks with me. Then, I think he must have listened and understood, must have changed his mind, because suddenly, he drops behind me.

Instinctively, I look back, and I don't understand what I am seeing.

He's standing at a slight angle, quite close, with one hand slightly raised, the other reaching down, pressed into his body, almost behind his back. He looks like—I struggle to find the image—a tennis player about to serve, about to bring his racket around to hit the ball.

It's quiet. The streetlights are half hidden by the trees. On either side of the road, the houses look empty. There's no one in sight. Our eyes meet, but his face is vacant, blank. He doesn't say anything. It's like time has stopped, and we're frozen in a tableau. I want to get away, but now I'm afraid that if I turn, I'll break the spell and time will start to move again.

I don't want it to. I don't want what will happen when time starts again.

It seems like minutes, but it can only have been seconds until someone appears around the corner and walks briskly past the place where we are frozen in our moment.

I'm off at once, walking up the hill closely behind this passerby, catching up with him, passing him, and keeping going. I want him between me and the stranger. Then, when I am far enough away to feel safe, I look back.

He's gone. The road is empty.

Ten minutes later, I'm home, the babysitter goes, and I tidy up, moving quietly so as not to disturb my sleeping son. We live in a bedsit with a shared kitchen. It's cramped, it's not very nice, but it's a roof over our heads. My good mood has gone.

I put the encounter with the stranger out of my mind and start preparing for tomorrow.

I sort out some new music tapes. The same ones, over and over again, are starting to drive us mad. And a book—something satirical, something surreal. Flann O'Brien and JP Donleavy are the authors Brian likes, but, though he enjoys reading, he can't concentrate for very long. Maybe some short stories, maybe some articles, some commentary, something funny. *I expect you're wondering why I called this meeting.*

Suddenly, my mood lifts and I find I'm laughing again.

•••

Six years later, and I no longer walked through Broomhall on my own at night, not anymore. We none of us walked on our own if we could help it. Thirteen women had been butchered by a man the press had dubbed "The Yorkshire Ripper." The photographs of the women he killed adorned the front pages, but what dominated these images was the unknown face, the face of their killer.

The official attitude was one of horror. The reality was different. The women who died—most of the women who died—were not innocent victims in the public gaze: they were women of loose morals, the kind of women who went to pubs and enjoyed a drink, or more significantly, they were prostitutes. The police were determined this killer was a man on a mission to kill such women. It didn't seem to cross the minds of the all-male team in charge of the investigation that prostitutes were simply more vulnerable, easier targets for a man who hated women so much.

These men, these senior police officers, thought they knew best. They thought they knew better than the women who survived attacks made by the killer, the women who gave them accurate descriptions of both his face and his voice, the women who produced photofits that were uncannily similar and close likenesses of the man who was finally convicted of these crimes. The women gave the police information that could have stopped him, but the men in charge knew better, and went their own, fatal way.

The attacks and the murders began in July 1975, a few weeks after my encounter with the stranger in the square. The first three women, who were savagely attacked as they walked home in the evening, were not prostitutes. In each case, the attacker approached them with friendly, casual remarks and walked with them for a while before attacking. In each case, he was interrupted and fled, leaving the women with terrible injuries. He carried out his first killing that August, when this time, he was not interrupted.

Of the thirteen women who were killed—the thirteen we know about—by this man with a self-proclaimed mission, less than half were prostitutes, but the image remains of him as a prostitute killer, a "street-cleaner," and it has never gone away. The legacy of this is that too many of the dead women are remembered by this one fact of their lives. Though they were mothers, workers, family women, friends, partners, women in their own right, they are forever Ripper victims, their evidence ignored, their stories discounted.

Women were murdered across the north of England, in Leeds, Halifax, Bradford, Manchester. The police narrative turned the investigation into a quest in which the Ripper made a challenge to a senior police officer, the senior police officer accepted it, and the dead women lay between them like discarded tokens as the two of them played out their game.

There were whispers of acts more dreadful than the ones we were told about, of secret rituals and acts of slaughter that were barbaric, horrific beyond belief, that were kept secret so that the police would know the culprit when they caught him. It was almost as if shattering a woman's skull and killing her by stabbing her repeatedly was too commonplace and wasn't in itself the very epitome of barbarism and horror.

Women were told to leave the streets, while men sang "There's only one Yorkshire Ripper" to the tune of "Guantanamera" at football matches.

And women started to get angry. The street-cleaner brought us out onto the streets.

•••

Just into the New Year of 1981, routine policing in Sheffield led to an arrest. It happened not far from where I lived, maybe ten minutes' walk from my encounter with the stranger. The woman in the car with the killer, his next intended victim, was someone I knew—not well, but we had met and exchanged casual conversation. I knew her name, Olivia, and she knew mine. She was working as a prostitute and told the police that she had been picked up by this man as he drove through Broomhall Street, just around the corner from Havelock Square.

When I saw the photograph of the man arrested for these killings, a West Yorkshire man called Peter Sutcliffe—I had a moment of recognition. This was the stranger from the square.

And I was back there again but not standing in the square looking into the blank face of the man who had spoken to me. I was back at the hospital, laughing with Miss Platts and her posse as Brian settled his glasses back on his nose and looked pleased with himself. I was listening to the Dubliners singing "Whisky in the Jar." I was making sardonic comments about Pan's People. I was back in the golden time.

Was it Peter Sutcliffe, in the early days of his life as a killer, who approached me that night? We know from his own accounts of his movements that he was familiar with the streets of Broomhall, that he sometimes went to the Hanover pub, not far from the square where I met the stranger. We know that he habitually prowled red-light districts, and that he had attacked at least one prostitute long before the so-called Ripper killings began. When I recall that night, a disturbingly familiar face looks back at me through the evening light, but I also know that memory paints its own pictures and like so much in this life, it can't be relied on.

I just don't know, and I don't think it matters. Maybe I was lucky that night, one bit of luck I wasn't even aware of in times that otherwise held no luck at all.

The golden time was drawing to a close.

•••

As the spring of 1975 moved into summer, a week after my encounter with the stranger, Brian contracted an infection. He died on the 14th of June of acute renal failure and septicemia. Looking back, we should have known. He had an open wound that wouldn't heal. It was simply a matter of time before something got him. That quiet time in the hospital was a wonderful interlude, but it was never more than that. The medical doctors and the nurses had been optimistic, but, as they told me after Brian's death, the surgeons had never held out much hope.

It would have been better, one of the nurses said, if he hadn't survived the first surgery, because it meant he went through so much more pain and suffering before he died. I could understand what she meant, but if he had died then, we would never have had the golden time. And we both valued that.

It's easy for me to say it was worth it. But it was.

Brian Patrick Keenan, October 9, 1946–June 14, 1975, buried in Thetford, Norfolk.

The Kičevo Monster

Mitzi Szereto

.

"The people of Kičevo live in fear after another butchered body has been found in the town. The corpse strongly resembles one discovered twenty kilometers outside Kičevo last year, and there is a possibility that these monstrous murders are the work of a serial killer."

—from *Nova Makedonija* in an article by Vlado Taneski, May 19, 2008

Macedonia, which is only slightly larger than the US state of Vermont, is one of the poorest countries in Europe. Nearly a third of its approximately two million citizens live in poverty. Government corruption, political and ethnic tensions, and unemployment are all contributing factors. A recent UNICEF study shows that poverty rates are even on the rise, particularly among families with young children, with small farmers hit the hardest. Like many countries in the region, Macedonia has struggled with the transition from communism to capitalism.

The country has a long history of being taken over by others, including the Ottoman Empire, Serbia, Italy, and Albania. At the end of World War II, Macedonia became part of communist Yugoslavia, and it remained so until 1991. With the breakup of Yugoslavia, the

Republic of Macedonia was formed. However, still more change was to come for this small landlocked nation. After a twenty-seven-year dispute with its southern neighbor, Greece, over history and national identity, the Macedonian parliament officially changed the country's name in 2019 to the Republic of North Macedonia.

Set in a picturesque valley formed by the southeastern slopes of Mount Bistra, the small provincial city of Kičevo is about seventy road miles southwest of the capital Skopje and under two and a half hours' drive to the Albanian border. Ethnic Macedonians make up the bulk of the city's 27,000-plus population, followed by Albanians, Turks, and Roma. About 60 percent of residents are Orthodox Christians, with Muslims being the second largest religious group. Kičevo's communist past can still be seen in its drab apartment blocks, faded murals, and beat-up old cars, all of which are juxtaposed against a Kičevo that wants to move forward into the future. This humble Balkan city isn't a place most people are likely to have heard of, let alone visit. It's not listed as a "must-see" destination in tourist guidebooks. People usually bypass Kičevo on their way to somewhere else—somewhere *better*—such as Skopje, the resorts of Lake Ohrid, or Sveta Bogorodica Precista (Holy Mother of God), the Christian Orthodox monastery nestled high in the mountains.

Yet Kičevo can claim some status. Not only was it the first Macedonian city to be liberated after World War II, but it also serves as the seat for the municipality of the same name. It has even produced a couple of saints, a handful of professional footballers, and a singer who represented the nation on the Eurovision Song Contest. Kičevo has also produced a serial killer.

•••

Mitra Simjanoska, aged sixty-four. Found dead in 2005.

Ljubica Ličoska, aged fifty-six. Found dead in 2007.

Živana Temelkoska, aged sixty-five. Found dead in 2008.

•••

Three women who'd lived in Kičevo their entire lives. But someone decided they'd lived long enough.

Mitra Simjanoska vanished on November 16, 2004. Her nude body was found stuffed inside a nylon bag at the construction site of an athletic complex. She'd been placed inside a deep hole with her legs tied together with telephone cable, then covered over with stones and refuse. Simjanoska had been beaten and raped, sexually violated with foreign objects, and strangled with the same telephone cord used to bind her legs. By the time she was discovered, she'd been missing for nearly two months.

Ljubica Ličoska disappeared on November 10, 2007. Her nude body, also stuffed inside a nylon bag, was dumped in a ravine near a service station on a mountain pass outside Kičevo. A truck driver who'd stopped happened to notice a hand sticking out from the surrounding refuse. Ličoska had been beaten and raped, sexually violated with foreign objects, and strangled with the same telephone cord used to tie her legs. She was found nearly three months after she went missing. She lived in the same part of town as Mitra Simjanoska.

Živana Temelkoska vanished on May 7, 2008. Her mutilated body, naked but for a dressing gown, was stuffed inside a nylon bag, then left at a dump site near the town's football field. She had thirteen wounds on her skull and several broken ribs. She'd been beaten and raped, sexually violated with foreign objects, and strangled with the same telephone cord used to bind her legs. Temelkoska lived in the same area as the other two murdered women. She was found a few days after she disappeared.

And then there was seventy-eight-year-old Gorica Pavleska, who went missing on May 30, 2003. To this day she has never been found.

These four individuals had something significant in common: they all worked as cleaning women.

•••

In 2008, Vlado Taneski was at the top of his game. An ethnic Macedonian who'd lived his entire life in Kičevo, he loved his home. He'd penned many poetic paeans to the countryside, some of which were good enough to be published. The fact that he also wrote novels possibly indicated literary aspirations beyond those of reporting Kičevo's news. Taneski had been in journalism since his twenties. He'd even received awards. An old-school reporter who preferred to write his copy on a typewriter, Taneski's heart and soul were set solidly in the past, in the days before capitalism replaced communism. During his formative years, he was head of Kičevo's Communist youth organization, later going on to attend a political school, where he learned the principles of Marshal Tito's League of Communists. He'd also served in the Yugoslavian army.

Taneski's career as a journalist got its start with an editorship at Radio Kičevo. After that, he became a staff reporter at the national daily newspaper *Nova Makedonija* (New Macedonia)—a position he happily held for eighteen years, working from Kičevo until he was suddenly let go in 2003 after the paper changed hands.

Alas, 2003 was a very bad year for Vlado Taneski. Not only did he lose his job, but both of his parents died. With their deaths came the loss of their pensions, which had been helping to keep the Taneski household solvent. When his wife Vesna accepted a job promotion with the Ministry of Education, which necessitated her moving to the capital and taking their two sons with her, Taneski probably felt as if he'd been abandoned. For the first time in his life, he was completely on his own.

2003 was also a very bad year for elderly cleaning woman Gorica Pavleska. It was the year she disappeared.

•••

Taneski decided to turn his misfortune around by becoming a freelance reporter. Soon, he was busy writing articles for *Utrinski Vesnik* (Morning Herald) and the weekly newsmagazine *Vreme* (Time). He even wrote articles for the newspaper that had employed him for nearly two decades, then fired him. Things finally seemed to be back on track. Taneski was doing what he loved and was in demand. The people of Kičevo trusted him and relied on him to keep them informed about what was happening in their town. His editors in Skopje considered him their "to go" reporter for the area, their man on the ground.

Journalism was Vlado Taneski's life. He didn't sugarcoat the news or shy away from the uncomfortable or the unpleasant. He believed in the truth and the public's right to know, even if it put him at risk from some of the people he wrote about, particularly corrupt officials who weren't exactly pleased to have their wrongdoings made known. Macedonia was a country with plenty of corruption, and Kičevo wasn't immune.

It was Taneski who linked together the three grisly murders in his hometown. He'd already reported on the 2005 murder of Mitra Simjanoska and the subsequent trial, which resulted in two men (Ante Risteski and Igor Mirčeski) receiving life sentences for Simjanoska's murder as well as the murder of an elderly man named Radoslav Bozhinoski. Taneski had also reported on the 2003 disappearance of Gorica Pavleska. These women had been his neighbors; he saw their family members in the street and in the local shops. He made a persuasive pitch to his editors in Skopje. Who better to cover the murders than Taneski himself?

Serial killers were and still are rare in Macedonia. The fact that the small city of Ohrid, about an hour's drive from Kičevo, was terrorized by a serial killer from 1999–2008 was unusual enough, though the victims were street foreign currency dealers who'd been targeted specifically. Police had a full confession from the killer—a man with an extensive criminal record. The Ohrid murders had nothing in common with the Kičevo murders.

Vlado Taneski was now hot on the reporting trail of a serial killer in his hometown. The victims were all older women who'd suffered brutal deaths. Their work-worn hands and work-worn eyes were familiar to Taneski. His mother, Gorica, had been a cleaning woman at the local hospital. She'd even known the murdered women. What made the killings more poignant yet was that these women resembled Taneski's deceased mother.

A serial killer in Kičevo. This was a major step up from Taneski's usual beat of local events, school news, petty crime, and corrupt politicians. This was the big time for humble little Kičevo—and Vlado Taneski was determined to be THE reporter on the story.

Working closely with law enforcement, Taneski chased down every lead. He interviewed family members of the victims, often visiting them in their homes, where he'd be customarily served tea and cake as he gleaned whatever information he could get out of grieving relatives. Taneski had their trust. He was their neighbor as well as a respected journalist. In his articles, he provided as many details as possible about the town's local serial killer, dubbed by him the "Kičevo Monster." Since none of the other reporters covering the killings were privy to some of the information in his reports, Taneski had an extra edge. His reputation as a journalist was skyrocketing.

He had the scoop of a lifetime. By now, he was contributing pieces about the murders to several newspapers. His byline seemed to be everywhere.

The people of Kičevo were terrified and rightly so, their eyes glued to every word Taneski wrote as they hoped and prayed that the town's vicious killer would be caught before someone else's mother became the next victim. Taneski appeared to be of a similar mindset and had no qualms when it came to criticizing the police in print, declaring that they could've been doing a better job of finding the killer. It was Taneski's thoroughness and attention to detail that led editors to give his articles prominence and made Kičevo's local reporter a favorite with readers. It was also what eventually led police to his doorstep.

Taneski's newspaper reports contained a number of unattributed facts related to the murders, including details that hadn't been made public. Just where was he getting his information from? One might assume he had an inside source—perhaps someone in the police department who was leaking information to him. Good journalists always have inside sources. Or maybe his information was being supplied by the killer himself?

Police in Skopje compiled a profile of the Kičevo Monster. He had to be physically fit and likely younger, he had to be of above-average intelligence, and he had to be suffering from some form of deeply rooted sexual frustration, which had evolved into a pathology of sadomasochism. Furthermore, the killer was probably known to his victims due to the ease with which they were abducted coupled with the fact that the three women lived in the same general area.

In 2008, approximately eight-thousand males lived in Kičevo. However, many were too old or too young to fit the brief. After eliminating the least likely suspects, police conducted interviews with nearly 250 men, narrowing them down to a handful, which included a taxi driver, neighbors of the victims, and the Kičevo journalist who'd been reporting on the crimes. Finally, they could compare these men's DNA with the semen samples taken from the murder victims.

Vlado Taneski stood out from the others as if he were holding up a sign proclaiming his guilt. He was privy to details about the murders that hadn't been released. He knew the specific type of telephone cord the killer used as his "signature weapon" to strangle the women *and* that this cord had been used to tie up the victims. He'd even reported that Ljubica Ličoska had been abducted on her way to the supermarket by two men who claimed her son had been injured in an accident, though no one could substantiate this story. Once again, it appeared that the only source for Taneski's inside information was Taneski himself. Moreover, the victims' similarity to his deceased mother in appearance, age, job, and educational level had to be more than coincidence. Kičevo police and their colleagues in the capital's violent crime unit were convinced they'd found their man.

On the afternoon of Friday, June 20, 2008, Vlado Taneski was placed under arrest.

An official announcement from the Minister of Interior in Skopje followed: they had a suspect. That same day, Taneski's editors tried frantically to reach their star reporter in Kičevo. But Taneski was nowhere to be found.

A search took place of Taneski's Kičevo home as well as the ramshackle summer cottage that once belonged to his parents (he often took advantage of its secluded location to write). Here, police uncovered a collection of hardcore pornographic material along with ropes and cables. They found detailed notes on the murders, which Taneski had used for his newspaper articles. Shoes and other items of women's clothing were also found. At best, all of this could be seen as circumstantial evidence. But when three independent labs confirmed that Taneski's DNA was an exact match for the semen found inside the body of Živana Temelkoska, there could no longer be any doubt. Vlado Taneski was charged with murder.

During questioning by police, Taneski said little, though at no point did he request a lawyer or admit guilt. He was finally assigned a public defender.

The day after his arrest, Taneski was transported to a prison in the town of Tetovo, where he was to be held on a thirty-day detention order while investigations continued. By now, police were convinced that Taneski had not only murdered Živana Temelkoska, Mitra Simjanoska, and Ljubica Ličoska, but that he was responsible for the 2003 disappearance (and likely murder) of Gorica Pavleska. They believed he'd held the women at his summer cottage, torturing and raping them before finally killing them. They also believed he might have dressed his victims in his mother's clothing as part of some oedipal ritual.

Teneski arrived at the prison in good health. Because of overcrowding, he was forced to share a cell with three other men. He showed no signs of depression and didn't give prison officials other cause for concern. Could it be that Taneski knew his innocence would be proved?

"He ate all his meals and acted normally," Tetovo prison governor Nuriman Tefiki told reporters. "What happened later remains a mystery."

In the small hours of Monday morning, not even a full three days after his arrest, one of his cellmates found Taneski on his knees in the cell toilet with his head submerged inside a bucket of water. (Due to a water shortage, buckets of water for sanitary purposes had been provided to prisoners.) Attempts to revive him failed, and he was pronounced dead. Prison officials and police concluded it was suicide. "He put his head in a pail full of water," police spokesperson Ivo Kotevski told reporters. "It is unclear how none of his cellmates or guards noticed while he was doing so. He finished like in a horror movie."

Taneski was fifty-six years old.

•••

Vlado Taneski bore no resemblance to the Kičevo Monster he'd been writing about. The Kičevo Monster was a violent man, a brutal man, a sick and twisted man who enjoyed inflicting pain on his victims before taking their lives. But Taneski was a quiet man who enjoyed a quiet life. When he wasn't working, he liked nothing more than being a homebody. He was respected member of the community. He had a successful career, a family. The Taneskis were looked up to. Vesna, his wife of thirty-one years, was the first female lawyer in Kičevo. Zvonko, his eldest son, was a leading academic, poet, and writer in Slovakia. Igor, his younger son, served as a doctor in the Macedonian army. How could a man with so much to take pride in have committed such atrocities? Taneski didn't fit Kičevo's image of a serial killer at all. He was just a normal middle-aged family man. Some might even say he was handsome with his tall, solid build and dark, Slavic features.

So, how could a man without any precedent for this type of behavior (or any that were known) suddenly turn into a violent serial killer? "They can begin to kill at any age, although more typically they begin much younger than Taneski's age," says psychologist and criminologist Dr. Candice Skrapec, professor of criminology at California State University, Fresno. "But it would be possible for someone who has led a nonviolent life to become violent were he to develop, for example, a brain tumor in particular regions of the brain, or someone who develops symptoms of psychosis later in life."

Might this explain what happened to Taneski?

"Just because we do not know of any prior violent offenses, this does not mean that none occurred," says Dr. David Keatley, cold case consultant, criminal profiler, and senior lecturer in criminology at Murdoch University School of Law in Perth, Australia. "Many/most serial killers have a 'snap' event that is a proximal antecedent to their killing series."

"I would never believe that he is capable of doing something like that," Ljupco Popovski, Taneski's editor at *Utrinski Vesnik*, told *The Associated Press*. Indeed, Popovski's assessment seemed to be shared by most everyone. Described by colleagues and his wife as quiet, low-key, and mild-mannered, Taneski was the last person anyone would have imagined capable of murder, particularly murders as vicious and gruesome as those that had been perpetrated against the motherly figures of Mitra Simjanoska, Ljubica Ličoska, and Živana Temelkoska. Yet Taneski's relationship with his own mother had been troubled, the relationship worsening following the 2003 suicide, reportedly by hanging, of his father Trajče, a sawmill worker and World War II veteran. (Trajče took his life in the cottage where Taneski is believed to have tortured, raped, and murdered his victims.) Taneski's mother, Gorica, died that same year from an overdose of sleeping pills.

According to family members and others who knew them, Taneski's parents were highly authoritarian individuals who were not much missed after their deaths. Under the circumstances, Taneski's home life couldn't have been easy. His elder brother was disinherited and banished when he left home. Taneski's sister left soon afterward, leaving him on his own with his mother and father—a situation that continued long into his adulthood. In an interview with a local television station, Vesna Taneski said of her husband: "He was always quiet and gentle. The only time I ever saw him get aggressive was when we were living with his parents."

Taneski's difficult relationship with his mother coupled with the specific type of victim being targeted bears a similarity to another serial murderer. "One case did go through my mind when listening to Taneski—that of Edmund Kemper, a very famous serial killer who had issues with his mother and killed various women as a 'build up' to killing his mother," says Dr. David Keatley. "It's a very complicated case, but the overall premise is that he was killing women as substitutes for killing his mother—until, finally, he killed his mother. Now, I wonder if Taneski, who had known issues with his mother, felt that she may be responsible for his father's suicide—thus increasing the tension. Then, when his mother dies, he somehow loses that chance to kill her—leading him to attack women who looked similar and had similar jobs? In that sense, it almost mirrors Kemper."

The three murdered women had known Taneski from his infancy. None of these women had any reason to fear or distrust him. Lubjica Ličoska, who lived a short walk away, had even cleaned his house. Might there have been something "off" about Taneski that everyone had overlooked until it was too late? Had he managed to keep a more sinister side of himself hidden all those years?

Yet some in the neighborhood *did* sense something disconcerting about their journalist neighbor. Zoran Temelkoski (Živana's son) remembered Taneski as being "secretive and mysterious." Neighbor Cvetanka Ličoska (Ljubica's sister) held a similar opinion, describing Taneski as "a very strange type." Both Zoran and Cvetanka had been interviewed by Taneski in their homes about the then-missing women.

Although the heinous nature of the crimes Taneski is believed to have committed is egregious enough, the calculated nature of the abductions is likewise disturbing. Before Živana Temelkoska disappeared, she'd apparently received a telephone call alerting her of a local news report that her son had been in an accident. The

report was aired on the same radio station Taneski once worked
for and continued to sell stories to. Neighbors claimed to have seen
Temelkoska rushing from her home, undoubtedly on her way to see
her "injured" son. Yet her son arrived home *uninjured* later that day.
Zoran Temelkoski believed the radio story was a carefully planned
hoax perpetrated by Taneski. "The fact that there were no witnesses
to an accident, nobody's seen a thing—that was a sneaky trick," he
told British television. The next day, Kičevo's star reporter showed
up at the Temelkoski home to interview family members about the
missing woman.

"In the end, there were many things that pointed to him as a
suspect and led us to file charges against him for two of the murders,"
police spokesperson Ivo Kotevski said in an official statement.
"We were close to charging him with a third murder and hoped he
would give us details of a fourth woman who disappeared in 2003,
because we believe he was involved in that case, too." Nevertheless,
the investigation into the murders of Mitra Simjanoska, Ljubica
Ličoska, and Živana Temelkoska is officially closed, since Macedonian
criminal law doesn't allow for the prosecution of a deceased person.

Questions still linger as to the guilt or innocence of Vlado
Taneski. The truly damning evidence against him was the DNA match
with the traces of semen found inside Živana Temelkoska. There
were also DNA matches with the other two victims, though for some
reason these were never made official or publicly released. To further
cloud the waters, a jersey had been found near Temelkoska's body
that contained traces of blood a forensic examination revealed had *not*
come from the victim. Yet according to Taneski's military records, his
blood type didn't match the sample taken from the jersey either. So,
whose blood was it?

Macedonia isn't known for having a pristine criminal justice
system. Ante Risteski and Igor Mirčeski had already been sentenced

to life in prison in 2005 for one of the murders Taneski is believed to have committed—that of Mitra Simjanoska—as well as the torture/murder of Radoslav Bozhinoski. The men admitted to breaking into Bozhinoski's home and murdering him. The elderly man had been beaten, tortured, and raped (with foreign objects) in what was described as a frenzied attack apparently bolstered by drugs and alcohol. Yet Risteski and Mirčeski steadfastly denied any involvement in Simjanoska's murder. Nonetheless, they were convicted for both murders based on confessions Risteski later claimed had been beaten out of them by police. The case was considered closed.

It wasn't until the murders of Ljubica Licosksa and Živana Temelkoska came to light that a connection was made with the Simjanoska case. These two women had been abducted and murdered while Risteski and Mirčeski were locked up in a prison cell. It was later established that the DNA analysis that would have cleared both men of Simjanoska's murder had been suppressed. No explanation was forthcoming as to how or why this suppression occurred or who was responsible.

Had authorities simply jumped the gun? Taneski was already guilty in everyone's eyes. Even the procedure for collecting evidence during the search of his two homes was suspect. Questions remain as to how these murder investigations were handled and why pertinent information wasn't made known.

Why would Taneski include details of the murders in his newspaper reports that ultimately led straight back to him as the guilty party? "Writing those stories could be interpreted as him holding power over more people," says Dr. David Keatley. "A life of rejection and subordination, and he finally has power in the form of more knowledge. He can give the information no one else can. It also could act as a trophy of the kills—he gets to relive them vividly through writing and then keep the printed version."

At the time of his arrest, Taneski's journalism colleagues found it hard to imagine that the man they'd known and worked with could be the Kičevo Monster. His wife flat out refused to believe it. Describing her marriage as "ideal," she has stood by her belief that her husband wasn't responsible for the murders. "He looked at me straight in the eyes and said, 'I haven't done anything or killed anyone. One day, everything will come to light.' Those were his last words to me," Vesna Taneski told a British journalist. She dismissed much of the evidence in the case, such as the items of women's clothing found in the summer cottage—items police alleged belonged to the murder victims. She also dismissed claims that she and Taneski had been estranged. Despite relocating to Skopje for work, she returned home to Kičevo to spend weekends with her husband when he wasn't traveling to the capital to be with her. Her memories of Vlado Taneski are those of a loving husband and father.

Nevertheless, the timing of the 2003 disappearance of Gorica Pavleska with the recently unemployed and recently "orphaned" Taneski suddenly being left on his own cannot be dismissed. "Many serial killers can show a high level of restraint and management, for many weeks or months or years—especially if they have needs satisfied in other ways. In that way, Taneski's wife leaving him may have been another one of those factors in the sequence leading to his killings," says Dr. Keatley. "Many scholars refer to a 'recipe' of factors that lead to serial killing; but I take that a step further and suggest it's not just the 'ingredients'—the key factors that are in many serial killers' life histories—but it is the *sequence* of events that matter more. The sequence may be what predicts when, how, and who they kill," adds Dr. Keatley. "If we want to use the 'melting pot' or 'recipe' analogy, then we need to remember the order of adding ingredients is important too."

As for Taneski committing suicide by drowning himself in a bucket of water, this opens the door to still more questions. Although the autopsy showed that his lungs were filled with water, thereby indicating death by drowning, the crime scene had been compromised to the point where any potential evidence that might have helped with the inquest was ruined.

Was Taneski also a murder victim? The three men sharing his cell had no motive. They weren't violent or hardened criminals, nor were they facing any significant amount of time in prison for their crimes—and murdering Taneski would have put them at great risk of being locked away for a long time. Could someone in authority have been behind Taneski's "convenient" death? Though considering all the time and work that had gone into the case and the newly democratic Macedonia's desire to show that its judicial system was functioning at a high standard, who stood to gain from his death?

Suicide then?

"The majority of serial killers have psychopathy—a personality disorder not commonly associated with suicide," says Dr. Candice Skrapec. "If he did not have a history of antisocial, impulsive behavior, etc., he would not have psychopathy. But he could have had a more serious mental disorder that had a late-onset."

The drug paroxetine was reportedly found on Taneski at the time of his death. Sold over the counter in Macedonia, it's been used to treat depression and other mental disorders. Taneski might have been self-medicating with the drug rather than face the stigma of seeking professional help for mental health issues. The primary ingredient in paroxetine, a source of major controversy in other countries, is now considered dangerous, since it's able to stimulate and increase suicidal tendencies. Taneski's family history of suicide combined with the stress he was under from murder charges hanging over his head quite likely placed him at a high risk for having a negative reaction to the drug.

"I did not commit these murders." These were the words written on a note found beneath the pillow of Taneski's prison bunk. The note was verified as having been written by him.

If Taneski were truly innocent as he claimed, surely he would have wanted to prove it in a court of law. Yet perhaps he already knew the outcome should he stand trial and decided to save himself and his family from more misery and shame.

Vlado Taneski cannot speak from the grave as to his guilt or innocence. However, Macedonian authorities remain confident that he was the "Kičevo Monster."

Connecting the Dots

Marcie Rendon

There were close to six thousand missing and/or murdered Native American women in North America as of 2016, according to one estimate from the National Crime Information Center. The numbers are staggering when one considers that Native Americans are only about 1 percent of the entire population. Some of these are so-called random murders and disappearances, while others are women who have been trafficked. The question in the back of Minneapolis Native women's minds is always: how many of these missing and murdered are the work of another serial killer targeting Native American women?

Native American women spent 1986 and 1987 living in terror when Minneapolis police made a public announcement that a serial killer was targeting Native American women. Over one year, three women were found killed and left in grotesque positions after having been sexually violated.

Billy Glaze, a white transient also known as Jesse Sitting Crow, was convicted of all three murders following his arrest in August 1987. In 2009, the Innocence Project conducted DNA testing on evidence found at the crime scenes. Glaze's DNA did not match any found at any scene. The DNA did match a Minnesota Native man, a convicted rapist with the initials JAS. On July 3, 2018, a *City Pages* news article details the findings of the Innocence Project's attempts to clear Billy Glaze's name. Diagnosed with stage four lung cancer, he died in prison in 2015 without his name being cleared or another person charged.

Whoever killed the women back in 1986–87 arranged their bodies in a park, in a vacant lot, and then on the railroad tracks one block from where I lived during those years.

I was a single mom with three young daughters under the age of ten. I remember waking one spring morning to an urgency of voices that pulled me outside. From my ground-floor apartment window on 28th and 17th, I could see groups of people walking to the overpass above the tracks. I grabbed my house keys, locked my still-sleeping children in the apartment, and walked to join the group leaning over the concrete overpass a few blocks away.

I leaned on the wall and looked down. From our vantage point, I could see a covered body on the tracks below. A handful of police were standing around the body. I remember the body was covered, but rather than being flat like you see people laid out on TV, the body humped up. I don't remember how long we stood there, looking down, before more police arrived and cordoned off the overpass, moving us off and telling us to go home.

The railroad tracks ran parallel between the end of the 28th Street block and the beginning of 29th Street in a deep, man-made trench that ran east to west in the Phillips neighborhood. Phillips was also known as the "reservation in the city." It is where Native American families had been moved to during the government's Relocation Program, an assimilation work program to move us from the reservation to various cities around the United States. Phillips was home to the Minneapolis American Indian Center, the American Indian Movement, the Indian Health Board, the Minnesota Indian Women's Resource Center and the first ever Native-controlled housing projects, Little Earth.

On the south edge of the neighborhood runs Franklin Avenue. The infamous Corral Bar and Art's bar were on Franklin. The north edge of the neighborhood is bordered by Lake Street, known to be frequented by men and women who often used the railroad overpasses as evening business sites. On the east is Hiawatha Avenue running north-south, as does Chicago Avenue to the west. A square block of ten streets. The second poorest section of the city of Minneapolis, with health and poverty statistics vying with third-world countries.

I moved to the Phillips neighborhood in 1978 to find work to raise my family. The Native community within those ten square blocks was a small community—it seemed like everyone knew everyone else or knew someone who knew someone. While I spent time at both the Corral and Art's during my drinking years, by 1986, I had been sober for ten years.

When the first woman, Kathleen Bullman, was found in the summer of 1986 and I heard about the violence of her death, I was scared but I self-righteously thought, "I'm not at the bars, drinking. I'm safe."

When the second woman, Angeline Whitebird Sweet, was killed in the spring of 1987, the Native American community was warned by the Minneapolis police about a serial killer targeting Native women.

The American Indian Movement restarted the AIM Patrol. Much like the Guardian Angels, the AIM Patrol had been active in the mid-1970s to escort our men and women safely home from the bars on Franklin Avenue. Men and women were targeted both by over-aggressive police and thugs who looked for vulnerable people out on the streets late at night.

Eileen Hudon lived on 18th and Clinton Avenue in 1986, just on the perimeter of where the murders were taking place. She herself was abducted, raped, and held captive by a stranger during this time. She recounted the incident. "I was worried for my daughter, not so much for myself. The whole community was terrified. I was on a Saturday-night bowling team, and my brother dropped me off at my apartment complex. As I put my key in the door, I felt the gun at the back of my neck and I just stopped 'cause I had the keys in the door, and I could hear my children laughing. I didn't want anything to happen to my children. I was raped and beaten by the butt of a gun. This person had taken me near the Harriet Tubman Center for battered women. This happened during that time of serial killings."

Hudon was able to describe him to the police as "a nerdy-looking, kinda churchy-looking African-American guy" driving a brownish sedan. She looked at mugshots for one whole day, retraumatized with each drawer of photos she looked through. The man was never caught or charged for her rape.

After she was raped, Hudon joined the AIM Patrol. She remembers Billy Glaze as a white man who wanted to fit in with the Indians. "He always looked slightly confused," she said. "It was like he was searching for someone to talk to, and the Indians ignored him. He wanted some kind of attention from Native people and no one would pay attention to him. I remember wondering why he was with us. He was on the AIM Patrol—he hung out there. He called AIM after he was arrested and told them, 'I didn't do this—you better find out who did.' "

Hudon continued. "He was a dumbass about five-nine. He had that wannabe look. When I found out he was the one who was charged I thought, no. I knew Angela Green [the third woman Glaze was charged with killing] when she was thirteen, and she was jumped by eight girls. She beat them all off. I was working in the school, and I was running from the farthest distance to help her. She didn't need me... She knew the neighborhood. She understood the neighborhood. I thought, it had to be two people. There was no way that little scrawny-ass Glaze would have been able to abduct her. She would have hurt him."

Hudon was frightened by another man, one from Oklahoma who frequented Art's bar. He was an Indian man who would sit at the bar and just glare at the Indian women. "What was so terrifying was that we as Native women suspected many of our own men. This whole incident, that time of the serial killer, they, men in general, learned about our vulnerability as Native women. I worked one night a week as an advocate. Every time I was on duty, I'd get reports of rapes of women by taxi drivers. Men already knew about our vulnerability, but the killings magnified the visibility of our vulnerability."

TS was a nineteen-year-old woman who, at the time, had moved to the city from a far northern reservation. She moved for a job but started drinking. After she missed her first interview, she went partying, staying relative-to-relative. A cousin two years older told her that if they ever got separated, she should always keep cab fare in her sock for a safe ride home. This cousin told her about a guy whose name was M. "He used to hang around at the Corral and she told me, 'Don't ever go with him, the community thinks he might be the killer.' And so, um, in a way I felt really safe 'cause I thought if he is the one I am safe as long as I stay away from him."

TS continued her story. "One night I got separated from my cousin, but I didn't have a phone to call, no cell phones back then, and there was no payphones close by. I was walking and I saw a white guy coming and I went into one of those apartment buildings 'cause I was scared and he followed me and said, 'You don't live here do you? You shouldn't be here.'

"He said, 'I will walk you across the park, but after that you are on your own.' " Once the man walked her across the park and found a cab, she got in the front seat, as she wasn't familiar with cabs. "There was no window handles on the door or locks. He wouldn't let me out.

He kept driving me around. He undid his pants and made me touch him," TS said. "I talked and talked to him. I told him I needed to go or all my brothers and uncles will be out looking for me. I was by my boyfriend's house by the Indian Health Board. I told him to just pull up over there and let me run up there and tell them I am okay. I told him the bathroom window with the light on was my mom sitting up there waiting for me. He let me out. I ran to the door and my boyfriend's mom let me in to stay there until my dad picked me up."

Because that incident happened in a Yellow Cab, TS determined that her next cab would be a Red and White. The man drove her around the block repeatedly and didn't let her go until she gave him a phone number.

"So then the last one, all cab-related, I called a Blue and White; I don't know what my nineteen-year-old mind was thinking. I was at Art's bar with my cousin and we got separated. They had told me not to walk on Franklin Avenue and to never use the side street that led directly to the apartment because it was too dangerous. I had money, but my pants was real tight. I couldn't get my hand into the pocket to get the money. The cab driver thought I was trying to jump my bill. He got very angry and he drove me to the field where the second body was found. I was so drunk. I thought, 'Oh my fucking god, this is it, this is it.' I literally thought he was the serial killer when he took me to that field," TS said. Thankfully, a cop was there, and she paid the cab driver after explaining it was difficult to get the money out of her pocket. "I had to pay the cab and get home from that field. I ran home with keys and something else in my other hand, scared to death being in that field. No one said never go to the bars. Just that we were to always stay together. Our safety thing was the money in the sock to get the cab home. Some traumatizing-ass things happened."

TS said people around her thought the serial killer was a short, stocky Native Indian guy with a mustache, and they pointed him out to her. She said this man was always in the Corral Bar by himself. He hung out at the bar, not at the pool table where she and her cousins would hang out. She never felt unsafe being in the bar because there were always people around.

Glenda L. worked as a waitress at the Corral Bar. She remembers AIM giving women whistles to carry at all times and made sure her boyfriend was waiting outside the bar each night to drive her to and from work. She too isn't convinced that Billy Glaze was the killer. She said, "There was a guy, everyone knows when a white guy shows up. This guy would come in, and he would stand at the corner of the bar and always order one Tequila Sunrise and nurse it through the whole night. I would watch him, trying to determine if he was staking out any women or following any woman out." She said the police had said there were no footprints at the crime scene and remembered the man wore "Minnetonka slip-on mocs and no socks. I thought to myself, 'Is he one of the killers?' He made me nervous. I heard later he was killed in a shoot-out with the police and that someone who was in prison with him said he was the killer. I don't know. I never remember seeing Billy Glaze at the Corral. The cops didn't interview me. I always wonder if that guy was one of the killers, and Billy Glaze got nailed for it. The cops wanted someone. The whole community was scared."

I, too, was scared. I remember having conversations about the killings after AA meetings. In 1985, Southeast Asian refugees were moving into the Phillips neighborhood. With their waist-length black hair, it was hard to distinguish them from us from behind. We wondered how the killer determined which women were the Native women if he was stalking them at night. It had to be someone who knew us.

During the spring of 1987, we all lived in fear. Without cars, most of us were used to walking freely through the neighborhood, day or night. This changed. I became hypervigilant and wondered about every man, about every suspicious noise outside. A friend borrowed a large German Shepherd-mix for me to keep at the apartment, and the dog barked at anyone who came close to the outside walls inside the fenced-in yard. One night, the dog was lying in the living room, and he all of a sudden jumped up. Rather than running to the window, he staggered but kept going, a deep growl coming from his throat. Still staggering, he ran into the wall and slumped to the floor. He was breathing heavily with his tongue hanging out. I sat on the floor next to him giving him sips of water. It was clear he had been drugged or poisoned.

After the murder of Angela Green, the third woman killed and whose body I saw covered down on the railroad tracks just blocks from my apartment, the terror intensified. I worked out an agreement with my friend Janet. She would call me late in the evening, and I would put my phone by my pillow and fall asleep with her on the other end.

And then, on August 31, 1987, we got the news of Billy Glaze's arrest, and the community was assured by the police that the killer was caught. And, in fact, there were no more murders of a similar nature in the following time. There continued to be rapes and murders, but none with the signature claim of rape and degradation of the Bullhead, Sweet, or Green murders.

Fast forward to 2009, when the Innocence Project took on Billy Glaze's claims of innocence and DNA evidence supported his claim, and to today with the estimated six thousand missing and/or murdered Native women across the continent. The terror continues.

A woman who worked then and continues to work as a sexual abuse advocate for women said of that time, "I was an SA advocate working Southside Minneapolis when that happened. Days were filled with terror, sleepless nights, horror, sadness, fear, suspicion, anxiety, then anger, rage. I wanted to lash out to him, 'You will not win, you bastard.' I was angry with the media for saying the serial rapist was targeting women leaving bars. One woman didn't have any alcohol in her system. He raped and murdered Indian women because they were Indian and women. I did street outreach, posted flyers, did self-defense tips all over Southside, worked with the AIM Patrol. One thing kept crossing my mind, 'Who is this monster? Is he someone I know? Is he on AIM Patrol?' I'm not 100 percent convinced it was Billy Glaze."

Glenda, who also questions if Glaze was the killer, is a chemical dependency counselor today. She said, "As Indians, going all the way back to the atrocities of boarding schools, we are taught to keep secrets. The secrets we keep, about people in our own families and community, keep us in a place of vulnerability."

In 2009, Eileen Hudon started the Ogichidaquay Council (Women Warriors) to address the silence around sexual violence in the Indian community and legal issues regarding missing Native people. She asked, "What do mainstream strategies mean for Native communities? There are many good-hearted people, but they can't see even if they want to. Recently, in Wind River, Wyoming, it was happening at a man camp in the oil fields. In Canada, it is the Highway of Tears, where they find the bodies of our women. In the 1970s, it was Highway 66 through Oklahoma. There are any number of women missing from Minneapolis right now.

"One mother, whose daughter was missing, never gave up and eventually found where her daughter was buried in Chicago in a pauper's cemetery. The city had listed her as a white woman. We are still invisible to them… In March, a suspected serial killer was targeting Native women in South Minneapolis. He was caught recently because a group of women who had been trafficked formed an informal effort, and they found him and turned in all his information to the police. There is so much work to do."

TS, who now works in the field of corrections, agreed. "In this recent time of violence against our women, I have learned a lot about the state of our women. We started a women's group. I said, 'We can start something, do it our way.'… What was unanticipated for me was that the women didn't think we could do it. That we needed a white woman or a man to do it for us. We need Native women. We don't need a man to tell us what to do, and we don't need a white woman. Right now, with all the violence Native women are facing, it's like being a medic on the battlefield—trying to help the wounded while getting shot at—and the wounded don't want treatment."

All the women interviewed were living in the Phillips neighborhood in 1986 and 1987. They frequented the bars and hung around men they each suspected of being the serial killer. None of them thought it was Billy Glaze. Project Innocence doesn't think it was him. So many Native women are missing or coming up murdered, and we know it cannot be the work of one man. Is there one serial killer still out there targeting Native women or ten? We don't know. But women who work with sexual assault victims often have experienced a trauma of their own.

TS wishes more was being done to solve these cases. She said, "The thing that really bothers me is it is like an epidemic. So many women missing, but there is never anybody connecting the dots."

The First of Criminals

MARTIN EDWARDS

"When a doctor does go wrong," Sherlock Holmes once said to Dr. Watson, "he is the first of criminals. He has nerve, and he has knowledge." Holmes was talking about one of the great villains of English fiction, Dr. Grimesby Roylott, the murderer whose nefarious activities are chronicled in the masterly short story, "The Adventure of the Speckled Band."

To illustrate his point, Holmes cited a couple of examples from Victorian Britain. One was William Palmer, the Staffordshire doctor known as "the Rugeley Poisoner," who was hanged for murdering three people, but by some accounts killed as many as fifteen. The other was Edward William Pritchard, hanged in Glasgow for poisoning both his wife and his mother-in-law. Among Britain's most notorious murderers have been other medical men, notably Dr. Thomas Neill Cream, a serial killer hanged in 1892; Dr. Hawley Harvey Crippen, the American-born homeopathic practitioner whose flight from justice and subsequent execution in 1910 for the murder of his wife caused an international sensation; and Dr. Buck Ruxton, the Lancaster GP hanged in 1936.

Holmes's creator, Arthur Conan Doyle, was himself a doctor. He understood very well the threat that a dishonest member of the medical profession can pose. Not even Doyle, however—not even the sage of 221b Baker Street—could have contemplated the extraordinary scale of the crimes committed by Dr. Harold Frederick Shipman in the latter part of the twentieth century.

On January 31, 2000, Shipman was found guilty of the murder of fifteen patients under his care and of forging a patient's will. He was sent to prison for life, and the Home Secretary confirmed in 2002 that he should never be released. But following an exhaustive investigation, the first part of the authoritative official report into Shipman's criminal career concluded that he killed no fewer than 215 people. This figure was subsequently revised to an estimated 250 murders committed between 1971 and 1998; of these, 218 victims were positively identified. Further information might well come to light in future, but it seems likely that the definitive figure will never be known and may well be even higher than the estimate.

•••

In 1998, Shipman was perceived, in the words of another doctor in the town, Dr. Linda Reynolds, as "the best doctor in Hyde." He was well-established and widely respected within the tightly knit local community. A model citizen, or so it must have seemed.

Hyde is, on the surface at least, an unlikely setting for horrific criminal activities. A small town on the edge of Greater Manchester, it lies close to the boundaries of Yorkshire, Lancashire, Derbyshire, and Cheshire. Until local government reorganization in 1974, Hyde was in fact within Cheshire; it was then shifted to the newly created Metropolitan Borough of Tameside. Hyde grew during the Industrial Revolution, and, at one time, there were forty working cotton mills as well as a coal mine. The old industries have died away, and what is left is an unpretentious place, neither affluent nor desolate. There is no obvious reason why such a town should become the home of people capable of macabre and terrible killings. Yet the "Moors Murderers,"

Ian Brady and Myra Hindley, lived on an estate in Hattersley on
the edge of Hyde, and Dale Cregan, who in 2012 killed four people
including two police officers and attempted three other murders, grew
up nearby and handed himself in at Hyde Police Station. Shipman's
criminal activities were even more astonishing and conducted on an
almost unimaginable scale.

•••

In March 1998, some people in Hyde became concerned that a
number of Shipman's patients were dying in curiously similar
circumstances. Dr. Reynolds, who worked in a nearby surgery,
discussed the rumors with her colleagues and decided to alert the
South Manchester coroner, John Pollard. He referred the matter
to the police, and an investigation was undertaken. Regrettably,
the conclusion was that there was no evidence to substantiate the
concerns that had been raised. Shipman remained free to kill. And
that is what he did.

On June 24, 1998, Kathleen Grundy died at the age of eighty-
one. She was a Hyde woman of considerable distinction: she'd been
prominent in local politics and her husband had been mayor. At the
time of her death, she was still fit, alert, and active, and her passing
came as a considerable shock to those who knew her. A loyal patient
of Shipman's, she appreciated his willingness to make house calls
rather than insisting that she visited the surgery. Two friends found
her curled up on her sofa, fully clothed, as if she'd fallen asleep.
Shipman was called, and after a cursory examination, said she'd
suffered cardiac arrest. The cause of death he recorded on her death
certificate was simply "old age."

Grundy's daughter, Angela Woodruff, was a solicitor who had
always looked after her mother's affairs. She had in her possession

a will in which Mrs. Grundy left the bulk of her estate (valued at £386,000) to her family. She was therefore shocked to hear from another firm of solicitors that Mrs. Grundy had written to them a mere two days before her death, enclosing a new will leaving her entire fortune to Shipman and nothing for the family. Another letter had also been sent to the firm from someone called Smith, who claimed to be a friend who had typed out the will for her. Smith did not exist, and it emerged that the people who had witnessed the will had been duped by Shipman.

Angela Woodruff called in the police. Their enquiries led to a decision to exhume Mrs. Grundy's body, and forensic examination of the remains revealed large quantities of morphine. When questioned, Shipman claimed that his respectable patient had actually been a drug addict. Examination of her medical records revealed that Shipman had fabricated a series of entries designed to substantiate his wild allegation. In his surgery was a typewriter of the make used to type the will, which was plainly a forgery. It was also discovered that he had a criminal record, albeit dating back more than twenty years. He was arrested on September 7, 1998, on suspicions of the murder of Grundy, attempting to obtain property by deception, and forgery. Police investigations into other deaths he had certified led to fifteen specimen cases being identified, and he was charged with murdering those patients at a trial that began at Preston Crown Court on October 5, 1999.

•••

Harold Frederick Shipman was born in Nottingham on January 14, 1946, to a working-class family; he was one of eight children. When he was seventeen, his mother died; her illness brought him into contact with the medical profession, and he watched her being injected with morphine. Her death seems to have inspired him to become a doctor; conceivably, it also had a psychological impact that played a part in his becoming a serial killer.

Shipman was not an academic high-flyer; for all that, his upbringing seems to have imbued him with a sense of personal superiority over others. He failed in his first attempt to enter Leeds University Medical School, but a year later he was successful. In Leeds, he met seventeen-year-old Primrose Oxtoby; he married her on October 5, 1966, when she was six months pregnant. After qualifying, he worked at Pontefract General Infirmary; in 1974, he joined the Abraham Ormerod Medical Centre in the West Yorkshire market town of Todmorden.

The following year, his partners discovered that he had been dishonestly obtaining controlled drugs for his own use. In February 1976, he pleaded guilty at the Halifax Magistrates' Court to three offenses of obtaining pethidine by deception, three offenses of unlawful possession of pethidine, and two further offenses of forging a prescription. He asked for no fewer than seventy-four similar offenses to be taken into consideration and was ordered to pay a fine and compensation. However, the General Medical Council, which is responsible for maintaining the register of doctors and promoting the health of the public, decided to take no disciplinary action against him. Nor did the Home Office impose any prohibition on his future dealings with controlled drugs.

As a result, he was at liberty to continue practicing as a doctor without restriction or supervision. In October 1977, Shipman joined the Donnybrook practice in Hyde. He remained with Donnybrook until 1992, when he left the partnership and became a sole practitioner, moving into surgery premises at 21 Market Street, where he remained until his arrest.

•••

A key issue bedeviling the investigation of Shipman's crimes was and remains the inescapable reality that only in a few cases was physical evidence available to show whether he killed the patient in question. In addition to the fifteen counts on which he was tried, the police found three deaths where traces of morphine were found in body tissues. But Shipman pleaded not guilty. So, how could his guilt be established?

In a criminal trial, the jury is not usually allowed to draw an inference of guilt from evidence that the defendant has done something similar in the past. The crucial exception to this principle is that the jury may take past conduct into account if the similarity between the past conduct and the present allegation is so great or so striking that it would offend common sense not to do so. In the Shipman case, the "similar fact" evidence was not only crucial, it was overwhelming. The jury's verdict was unanimous.

Following his conviction, the British government established The Shipman Inquiry, which was tasked with the investigation of four issues:

1. The extent of Shipman's unlawful activities

2. The actions of the statutory bodies and other organizations concerned in the procedures and investigations which followed the deaths of Shipman's patients

3. The performance of the statutory bodies and other organizations responsible for monitoring primary care provision and the use of controlled drugs

4. What steps should be taken to protect patients in the future.

The Inquiry was conducted by a distinguished lawyer, Dame Janet Smith, DBE. Naturally, her terms of reference allowed rather more latitude than the strict requirements of a criminal trial. Her report made many highly important recommendations for improved public protection. In addition—despite all the difficulties she faced—she sought to cast light on Shipman's psychological makeup and to try to understand why he acted as he did.

Because the number of Shipman's unlawful killings was unguessable, Dame Janet decided it was essential to consider the available evidence in relation to every patient of Shipman's who died while he was in practice. Shipman's guilt in fifteen cases having been determined by the jury, Dame Janet originally considered 887 deaths. Since there was compelling evidence in 394 cases that the patient had died a natural death, the focus was on investigating the circumstances of the remaining deaths. Dame Janet reached a decision in each case and also in relation to one incident in which Shipman acted unlawfully but which did not result in the patient's death.

She concluded that Shipman committed serious criminal offenses throughout his professional career, regularly obtaining controlled drugs by illicit means. In August 1974, he unlawfully administered an opiate, probably pethidine, to a female patient, causing her to suffer respiratory arrest and putting her life at risk. In Hyde, his first victim was Eva Lyons, who died in March 1975. She was suffering from cancer and was terminally ill. Shipman gave her a lethal overdose and hastened her death. Initially, Dame Janet concluded that, in addition to the fifteen patients of whose murder Shipman was convicted, he killed two hundred others. After publishing her first report, Dame Janet identified three further victims and concluded that Shipman had started to kill people even earlier than had seemed to be the case at first, while he was still working at Pontefract.

The sheer scale of his crimes was such that establishing the precise truth was impossible. Eventually, after adding in the suspected deaths at Pontefract, Dame Janet concluded that the correct figure was approximately 250.

•••

There was a template for the "typical Shipman murder." Dame Janet described his characteristic method in terms that were straightforward, yet utterly chilling. "Shipman would visit an elderly patient, usually one who lived alone. Sometimes, the visit would be at the patient's request, on account of an ailment of some kind; sometimes, Shipman would make a routine visit, for example to take a blood sample or to provide repeat prescriptions; sometimes, he would make an unsolicited call. During the visit, Shipman would kill the patient. Afterwards, he behaved in a variety of ways and had a variety of typical explanations for what had happened. Sometimes, he would claim that he had found the patient dead when he arrived. If asked how he had gained entrance, he would say that the patient had been expecting him and had left the door 'on the latch.' Sometimes, he would stay at the premises and telephone relatives or call upon neighbors and reveal the death to them. He might say that he had found the patient close to death or he would sometimes claim that the patient had died quite suddenly in his presence. Sometimes, he would leave the premises after killing the patient, closing (and thereby locking) the door behind him. Either then or later, he would go in search of a neighbor who held a key, or to the warden if the patient lived in sheltered accommodation, and together they would go to the premises and 'discover' the body. On other occasions, he would leave the body unattended and would wait for a relative or friend to discover the death."

He had a standard *modus operandi*. According to Dame Janet: "His usual method of killing was by intravenous injection of a lethal dose of strong opiate. Sometimes, mainly if the patient was ill in bed, he killed by giving an intramuscular injection of a similar drug… There is no reliable evidence that he killed other than by the administration of a drug."

With a few victims, most of them terminally ill, he gave an intramuscular injection, which would take effect and result in death within the hour. It seems likely that he sometimes gave large doses of sedatives, such as Largactil, to elderly patients with reduced respiratory function. The effect of this was to induce deep, prolonged sleep and to make the patient vulnerable to death by bronchopneumonia.

What was more, Dame Janet concluded that "Shipman must have committed drug offenses virtually every day he was in general practice, in that he was almost always in possession of controlled drugs without lawful authority. He obtained large quantities of pethidine and diamorphine [heroin] by illegal, dishonest means, using deception and forgery."

Displaying a mastery of a lawyer's understatement, Dame Janet said, "It is deeply disturbing that Shipman's killing of his patients did not arouse suspicion for so many years…It was not until March 1998 that any fellow professional felt sufficiently concerned to make a report to the coroner. Unfortunately, Dr. Linda Reynolds's report of 24th March, 1998, came to nought."

Most frighteningly of all, she added, "Had it not been for Shipman's grossly incompetent forgery of Mrs. Grundy's will, it is by no means clear that his crimes would ever have been detected."

•••

How was Shipman able to get away with multiple murders for so
long? The answer is that superficially sensible legal safeguards proved
to be lamentably unfit for purpose. Most of his victims were cremated,
and the rules required a second doctor to confirm the cause of death,
while the cremation documentation had to be checked by a third
doctor at the crematorium. Appallingly, the system failed to lead to
anyone suspecting what Shipman was up to.

A depressing feature of the case is that Shipman's patients
frequently died suddenly and at home without any previous history
of terminal or life-threatening illness. The law requires such deaths to
be reported to the coroner, but Shipman contrived to avoid a referral
to the coroner in all but a very few cases. Quite simply, he claimed
to have diagnosed the cause of death and to be able to certify its
cause. Such was the strength of his reputation in the community that
he was able to persuade relatives that there was no need for a post-
mortem examination.

Following his convictions in 1976, Shipman declared an intention
never to carry controlled drugs again. One can well understand the
desire on the part of the authorities to rehabilitate a young doctor, but
in practice, forgiveness and an opportunity for redemption coupled
with lax regulation created the conditions that allowed industrial-scale
murder by a man with a second nature for betraying trust. Shipman
was not obliged to keep a controlled drugs register, and he managed
by various means to obtain and stockpile large quantities of controlled
drugs. In truth, the so-called "controls" were utterly useless. In 1996,
Shipman used the name of a dying patient to prescribe and obtain
12,000 mg of diamorphine on a single occasion. That *alone* was
enough to have enabled him to kill about 360 people.

The age profile of his victims was significant. The oldest, Ann Cooper, was ninety-three years old when she was killed. Most were elderly, although he did kill some younger people. There was a tendency, even in the case of generally healthy older people, to take the view that they had "had a good innings," and that at their age, death was not unlikely. The case does raise questions about society's attitudes toward older people far beyond the scope of Shipman's crimes.

The victims' gender profile was equally noteworthy. In her first report, Dame Janet noted that 171 of the victims identified at that point were women and forty-four were men. Given that women generally live longer than men and that Shipman's typical victim was an elderly person living alone, she thought it unsurprising that most of his potential victims were female. He was opportunistic and did kill men and younger people when the chance came his way. And, as Dame Janet said, "Whilst the majority of the deaths for which Shipman was responsible occurred while he was working as a single-handed practitioner, it is nevertheless clear that, even while working in a multi-handed practice, he was able to kill undetected over a period of many years." Similarly, she later concluded that he had been able to commit murder while working in a hospital.

More than a decade after Dame Janet made extensive recommendations for reform, they had yet to be fully implemented. Beginning in April 2019, a new, medical examiner-led system began to roll out within hospitals in England and Wales. The non-statutory system will introduce a new level of scrutiny whereby all deaths will be subject to either a medical examiner's scrutiny or a coroner's investigation. At the time of writing, it remains to be seen how the new regime will work in practice.

•••

Why did Shipman become a serial killer? Dame Janet was not required to answer the question, and Shipman refused to cooperate with her. She did not intrude upon the privacy of Shipman's wife or children. Nevertheless, her report contains much helpful material on the subject, as she sought to identify issues that might affect changes in the regime regulating how doctors practice. She even engaged a team of psychiatric experts to advise her.

Shipman's killings were not motivated by financial gain. Few of his patients left him any money, although he sometimes asked for an item of property belonging to a victim. In 1985, for instance, he asked the family of Margaret Conway if he could have her budgerigar, a variety of parrot, for his aunt, but they declined. Dame Janet noted that there was "much suspicion that Shipman pilfered money and items of property from the homes of his victims," but felt that did not constitute a motive for murder. He seems to have done it simply because he could.

The case of Grundy represented a perplexing exception to this general rule. Dame Janet said: "Shipman could not rationally have thought that he would get away with Mrs. Grundy's estate. The whole venture was grossly incompetent. Discovery was inevitable. I am not convinced that Shipman decided to kill Mrs. Grundy because he wanted her money…his thought processes must have been much more complex than that."

Shipman did not interfere with the bodies of his victims. Dame Janet noted that "He might on occasions have 'arranged' them, for example by putting a book or newspaper on the victim's knee to create the impression that he or she was reading just before death… There does not appear to have been any overtly sadistic or erotic motivation for his crimes…if one defines motive as a rational or conscious explanation for the decision to commit a crime, I think Shipman's crimes were without motive."

Shipman had a good name in Hyde, and his patients felt he always had time for them. Yet there was something sinister in the way he cultivated a caring image; he liked to be regarded as "an old-fashioned family doctor" and made no secret of his belief that elderly patients should be allowed to die at home "with dignity" rather than in a hospital. As Dame Janet said: "His reputation in respect of these matters was a useful 'cover' for his killings."

He was hard-working but had few friends and none among his professional associates. His patients appreciated his bluff bedside manner, and many thought of him as their friend; this did not stop him killing them. Dame Janet cited a poignant example in the case of Mavis Pickup. After her husband, Kenneth, died of a heart attack, "Shipman was curiously brisk about Mr. Pickup's death but showed great concern about his widow. He asked after her in a most sympathetic way and told her son that, if there was anything he could do, if she needed any kind of help, not limited to medical matters, he 'would always be there for her.' He killed her three weeks later after she had telephoned the surgery, upset because children had been knocking on her door and running away."

Shipman was blunt to the point of rudeness, but patients seem rarely to have been offended. As Dame Janet said, "When Mr. Stephen Dickson asked Shipman on 28th February, 1998, how long his father-in-law, Mr. Harold Eddleston, who had cancer, was likely to live, Shipman replied, 'I wouldn't buy him any Easter eggs.' Mr. Dickson did not take offense because he thought this kind of remark was typical of Shipman's style. Shipman killed Mr. Eddleston four days later."

A striking feature of his behavior was that patients' families found that "his usually kind and sympathetic attitude disappeared when their relative had died. They would naturally be very distressed. He would be curt and dismissive and would sometimes say the most inappropriate and hurtful things. When he had just killed Mrs. Mary Coutts in April 1997, and her son- and daughter-in-law, who were in a state of grief and shock at the suddenness of her death, were asking him about the circumstances, Shipman said, 'Well, I don't believe in keeping them going.' Often, he seemed unable to empathize with the bereaved."

Shipman's much-admired bedside manner was not displayed so often away from the bedside. He could be aggressive, vain, arrogant, and scornful of those he regarded as his intellectual inferiors. He liked to challenge officialdom and humiliate subordinates whom he thought were not performing well. His defining characteristic was deviousness. Dame Janet regarded him as "an accomplished and inventive liar. He could lie spontaneously to get himself out of a difficult situation and did so on countless occasions."

In the 1970s, Shipman became addicted to pethidine. He gave the excuse that he had taken to it because he had become depressed and unhappy about his work and his relationships with his partners. His partners were unaware of any signs of depression and did not think there were difficulties within the practice. In Dame Janet's opinion, it was "likely that whatever it was that caused Shipman to become addicted to pethidine also led to other forms of addictive behavior. It is possible that he was addicted to killing."

The psychiatrists thought his arrogance and overconfidence were a mask for poor self-esteem, and that he was probably angry, deeply unhappy, and chronically depressed, with a deep-seated need to control people and events. But this in itself does not explain why he became a serial killer. One possibility noted by Dame Janet was that he "might have developed a fear of death and a need to control death." Perhaps he had a morbid interest in death or experienced a "buzz" of excitement from close encounters with death. Possibly, the death of other people gave him a sense of relief from personal stress.

Dame Janet concluded that "after a death, when the relatives had assembled, he would enjoy acting as 'master of ceremonies.' He would be the center of attention and would take control. He would present himself as omniscient. He would give instructions about the removal of the body. He would give his explanation for the death, often saying that, although it might have been a surprise to the relatives, it had been no surprise to him. He might add remarks such as 'she was riddled with cancer'… Relatives would often be grateful to him and pleased that he had been present at the death…[he] seemed to think that he knew when a patient ought to die. He quite often said that it was 'for the best' that the patient should have died when he or she did…it may be that he persuaded himself that what he had done was in some way justifiable. The fact that most of the early killings were of people who were either close to death or very ill lends support to that view."

His early victims were generally those whose deaths presented the least danger of discovery. Dame Janet said, "He might have persuaded himself that he was doing his patients and their relatives a favor. The psychiatrists say that these apparently logical explanations for the early killings are not inconsistent with the theory that Shipman killed in response to a need within himself… Shipman seems to have been particularly willing to kill the bereaved…[and there were] some patients whom I think Shipman regarded as a nuisance."

Although Shipman's killings gradually became more frequent, the trend was interrupted from time to time, probably due to his fear of detection and desire for self-preservation. In a memorable passage, Dame Janet said, "When he resumed killing, he did so gradually, sometimes beginning with a terminally ill patient. It was as if he were entering the pool at the shallow end to see if he could still swim."

Shipman's rate of killing steadily increased, peaking in 1997 and early 1998. Perhaps this supports the theory that he had become addicted to murder. By this time, he was also more confident, not least in his ability to talk his way out of trouble. Dame Janet thought that "In forging Mrs. Grundy's will and killing her, Shipman must have been raising a flag to draw attention to what he had been doing. No longer in touch with reality, I think he might then have devised a fantasy plan, by which he could obtain Mrs. Grundy's money, run away and stop being a doctor. The killings would cease. This plan, rationally considered, was bound to fail, but it would offer him a fantasy future and a way to stop himself from killing."

Nonetheless, he did not confess and continued to protest that all he had ever done was to give appropriate treatment to his patients. Dame Janet concluded, "It may be that he has convinced himself that he is innocent. The psychiatrists say that such a degree of self-deception, which involves compartmentalization of ideas and dissociation of thought processes, is not uncommon following the commission of very serious crimes. It is a mental mechanism by which the criminal defends himself from the overwhelming anxiety which facing reality would cause… It may be that he knows what he has done and that it was wrong but chooses, possibly as a form of self-protection, to maintain a complete denial. I doubt that we will ever know."

Shipman hanged himself in his cell at Wakefield Prison on January 13, 2004, the day before his fifty-eighth birthday. Far from offering an explanation of his crimes, he went to his grave still in denial about what he had done. As Dame Janet said: "The bare statement that Shipman has killed over two hundred patients does not fully reflect the enormity of his crimes. As a general practitioner, Shipman was trusted implicitly by his patients and their families. He betrayed their trust in a way and to an extent that I believe is unparalleled in history. We are all accustomed to hearing of violent deaths, both in the media and in fiction. In some ways, Shipman's 'non-violent' killing seems almost more incredible than the violent deaths of which we hear. The way in which Shipman could kill, face the relatives, and walk away unsuspected would be dismissed as fanciful if described in a work of fiction."

To return to fiction and to Sherlock Holmes's pithy phrase, Shipman had the nerve, and he had the knowledge. So far as we know, no other murderer in Britain has ever killed so many people. He is indeed the first of criminals.

The Beast of BC

MIKE BROWNE

C lifford Olson's depravity horrified Canadians a decade and a half before Paul Bernardo and twenty years prior to Robert Pickton. Over a nine-month period, from November 1980 to July 1981, this man who called himself "The Beast of BC" abducted, raped, and murdered eleven boys and girls, aged between nine and eighteen.

Clifford Robert Olson Jr. was born on January 1, 1940, at around 10:10 p.m. in St. Paul's hospital in downtown Vancouver. Clifford's mom worked in a cannery, and his dad was in the Canadian Armed Forces during World War II. Unmarried when Clifford was born, they didn't legitimize their union until he was three. Since his dad was in the military and gone much of the time, Clifford didn't receive much discipline.

Olson claimed that one of his earliest memories was at age four of his fifteen-year-old uncle playing a game with he and his sister. The trio would strip, and the uncle would lay on top of each child who was facedown. They were then given nickels to keep their mouths shut. Clifford said he later played the game with other kids, with himself playing "uncle." He began lying early on to deflect trouble or prop himself up in the eyes of others. He'd tell people he was the first baby of the new year and much celebrated. This was a lie; there were six in the hospital before him.

At school, Clifford was defiant and rude and routinely lied to his teachers. As early as age ten, it's reported that he began flashing knives at little girls and forcing them into the bushes so he could ogle and grope them. He often skipped class and stole. Olson took up boxing and got fairly fit and strong for his smaller stature. He started selling newspapers at Lansdowne Park racetrack, where he met all kinds of interesting characters. Sick of being told what to do, he left school in 1956 and worked at the track more often.

Then, his career as a criminal began in earnest.

Between 1957 and 1981, Clifford Olson was arrested ninety-four times for crimes such as fraud, armed robbery, sexual assault, firearms offenses, escaping custody, and burglary. By the time he was forty-one, he'd spent only four years of his adult life as a free man.

On his release from prison in 1980, Clifford met Joan Hale, who bore him a son, Clifford Olson III.

•••

On the afternoon of November 17, 1980, twelve-year-old, dark-haired, blue-eyed tomboy Christine Weller was walking a friend's bicycle along what was then called King George Highway. Christine hated Surrey. She'd run away from home before, especially when her parents were drinking and fighting (they were separated now). Christine, her dad, and her grandmother were temporarily living in the low-rent Bonanza Motel on the highway. Richard, her dad, had promised they'd move into an apartment soon.

Christine had just walked with her dad to the Surrey Inn, where he was going for a few drinks to celebrate turning forty-seven. Richard asked where she'd gotten her bike, and she said her friend Clive had loaned it to her. He told Christine to "be careful with that boy." When they reached the Surrey Inn, Richard Weller kissed his daughter and said he'd try not to be late, and to make sure she rode straight home.

"Sure, Dad," Christine said, and began riding the bike in circles.

It was close to six o'clock, and Christine was making her way home when a man called to her from an open car window. He was parked in the lot of the Surrey Animal Hospital across the street from the Surrey Village apartments. "Hey!" he yelled. "Do you know where the employment office is around here for hiring kids?"

Christine rode over to the man and, after a brief conversation, left Clive's bike leaning up against the wall of the animal hospital and got into the front seat of the car. She was later seen in the same car around ten o'clock by a security guard at the Surrey Village Apartments. She looked as if she were drunk or drugged. The male driver, a resident of the apartment complex, said, "It's okay. She's my niece." The guard bought the story and walked away. The man drove off with the drunk girl beside him. Two and two would not be put together until much later on.

When Christine didn't come home that night, her grandmother and father assumed she was with friends. Her family reported her as a possible runaway to authorities on November 19, two days later.

There were reports of Christine being seen around Surrey, but nothing conclusive. Although Clive's dad had made a stink about the missing girl and his son's bike, the police said they were treating the case as a "low priority." After all, she had previously been reported as a runaway.

•••

On Christmas Day, 1980, it was sunny and warm in the Lower Mainland. Just off River Road in the brush near the Fraser River, Christine Weller's body was discovered by a man out for a walk.

She was nude, and she'd been drugged (at least with alcohol), sexually assaulted, strangled, and stabbed. It was determined she may have been there since the day she disappeared or very soon after. The press announced that Christine had been found. Police asked the public for help in finding Clive's red, ten-speed bike and gave Christine's description. The bike was found the following Saturday in the brush behind the Surrey Animal Hospital.

At Christine's memorial at the Burquitlam Mortuary, the reverend officiating said that God's wrath was waiting for this killer. Police were stumped as they tried to connect the case to other child slayings that had taken place previously. They had no idea of the hell about to be unleashed.

One man, who lived right across the street from the Surrey Animal Hospital, became obsessed with Christine's case and talked about his "theories" every chance he got. His friends thought he was crazy and a braggart. His girlfriend told him often to shut up and stop talking about it. But he kept on. Even though he was well known to police, they didn't speak to him about Christine. That man was Clifford Robert Olson.

•••

On April 16, 1981, thirteen-year-old, five-foot-one, one-hundred-pound Colleen Marian Daignault was enjoying the warm spring day on her skateboard. She'd been staying with her grandmother in Surrey while her parents were breaking up. Colleen, who'd spent the night with a friend in Delta two buses away, promised her grandmother she'd be home at four that afternoon. While waiting at a bus stop in North Delta, a car pulled up, the male driver asking, "Do you know where the employment office is? I'm looking to hire kids at ten dollars an hour to wash windows." Colleen got into the car and it drove off.

Colleen was also assumed to be a runaway and was, again, a low-priority case for police, who were overwhelmed with three hundred missing persons' cases monthly. Her family hoped for the best but knew something was wrong—this was out of character for the girl. Coleen was never seen alive again.

•••

On April 21, 1981, sixteen-year-old Daryn Todd Johnsrude was on Easter break. He'd come from Saskatchewan to visit his mom and her new husband in Coquitlam. Daryn was five-foot-five, weighed ninety pounds, and had shaggy, shoulder-length hair. He'd only been in town for two days and was unfamiliar with the area. His plan was to get a feel for the place and return permanently in the summer after finishing school back home in Regina. Daryn was a bit rebellious and tended to hang with people his parents didn't like. On his way to the store to buy a pack of smokes—something else his folks didn't like him doing—a car pulled up. Daryn and the male driver began to chat. The man offered him a job at ten dollars an hour and a bottle of beer. Daryn got into the car and it drove off.

Daryn's mom and stepfather were worried to death when he didn't show up that night. He'd left that morning at eleven thirty. Where could he be? He didn't know anyone in town as he'd only been there briefly.

•••

On May 2, 1981, near the small community of Deroche about sixteen kilometers east of Mission, two men were out running their dogs in the forest. One of the dogs became agitated just down a trail near the river. Upon investigating, the men found the naked body of a young male slumped over a stump.

After a few days and some confusion between police and Daryn's family, a positive ID was made. Daryn Johnsrude had been found. He'd been beaten to death with what appeared to be a hammer after being drugged and sexually assaulted. Due to the variance in age and gender, police had yet to make any connections between the two murders and Colleen Daignault's disappearance. Clifford Olson knew they were very much related, but he had other things to take care of. On May 15, 1981, he was set to marry the mother of his newborn son.

•••

On May 19, 1981, only four days after his wedding, the monster was cruising for his next victim. Sandra Lynn Wolfsteiner, sixteen, a pretty brunette with hazel eyes, was living with her sister in Langley. Not having a car, Sandra hitchhiked when public transit wasn't a viable option. That day, she was off to visit her boyfriend, Keith, in Surrey. She wanted to drop in on him at the auto-body shop he worked at to take him to lunch nearby on Fraser Highway. First, she stopped in to see Keith's mom. After a brief visit, she headed to the highway around eleven thirty to hitchhike to the body shop. Keith's mother saw Sandra get into in a silver-gray, two-door, medium-sized car with a male driver.

Sandra, or "Sandy" to her friends, was late for lunch with Keith. Worried, he called her home, but she wasn't there. His mom told him that Sandy had left her place before noon; she'd seen her get into a car. Keith called police and was told he'd have to wait forty-eight hours to make a missing persons' report. As the days passed, police suspected if something had happened to Sandy, Keith was involved. He agreed to, and passed, a polygraph test.

Sandy was placed on the missing persons' list.

•••

On the morning of June 21, 1981, thirteen-year-old Ada Anita Court
had just finished up a babysitting gig at an apartment rented by her
brother and sister-in-law. She loved the kids, and the kids loved her
back; some even called them "Ada's babies." Ada was going to take
a bus home to Burnaby, where she planned to visit her boyfriend,
but vanished on the way. What no one realized at the time was that
Ada had been picked up by the apartment caretaker's son in a black
pickup truck.

Clifford Olson.

After Olson admonished Ada for getting into a car with a
stranger, he'd plied the youngster with beer and the promise of work.

•••

Around eight o'clock that night, a White Rock man we'll call Jim was
out for a drive near Weaver Lake in the Agassiz region, a popular
park and picnic area. As he rounded a corner, he saw a man hunched
over something beside a black pickup truck. When Jim approached,
he saw the man bending over a girl wearing a multicolored sweater.
She wasn't moving. Jim got out of his car and asked if he could be of
assistance. The short, mop-haired man with the girl at his feet simply
stared at Jim, not responding.

Thinking something was off, Jim hopped back into his car
and took off. The other man got into the pickup and briefly gave
chase but Jim, who knew the logging roads, managed to lose his
pursuer. Although terrified, Jim didn't report his encounter to
police, not realizing what he'd seen until months later when the news
broke on TV.

Who knows what might have happened had he talked to the cops right away? Perhaps July 1981 would not have been as bloody. Olson went on to kill six more children and teens in a span of only thirty days.

When detectives began looking into the disappearance of Ada Court, Clifford Olson's connection to the property and previous criminal history, specifically that of sexual assault, finally caught their eye.

•••

On July 2, 1981, Olson struck again. This time, he took his youngest victim.

Simon Partington, aged nine, lived at 13141 96th Avenue in the Cedar Hills neighborhood of Surrey. Dressed in a blue T-shirt and jeans, the angelic-looking blond, blue-eyed Simon was slightly built at four-foot-two and eighty pounds. After scarfing down a big bowl of cereal, he grabbed his new Snoopy book, tossed it into the basket of his bike, and rode off to a friend's just blocks away at 9555 128th Street.

Simon never arrived. Within a few hours, he was reported missing. He had not done his paper route that afternoon.

A massive search that grew to two hundred volunteers combed Surrey looking for the boy. As Simon was only nine, it was tough to dismiss him as a runaway. Foul play was suspected. He disappeared only blocks from where Christine Weller had vanished in November of the previous year. The police, the media and the public began to wonder if these cases could be connected. Could there be a serial killer stalking Surrey?

The search was scaled down after six days. There was no sign of Simon. He'd vanished.

•••

Olson, unmoved by the heat that had been turned up with the press coverage and public interest in the disappearances, was on the hunt again only a day after Simon's disappearance. He approached two girls, sixteen-year-old Sandra Docker and her friend, Rose Smythe, in an arcade at Lougheed Mall on North Road in Burnaby, asking them if they wanted jobs cleaning carpets.

The girls got into the man's silver Pinto, and they drove around the block to Cameron Street to a building with construction signs on it. Olson told them this was where they'd be working. He was setting his trap.

The trio made plans to connect on the next Monday, July 6, 1981, and the girls drank beer with the man in his car before he took them back to the mall.

On July 6, as agreed, Olson picked up the pair at Lougheed Mall. They drove around while Olson tried to work out how he could take two girls at once. He decided on one, and Sandra looked like the easiest mark. He told the girls he only had enough work for Sandra and dropped Rose back at the mall. Sandra was a little concerned being alone with a strange man but tagged along anyway. They drove around the Lower Mainland, and Olson picked up whiskey at one point, feeding it to Sandra.

In Surrey, Olson exchanged the Pinto for a green Ford Granada at a rental lot. As he drank the whiskey, his demeanor darkened. Sandra didn't want any more booze. She was feeling sick and quite drunk, but Olson forced it on her angrily. Thinking she was now drunk enough to manage, he drove to a secluded location in Surrey. "This is my newest job site," he said, crawling into the back seat to sexually assault Sandra Docker. She fought, and Olson grew frustrated. Unable to perform, he said drunkenly, "You're fired." He took Sandra back to the mall and kicked her out of the car.

Sandra then flagged down an approaching Royal Canadian Mounted Police (RCMP) vehicle. "The driver of that green car just tried to rape me," she told Constable Smith.

She sat in the police vehicle while Smith broadcast: "Burnaby, all cars, green Ford Granada, BC license JBH 616, departing Lougheed Mall. Proceeding east on Cameron. One male occupant, Caucasian, forty years, brown hair. Wanted [for] sexual assault. It just happened."

Police gave chase and picked up Clifford Olson.

•••

Olson talked endlessly in the interrogation room, but only to deny or say the girl was into it at first. He reminded police that he'd helped them get a child rapist convicted. Since he'd been their jailhouse snitch, he felt they owed him.

Sandra's credibility was questioned. As there were no other witnesses, and she'd been drunk at the time of the alleged attack, Olson was released.

•••

On July 9, 1981, a day after getting away with attempted rape, Olson was out cruising again like the shark he was. This time, he had an eighteen-year-old male in the car. He did this often; it was easier to lure younger people with good-looking bait. The passenger's name was Randy Ludlow.

Ludlow later gave his account of what happened that night.

Olson had spotted a pretty girl leaving a phone booth on Columbia Street in front of the Royal Columbian Hospital. It seemed

like he knew her because when he waved, she smiled and came up
to the car.

Her name was Judy Kozma; she was fourteen and a part-time
cashier at McDonalds.

Judy was heading to a job interview at Wendy's in Richmond.
Olson offered her a lift. The trio drank beer in the car on the way.
Arriving too early for Judy's interview, they stopped at a liquor store
to buy more booze. Olson gave Randy a fistful of cash, meaning to
impress Judy. Randy went inside. When he returned, Judy was now in
the passenger seat, laughing and chatting with Olson. He was offering
her a job cleaning carpets. He told her she didn't need the jobs at
Wendy's or McDonald's.

Olson and Randy gave Judy more booze. Olson also gave her
pills "to keep her from getting too drunk," but the sedatives had the
opposite effect. Olson drove back to Coquitlam and dropped Ludlow
off at the Lougheed Mall, saying he had to get Judy to her interview,
then drove away.

Judy was never seen again.

The next day, Clifford Olson took his wife and young son to
Southern California to visit the Knott's Berry Farm theme park,
staying until July 21, 1981.

•••

On July 15, 1981, the police met in Burnaby to discuss the case of the
missing Lower Mainland children. Twenty-four police investigators
attended from Vancouver Police Department, New Westminster
Police Department, and RCMP members from Burnaby, Surrey,
Coquitlam, Richmond, Squamish, and Vancouver headquarters'
Serious Crime Section. What police didn't tell reporters that day

is that one man had jumped to the top of the RCMP's suspect list: Clifford Olson.

•••

Clifford Robert Olson Jr., formerly of Surrey, BC, now living in Coquitlam. He stood five feet and seven inches tall, weighed 175 pounds, and had brown hair and brown eyes.

Some of the police officers who'd dealt with him over the years felt there was something not quite right with Clifford. He seemed empty.

Police talked about the Christine Weller murder, the sexual assaults in Squamish, Daryn Johnsrude, the recent attack on Sandra Docker, and Olson's proximity to all the abduction sites. Everyone agreed that all these things together—Olson's recent history, including his access and proximity of residences to crime scenes— were too much to ignore.

Burnaby RCMP would keep an eye on Olson using their surveillance unit, Special "O" Section.

But where was he?

One investigator, pretending to be an insurance agent, visited Clifford's folks. They told the undercover officer that Clifford and his family were vacationing in the US.

On July 23, 1981, two days after returning from the US, Clifford Olson was on the hunt again. Having committed murders of seven Lower Mainland children and young people in seven and a half months, Olson was not finished. Four more Lower Mainland youths were yet to be slain in the bloodiest week the region had ever seen.

•••

Raymond King Jr., fifteen, hopped on his bike to head over to the
Canada Manpower Youth Employment Centre in New Westminster.
He dreamed of earning his own money, maybe enough to have his
own car one day. As he chained up his bike behind the building, the
slightly built, sandy-haired boy with the impish smile was approached
by Clifford Olson. Olson used his tried-and-true lure of a promise of
work, exactly what Raymond King was looking for.

Raymond got into Olson's car, another rental from Metro Motors
in Port Coquitlam.

Olson drove them down Highway Seven toward Harrison Mills,
offering beer and pills to the youngster. They ended up on a bumpy
logging road that led to a provincial campground near Alpine Link.
Here, Olson sexually assaulted Raymond numerous times before
driving a three-inch spike into the top of the boy's head. Clifford
dragged Ray up a cliffside trail and dumped him over, throwing rocks
down onto the boy, ensuring the large stones hit him in the head and
chest. Raymond King was dead.

When Raymond didn't come home, Ray King Sr. knew something
was wrong right away. Raymond was a happy boy and would never
run away. When his bike was found behind the Manpower building, it
appeared the boy was another victim of foul play.

•••

That evening, police spoke with Clifford Olson at his Coquitlam
home, not knowing what he'd just done. They told him they wanted
to know if he'd inform for them—for cash. He'd informed for them a
few times before. This time, Olson claimed he had information about
robberies and murders. Cops thought this would be the best way to

justify being around more. They didn't want to let Olson know they were on to him.

Olson told investigators his thoughts about the disappearance of nine-year-old Simon Partington. According to the book *Where Shadows Linger: The Untold Story of the RCMP's Olson Murders Investigation* (W. Leslie Holmes and Bruce Northorp), Olson gave theories about what he "thought" had happened to Simon. He said it might be a hit-and-run where the driver, scared of what he'd done, had disposed of the body, or it was a kidnap for ransom, or the kidnapper was "a pervert."

Olson offered to do his own investigation but told police they needed to pay him for his efforts. They agreed, having set their trap to get the man they thought a predator to slip up. Olson was greedy and couldn't keep his mouth shut.

•••

The recommendations to surveil Olson were bogged down in red tape and bureaucracy. He was still able to prowl at will.

On July 25, 1981, Judy Kozma's body was found near Weaver Lake, only two days after Raymond King disappeared. Judy, missing since July 9, was sexually assaulted and viciously stabbed in the torso, neck and head. She was found close to where Daryn Johnsrude had been discovered in May.

While police were recovering Judy Kozma's remains a mere two days after his last murder, Olson was hunting again.

His next victim would be eighteen-year-old Sigrun Arnd, a German student touring in Vancouver with a larger group. Sigrun was from Weinheim, a small Rhine Valley town near the Swiss border. Her father was the owner of a watch shop there. She was visiting Canada because she relished the opportunity to learn about the culture and speak to native English speakers. Sigrun had gone to visit a cousin in Coquitlam while the rest of her group was on a day cruise. Her cousin wasn't home, so she started to make her way back to Burnaby, where she was staying in youth hostel. She was frustrated that she'd have to take several bus connections.

Olson saw the pretty girl waiting for the bus and pulled over to chat her up. Sigrun was small and bespectacled, looking younger than her eighteen years. He offered her a ride. As she got into the car, he invited her to have a drink with him. The brazen Olson took Sigrun to a busy pub in Coquitlam. She seemed happy to be experiencing real local culture as she drank beer with Olson and some business associates who'd joined them. After a few pitchers, Clifford offered to take her back to Burnaby after showing her around. Once in the car, he gave Sigrun another beer, grinning to himself as she drank. He'd dosed the beer with three chloral hydrate sleeping pills, his favorite rape drug. Their destination was the peat bogs near Richmond, where Olson had dumped Christine Weller and the yet-to-be-found Simon Partington.

As they got out of the car, Sigrun felt woozy. Olson gave her a fourth pill, lying that it would perk her up. The pair walked toward the river, Clifford bringing up the rear. Near the train tracks, when Olson was sure the coast was clear, he produced a heavy framing hammer from inside his coat and brought it down on the back of Sigrun's skull. She collapsed, barely conscious. He quickly stripped her and, while taking off his shirt, a train whistle sounded. As the train went slowly by, the brakeman running behind it saw what he believed to be a couple engaged in consensual outdoor sex. The brakeman and Olson made eye contact. Olson waved and smiled at the unsuspecting man. Weeks later, the railroad employee became aware of what he'd seen and reported it to the police.

Once the train was out of sight, Olson finished his brutal sexual assault. Before he beat Sigrun to death with more blows from the hammer, he asked her if she believed in God. He then implored her to pray for him as he went to work crushing her skull. Olson dumped her in a ditch filled with stagnant water, covering her with sticks and leaves.

•••

July 27, 1981 was the day that RCMP surveillance was to begin in earnest. But Olson was up early and on the prowl before the police could get set up.

When fifteen-year-old animal lover Terri Lyn Carson left home that morning, she was on her way to apply for a part-time job at a local pet shop called Fin N' Feathers. Cruising in the Guildford area, Olson spotted Terri, barely five-foot-tall and just over one hundred pounds, at the bus stop. He pulled over and went into his usual spiel, offering her a ride and the possibility of a job. Once in the car, Terri celebrated her job offer with a beer Olson gave her. He'd laced it with chloral hydrate.

They drove east toward the city of Hope about two hours away. Once there, Clifford cashed traveler's checks he'd stolen from Sigrun, signing them "Robert Johnson." The bank teller didn't notice the crude forgery.

On the way back, Clifford pulled off onto a logging road near Agassiz. Here, he brutally raped Terri Lyn, hammering a screwdriver into her head, breaking it off in her skull. Still alive, Terry Lyn was dragged to a ditch, where Olson dumped her facedown in the water and stood on her back until she drowned. He left her there.

That afternoon, the RCMP set up their surveillance on Clifford Olson's residence, though by then, it was too late for Terri Lyn

Carson, his tenth murder victim. Police saw Olson pull up in his car, freshly through the car wash. He went inside, showered, and went to bed.

Terri Lyn's mom called around when her daughter didn't come home. None of Terri Lyn's friends had seen her even though they'd made plans. She had not shown up for her job interview at the pet shop. Her mom called the police.

Police again treated the case as a runaway. Terri Lyn was fifteen, lived in Surrey, and came from a broken home. Perhaps they didn't want to believe that Olson could commit another murder right under their noses, but he had.

•••

Cops believed Clifford knew he was being followed. He zigged and zagged all over town, losing them multiple times, only to show up minutes later to have the whole thing repeat itself. Frustrated, the surveillance team gave up, deciding to regroup and work out better tactics. In truth, Olson wasn't on to them at all. He was just doing his thing.

On Tuesday, July 28, 1981, police met Olson in the parking lot of the Caribou Motel. Delta Detective Dennis Tarr told Olson he might be able to make as much as $100,000 for information on the child killings.

Clifford bit.

"Pick a number between one and ten," Olson said to Tarr.

"Nine," said Tarr.

"I tell you what," a grinning Olson said. "I'll give you a letter and, in that letter, will be nine numbers, each one corresponding to a location. What you find there will be your business."

Tarr pressed Clifford for more information about what they would find at the locations. Clifford said he didn't want to testify and be seen as a snitch; he had his family to worry about. The meeting ended with Tarr pretty much thinking, "Gotcha," as the two planned to meet in another two days.

On Wednesday, July 29, 1981, Clifford Olson was arrested and detained after he and two other men picked up a couple of teenage girls and got them drunk. Cops moved in before anything more serious occurred. Olson was released at three thirty in the morning without charge and was off to meet his lawyer.

But one more young person was to die.

•••

Seventeen-year-old Louise Chartrand, described as young-looking and small for her age, hitchhiked into Maple Ridge, where she worked at Dino's Place on Lougheed Highway. Arriving early, she stopped at a corner store to buy a pack of smokes and kill some time before her shift.

A car pulled up to where Louise was sitting smoking. Rolling down the window, Clifford Olson went into his manpower/hiring-teenagers lure. She got into the car.

Plying Louise with booze and pills, Clifford drove them toward Whistler, presumably away from the prying eyes of the cops. He took Louise to a gravel pit just off the highway near Whistler, where he raped and sodomized her for hours. Olson smashed her in the back of the head with his hammer, then covered the dying girl with sand and gravel. He cleaned his hands with the whiskey they'd shared, got into the car and left.

Olson washed his car at a garage, making it home at six fifteen in the morning. He had a bath and told his wife, Joan, to pack. They were going to Alberta. The cops were trying to frame him.

•••

Olson had committed four brutal murders in the span of seven days. What drove him to kill at such a rate? Perhaps it was the stress of being under the microscope. Maybe he knew his time was short? "We have found that a person with paraphilias is more likely to commit one of these types of activities when he's under a great deal of stress," says Roy Hazelwood in his book *The Evil That Men Do: FBI Profiler Roy Hazelwood's Journey into the Minds of Sexual Predators.*

As Louise's sisters were talking to police about their missing sister, Clifford lammed it to Calgary with family in tow. While there, he tried to lure another girl living nearby into meeting him. He'd hurt her before, so she refused.

On August 5, 1981, the body of another young male was found in a ravine near Weaver Lake. This was Raymond King, missing since July 23, 1981.

Olson returned home to Coquitlam that week, now under twenty-four-hour surveillance. He was tough to follow, randomly zipping all over and never driving the same car for long. He had a habit of continually changing rental cars. Police watched him commit property crimes. Although the task force needed information about murders, they were also learning a lot about Clifford Olson.

On August 12, 1981, Clifford took the ferry to Victoria on Vancouver Island. After burgling two houses there, he drove north toward Nanaimo, where he picked up a couple of girls hitchhiking. The surveillance team grew worried for their safety. When Clifford pulled into a secluded spot and got out of the car, police closed in. They couldn't risk endangering the girls any further.

Clifford had only stopped to pee.

Regardless, when he saw the cops, he bolted. After a quick chase, he was apprehended and handcuffed. Olson was indignant, claiming he'd done nothing wrong. Searching him, police found his notebook. In it was the name Judy Kozma. This piece of evidence finally linked him to one of the murder victims.

Olson was charged with two counts of breaking-and-entering and two counts of contributing to the delinquency of a minor. He was taken to Burnaby, and it's behind bars where the rest of Clifford Olson's story plays out.

He was nowhere near done hurting people.

•••

In August 1981, Clifford was in jail, and cops were talking to him as often as they could. They'd interviewed many people in Surrey, Coquitlam, and Burnaby, and there were multiple instances of other children being approached by Clifford in 1980 and 1981. He'd even molested a seven-year-old girl on his wedding day.

The cops needed Clifford to talk specifics to keep him behind bars for the murders. What came next was what some Canadians point to as one of the most controversial arrangements ever made with a criminal. This transaction was definitely a deal with the devil.

Olson would only talk for one thing: money.

Clifford wanted cash to take care of his young son and estranged wife, as he knew he'd never get out of jail again. He wanted $100,000, or $10,000 per body, and he would throw one in for free.

The RCMP took Olson up on his offer and made the "cash for bodies" deal, ensuring the money would go to his family. Clifford was later overheard in a phone call to his wife saying, "Honey, you're going to be rich." The $100,000 was put into a trust, and $10,000 would be released for evidence on each of the murders and the still-missing bodies.

Olson began talking, loving every moment of the control he felt he had. He relished in serving a big old shit sandwich to the cops. He felt in his twisted way like he'd won.

Simon Partington's body was found where Olson had said it was, by the Fraser River in Richmond where Christine Weller had been found.

Louise Chartrand's body was uncovered and removed from the shallow grave where Olson buried her near Whistler.

Ada Court and Terri Lyn Carson's skeletal remains were found near Weaver Lake.

Cops took pictures of a grinning Clifford showing them where the remains were. He coldly pantomimed each crime in detail, embellishing as he went.

After some searching, Sandra Wolfsteiner's bones were found off the road near Chilliwack.

The last body found on September 17, 1981 was Colleen Daignault in the woods of South Surrey.

Police still had not officially identified Clifford Olson as the man they had in custody, though he was mentioned by name in previous articles about the missing and murdered children in the Lower Mainland. When the press finally did name him as their suspect, no one was surprised.

The deal between Olson and the RCMP was kept secret for a time, but, like most secrets, it eventually saw the light of day. Many people were enraged; some thought the price was right—get the families' children back for a proper burial.

Clifford Olson was competent to participate in court proceedings, though he had to be kept clear of other prisoners. Child rapists and killers, known as "skinners" in penal lingo, are not looked upon fondly. Other prisoners, seeing Olson, would routinely throw things at him, including lit cigarettes.

In January 1982, Olson pled guilty to eleven counts of murder and was given eleven concurrent life sentences. Throughout the rest of his years, Olson, an escape risk and dangerous offender, spent his time in super-maximum prison special handling units.

During Olson's sentencing, trial judge HC McKay said, "I do not have the words to adequately describe the enormity of your crimes or to describe the heartbreak and anguish you have caused." He added, "My considered opinion is that you should never be granted parole for the remainder of your days. It would be foolhardy to let you at large."

There were other murders as yet unsolved that took place during Olson's brief stints of freedom over the years. Some people believed these were his crimes as well, though he never admitted to them.

Olson sent graphic letters to some of the victims' families detailing his crimes, taunting them from his prison cell. He also pestered government officials and reporters by phone and mail until his access was restricted. Every time he came up for parole, the families cringed at having to deal with the monster face-to-face again.

One of the psychiatrists who interviewed him over the years was Stanley Semrau. In his book *Murderous Minds on Trial: Terrible Tales from a Forensic Psychologist's Casebook*, Semrau talks about applying the PCL-R, or psychopath test, to Olson. "Out of a maximum score of 40, 30 is considered the cut-off for formal designation as a psychopath. Clifford Olson scored 38, the highest score I have ever given and placing him in the 99.7 percentile among male prison inmates."

The "Faint Hope Clause" in Canada said an offender, no matter how dangerous, can apply for parole after serving fifteen years of a life sentence. Olson, representing himself, applied for and was denied this type of parole. In fact, outrage at Olson's abuse of the system and the pain he caused families again and again led to federal Bill S-6, repealing the Faint Hope Clause from the criminal code. Multiple murderers are no longer eligible for early parole. No other families will be subjected to this kind of appeal.

In his cell, Olson had cable TV, books, magazines, and a small tape player and radio. Some claimed the money for these things came from "fans" all over the world. Perhaps his ability to afford luxuries was also due to his being paid his $1,169.47 Old Age Security pension when he turned sixty-five in 1995. This was disclosed to the media in 2010, and there was an uproar that this monster would then be eligible for another payment by way of the GIS (Guaranteed Income Supplement) for low-income Canadians who reach seventy, which Clifford had just turned. After petitions and much public outrage, the payments to Clifford Olson were cut off in June 2010.

In September 2011, Corrections Canada reported that Olson was in the hospital suffering from terminal cancer. He died on September 30, 2011.

Trudy Court, Ada Court's sister, said that when she heard he was dead, she cried "tears of happiness, because justice is done for the children. Our justice system couldn't do it for them. But life has. He's gone now."

Australia's Brownout Murders

ANTHONY FERGUSON

When considering Australian serial killers, many readers are drawn to the myth of Mick Taylor, the psychopathic Vietnam War veteran made famous by the *Wolf Creek* films. Thoughts of Australian murder can conjure images of the vast empty spaces of the outback, into which unwitting travelers might descend and disappear. However, the mythology is far from reality when it comes to Australian serial killers. Mick Taylor is a fictional monster based loosely on the "Backpacker" murders perpetrated by Ivan Milat in the early 1990s, and the disappearance of British traveler Peter Falconio in 2001.

The truth is that most Australian serial killers operate in urban settings, a trait they have in common with their international counterparts. Perhaps the pressures of urban life, work, and relationships drive these already unstable individuals over the edge. It is also notable that several Australian serial killers have been immigrants rather than Australian born. This isn't to suggest that Australia does not breed its own psychopaths, but rather to emphasize that many psychologically troubled migrants who came to make a new start in the Antipodes brought with them demons they could not escape.

Foreign-born Australian serial killers include the English-born homosexual "Mutilator" William MacDonald (who liked to cut

off his victims' penises and sleep with them); fellow Englishman
"Granny Killer" John Wayne Glover; and the subject of this story,
the American GI Private Eddie Leonski, Melbourne's wartime
"Brownout Strangler."

During World War II, Australia experienced a series of serial
murders that were abetted by circumstances that afforded the
opportunity for foul play. Consider the ingredients: a society thrown
off kilter by global conflict and the fear of a vicious enemy lingering
on its doorstep; a plethora of lonely, love-starved women left behind
by their men as they fight overseas; a military camp full of cashed-
up, homesick, young American soldiers; the government imposition
of a "brownout" (the dimming of public lighting after dusk to deter
bombing raids); the thrill of illicit public sex in darkened alleyways
with exotic strangers; a clash of two disparate cultures—one brash
and forward-looking, the other chained in Victorian morality;
copious amounts of alcohol; and a shy introvert emboldened by
drink displaying party tricks in pubs by walking across the bar on his
hands—a handsome young psychopath and serial killer who loves the
sound of women's voices so much he just wants to rip them out of
their throats.

The early months of 1942 were traumatic times for Australia.
Global conflict had raged for more than two years and showed no
sign of abating. Large numbers of young men had been shipped
to foreign shores to fight the Nazis and the Japanese, who were
advancing through the Asia-Pacific region. Australians lived in
mortal fear of invasion. Professor Kate Darian-Smith of Melbourne
University noted in her book *On the Home Front: Melbourne in
Wartime 1939-1945*: "Civilian morale plunged to an unprecedented
low [after military disasters]… Australia was a nation living in fear in
1942… The separation of families, the nightly blackout and air-raid
drills, and the constant uncertainty about the future contributed to

feelings of stress and heightened emotions." When Singapore fell and Darwin was bombed in quick succession, it seemed the enemy was on our doorstep.

With Australia's traditional protector, Britain, otherwise occupied on several fronts and seemingly ambivalent to the fate of its former colony, the Australian government took the momentous and far-reaching decision to look elsewhere for help. Prime Minister John Curtin ordered his cabinet minister in Washington, RG Casey, to seek an urgent audience with President Franklin D. Roosevelt. The outcome of their meeting was a significant agreement that would allow a substantial number of American GIs to be stationed in Australia, ready for immediate deployment. The whole operation was supposed to be top secret—so secret that on their arrival in Melbourne on February 2, 1942, an enormous crowd turned out to cheer. Among them was Private Edward Leonski, fresh out of New York City, an individual who would leave his mark on Australian society in a manner nobody would forget.

Around fifteen thousand American GIs arrived in the Victorian capital in February 1942. Most troops went to the large encampment of tents set up in North Melbourne at Royal Park, renamed Camp Pell in honor of a late American pilot. The American servicemen soon made their presence felt. They brought with them a certain Hollywood swagger; with their smart uniforms, polite manners, and better pay, they soon impressed the local women. This led to social tension of course, and newspapers of the day carried occasional reports of mass brawls erupting in the streets between Australian and American troops. Hence, there arose the echo of an infamous slogan coined by British servicemen about American troops stationed in England, that they were "overpaid, oversexed, and over here."

As the war raged closer to Australian shores, the government felt the need to introduce a nighttime "brownout," a less stringent version of the blackout imposed on London. It was a bit of a culture shock, but nevertheless effective. All windows were covered after dark, street and car lights were dimmed, and a speed limit of twenty-miles-per-hour was imposed.

The changes had no adverse effect on the GIs. The brownout only served to assist them in their favorite hobby of courting the local women. It might be said that some of them abused the hospitality. In a short period of time, the social fabric of Melbourne changed inexorably. Traditionally known as a quiet, respectable town, Melbourne rapidly segued into a den of sly grog shops (unlicensed barrooms) and bawdy houses. The local population took their moral cue from the free-spending Americans to let their hair down in defiance of the national mood of fear. Melbourne's prostitutes never had it so good.

The cultural impact of this small-scale American invasion cannot be understated. Most Australians at the time saw themselves as loyal British subjects. They were shocked when British Prime Minister Winston Churchill refused to divert any troops or resources to help Australia. Hence, they came to grudgingly accept the brash young Americans. By 1943, there were 250,000 stationed in Melbourne, Sydney, and Brisbane. Over the course of the war, around one million American servicemen would walk on Australian shores, and they left an indelible mark on our society. They spread new ideas about music, food, language, and manners and, more importantly, forged the basis of a strategic political alliance that is still in place today.

The brownout, which would give Leonski his serial killer pseudonym, stayed in place until the war ended in August 1945. The social impact was significant. It disrupted activities and shopping hours and caused a notable increase in traffic accidents and all sorts of crime. The authorities were concerned it would encourage immoral behavior like illicit public sex. Which it of course did. Crime and sex were key elements of blackouts and brownouts.

Among the GIs stationed at Camp Pell, Private Edward Leonski was a man of contradictions: tall and powerfully built, yet boyish and baby-faced. His mood could swing rapidly from despair to joy. Despite his hulking physique, he sang frequently in a high soprano voice. A brooding introvert, he came out of his shell when he drank, and Eddie drank frequently. He was an alcoholic with a family history of alcoholism and madness. Most importantly, Leonski was emotionally immature: a boy in a man's body. Those who knew him thought he didn't know how to relate to other people, particularly women. It is said that his early sexual experiences may have been restricted to prostitutes. To cover his inadequacies, he resorted to boasting, goading his fellow conscripts into feats of strength that often ended in violence. When in Melbourne bars, his voice grew louder as he drank, and he became known among locals for a particular party trick. When intoxicated, he would show off by walking along the bar on his hands, drawing rounds of applause from other patrons.

Leonski was born in New Jersey on December 12, 1917, into a poor Russian immigrant family. For most of his life, the family lived in a tenement building on East 77th Street in Manhattan, a working-class suburb on the edge of the more prestigious East Side of New York. Eddie was a shy boy with few friends. While he was a good student, his main passion was bodybuilding. He grew up to be a tall, muscular figure with blond hair and blue eyes.

Although considered fairly bright, young Leonski rejected the notion of a desk job, choosing physical labor where he could display his strength. He liked to show off his body and had a down-to-earth charm, which attracted women. However, he apparently had little experience with the opposite sex, much preferring the company of his mother, whom he adored. That love was reciprocated. Eddie was his mother's favorite among several children, and their love was his only bright spot in a lonely childhood. Consequently, the young man developed a deep attachment to her.

Leonski succumbed to the family habit of heavy drinking in his youth. His mother married twice during Eddie's childhood, and both husbands were violent drunks. His Russian-born father, John, died from alcohol-related conditions in 1924. The second marriage fared no better, and Amelia Leonski was twice committed to an asylum in 1928. By then, she was a chronic alcoholic herself, suffering from manic depression and suspected schizophrenia. Eddie had three brothers; one was committed to a mental asylum in 1940, another ended up in the penitentiary with a long criminal record, and the third was described as shiftless. His sister, Helen, was apparently the only family member not afflicted with the Leonski flaw.

Eddie was drafted into the US Army against his will on February 17, 1941. He seemed worthy military material—well-behaved, with a good physique and no prior criminal record. It was not until his military service commenced that the first chinks appeared in Leonski's veneer. He started to drink heavily again and began to display the erratic behavior that led to his eventual downfall. He would easily break into tears and was prone to violence. In retrospect, it is possible to surmise that separating him from his mother was too much of a strain on his fragile emotional state.

Like many individuals who go on to become serial killers, Leonski gave the authorities an early indication of his true nature when stationed in San Antonio, Texas, for basic training. During Rest and Recreation Leave on April 13, 1941, Leonski had a few drinks and made an unsuccessful attempt to strangle a local woman. However, she neglected to press charges, and the official report listed the crime as a simple assault and not an attempt at murder. Leonski spent a short spell in a military prison.

By this time, Leonski's behavior was well known throughout the battalion. Many of his colleagues would later confess they were afraid of Eddie. He drank a lot, wept the night before the troops disembarked for Australia, and had to be forced onto the ship in tears. It was also common knowledge that Leonski regularly visited the red-light district in San Antonio. Leonski's troubled mind likely developed a Madonna-whore complex (Freud). The women he encountered in bordellos and bars could never meet the romantic ideal he embodied in his mother. Rather, they were reviled as objects of lust.

According to his later confessions, in March 1942, Leonski made two attacks on Australian women which did not come to light until after the subsequent murders. In the first, he tried to strangle a young woman in her flat. Fortunately, the woman escaped and alerted a neighbor. As Leonski fled, he left behind a compelling piece of evidence—a US Army-regulation singlet marked with the initials EJL. However, the woman didn't report the assault until much later, when she read of the Brownout Strangler in the press.

Later that month, Leonski approached another woman at a tram stop. After some polite conversation, the woman rebuffed his advances and the GI casually told her, "I'm thinking of choking a dame—and it might as well be you." He had almost choked the woman into unconsciousness when a tram came by and Leonski fled into the darkness. Just like the previous victim, this woman also failed to report the attack until after the subsequent murders.

By this stage, Leonski had resumed his heavy drinking. He was homesick and deeply depressed by the enforced separation from his mother. His shy nature made it difficult to make friends under normal circumstances, but his behavior showed an alarming contrast under the influence of alcohol. Drinking increased his self-confidence. After imbibing to excess, he became garrulous and aggressive. He would paw women in an offensive way and then laugh it off as a joke.

Leonski would say himself he was like Dr. Jekyll and Mr. Hyde. Drink released him from his inhibitions, and he became a different person.

Eventually, Leonski snapped and went on a bender, disappearing for six days. He was dragged back to Camp Pell and placed under military arrest of his own volition. He spent the next thirty days in the guardhouse. Upon release, Leonski went on another drinking spree. The emotional strain was driving him over the edge. He committed his first murder in the early hours of Sunday morning, May 3, 1942. Wandering the streets alone, anger and resentment boiling up within, he saw a figure through the winter drizzle, standing in a doorway. He struck up a clumsy conversation with forty-year-old Ivy McLeod as she waited for the night bus. As they chatted, Leonski maneuvered the small woman into a recess between two shops and suddenly lunged at her, forcing his strong hands around her throat. The woman fell back with the GI on top of her. In a frenzied state after choking her to death, he beat her around the face and tore at her clothes but had some trouble with her belt. Hearing footsteps approaching, Leonski fled.

The witness was on his way to his job of hosing down the pavement outside one of Melbourne's many pubs. For many years, Australian taverns were subject to early closing hours, which in turn led to the tradition of the "six-o'clock swill," where drinkers would see the deadline approaching and swallow as much booze as possible. This resulted in copious amounts of vomiting, inside and outside the bars. Hence the need to hose them down.

The witness saw a large figure in what looked like an American uniform rise from a squatting position and run away. He didn't get a look at the face but could tell the man was powerfully built. The victim was left with her legs spread and genitals exposed. There was severe bruising to her face and around the throat. It was apparent the killer had attacked in a post-mortem frenzy and had possibly intended an act of necrophilia.

Rumors quickly spread around the city that the perpetrator of the crime may have been an American GI. This led to heightened social tensions between the Americans and locals. At an official level, the US military hierarchy at first tried to brush off the incident as an anomaly. They refused to accept that one of their boys was a killer. They didn't want the bad publicity and feared an international incident.

The second murder took place within the week on May 8, on the steps of a popular boarding house at 13 Spring Street. It mostly catered to young women who had moved to Melbourne from the country. The victim, Pauline Thompson, was an attractive, thirty-one-year-old married woman with two children. Her husband was a police officer stationed in rural Bendigo, several hundred kilometers away. He was waiting for a transfer to the city. Mrs. Thompson was a part-time singer who spent a lot of time entertaining in bars. On the night in question, she'd arranged to accompany an American soldier to a dance, but he was late meeting her.

Growing more confident after getting away with his first kill, Leonski approached the woman in a restaurant and engaged her in conversation. He convinced her to accompany him to a sly grog house for something stronger. Witnesses would later recognize Pauline Thompson but not the GI she was with. They said she seemed relaxed and was openly flirting with the man. They could not even pick Leonski out of a line-up. With their regulation uniforms, accents, and haircuts, a lot of the American servicemen looked alike to the locals.

Around midnight, Mrs. Thompson took the GI back to her hotel. It is not known if she invited him in or politely refused him entry. As she turned the key in the door and made to walk up the stairs, Leonski attacked her. He would say later that she had been singing in his ear all night, and it drove him mad. He just wanted that voice—he had to take it from her and keep it for himself.

Her body was found in the doorway the following morning. The *modus operandi* was similar. She had been strangled, her clothes torn asunder in a frenzied assault, legs splayed, genitals exposed, and severe bruising around the face where she had been beaten. Once again, there was no evidence of sexual assault.

A wave of fear spread across the city, and many women started to think twice about associating with American servicemen. The Brownout Strangler was more feared than the Japanese. The police net inevitably tightened around the camps. It was around this time that the police received one of many anonymous tip-offs suggesting they look in the local pubs for a guy that walks on his hands.

The American authorities, meanwhile, were in a bind. They desperately wanted to apprehend the culprit themselves before the Australian police caught him. This was because they feared that Australian law would not apply the death penalty that they could apply under US military law. They wanted a culprit, any GI would do, and they wanted to hang him and have the whole thing blow over.

Leonski, meanwhile, had drunkenly confided in his only friend at camp, his tent companion Private Anthony Gallo, that he was the killer. Gallo would eventually turn his friend in, but at first, he refused to believe the confession, hoping his maudlin colleague was just making it up. Gallo would state that Leonski likened himself to a werewolf or Dr. Jekyll and Mr. Hyde, and the potion turning him into a monster was alcohol. Leonski also boasted to Gallo that Pauline Thompson had told him while they made love, "You have a nice baby face, but underneath, you are vicious." In retrospect, it was considered unlikely that Leonski had sex with her.

The Brownout Strangler claimed his third and final victim on another cold wintry night on May 18. Forty-year-old Gladys Hosking set off for home in the early evening gloom from her job at Melbourne University near Camp Pell. Watching her through the drizzle, a friendly GI approached and asked to share her umbrella. Gladys knew the Americans could be a little brash, but the young man seemed friendly enough, if a little drunk.

The GI walked her toward her lodgings, then asked if she could point out the way back to Camp Pell. Traversing a little farther into the brownout darkness, she began to give directions when he attacked her, his powerful hands sliding around her throat. Later, Leonski would say, "She had a lovely voice. I wanted that voice."

Leonski dragged the body under a fence into a secluded park. Picking her up, he carried her, slipping in the mud. When she suddenly gurgled, he panicked and flew into a rage, tearing at her clothes and beating her. He pulled her dress up over her face and fled, leaving her facedown in a pool of thick yellow mud.

Encountering an Australian private guarding some army vehicles, Leonski asked him for directions to his camp. The private noted the muddy state of his uniform. When Hosking's body was discovered early the next day, it was close enough to Camp Pell for word to spread around the camp.

A definite signature was now evident in all three murders—all of the women were old enough to be maternal types in societal terms; all were strangled; all had their clothes torn and ripped above and below their waists, exposing their breasts and genitals; and all had been savagely beaten around the face.

The fact this murder had taken place on the cusp of Camp Pell gave further credence to the suspicion that an American serviceman was the killer. As the police looked across toward the camp, Private Anthony Gallo looked back at them, his heart palpitating.

Gallo confronted Leonski on the quiet. Eddie now insisted it wasn't him. He had just been drunk and telling tales. All of

Melbourne's American camps were sealed off and placed under military guard. The local detectives were increasingly stressed. They still had no solid lead, and rumors abounded that the Yanks were about to be mobilized and shipped out into action. Their killer could be about to get away.

Then they got a break. On May 20, Gallo came forward and expressed his suspicions. Then, two local women came forward to state that they'd been attacked by a GI in the second week of May, between the second and third murders. One of them told how a GI had approached her in the street, followed her, and forced his way into her apartment, only to be chased off by her uncle. The uncle was called in, and he identified Leonski.

It wasn't enough to go on, but Leonski was now isolated and subjected to intense questioning. Grilled about the mud stains on his uniform and bedding on the night of the Hosking murder, and taken to each murder scene, the GI eventually broke down and confessed. The whole city heaved a sigh of relief, as indeed did Private Gallo.

The subsequent trial of Eddie Leonski gained a certain notoriety and led to an impasse between the American and Australian governments, both of which wanted to deal with Leonski under their own laws. Eventually, the Americans held sway, and the Australian authorities had to butt out of the subsequent judicial procedure. This aspect of the Brownout murders is covered in the 1986 film *Death of a Soldier*. Leonski's was the first case ever on Australian soil where a person was tried by foreign military tribunal for crimes committed against civilians.

He was duly charged with a violation of the 92nd Article of War and court-martialed in the second week of June 1942. The main issue in verifying Leonski's guilt lay in proving he was sane and how much of a role alcohol played in his decision-making when he committed the murders.

Colonel Spencer Eddy was reluctantly appointed as Leonski's defense lawyer. He did his best to convince the jury his charge was insane—Leonski was a narcissist and attention-seeker. Like an emotional, testosterone-filled teenager, he would do anything to draw attention to himself, even confessing to crimes he did not commit.

Leonski meanwhile carried on in his usual boisterous manner, acting as if he had done nothing wrong. He made inappropriate remarks about the crimes and treated them like a joke. Eddy suspected that Leonski might not be mentally sound, as he appeared to live in a fantasy world.

The unstable Leonski family background was taken into consideration and debated at length by several Australian and American psychiatrists. They concurred that Leonski was egotistical and insecure and that he would display his immense strength on the slightest provocation. Even during the trial, he continually tried to intervene, desperate to be the center of attention. The mental instability and alcoholism that peppered his family history was taken into consideration, along with one of his brothers' criminal tendencies.

After a lengthy deliberation, the psychiatrists concurred that the accused was sane and aware of his actions at the time of each of the crimes. Pointing to Leonski's written confessions, they alluded to the care he took to avoid detection after the commission of each crime, despite his apparent level of drunkenness. This, they suggested, indicated a rational, calculating mind carrying out premeditated murders. Leonski was diagnosed as sane but emotionally unstable.

Eddie Leonski was found guilty of the brownout murders and sentenced to hang—a decision fully supported by President Roosevelt in his role as Commander-in-Chief of the US Armed Forces.

Expounding on the case in his book *Private Eddie Leonski: The Brownout Strangler*, Australian writer Ivan Chapman drew on the later recollections of Lieutenant Hugh McHugh, one of the psychiatrists asked to assess Leonski's mental state at the actual trial in 1942. Looking back from the perspective of distance, McHugh suggested that Leonski had a strong love/hate relationship with his mother. The three women he strangled were older than himself, and forensic evidence suggested he did not have sex with any of them. It was proposed that Leonski had trouble resolving his oedipal feelings and resented the army for separating him from his mother.

Another American psychiatrist who took an interest in the Leonski case was Fredric Wertham. In the *Fredric Wertham Papers*, Wertham maintained that greater attention should have been given to the history of violence, alcoholism, and insanity in Leonski's family, and, that as far as he was concerned, Leonski was insane and should not have been held responsible for his crimes. Wertham suggested that Leonski had been overwhelmed by a "catathymic crisis." This resulted from a mother fixation that compels certain types of frustrated men to kill the person they love most of all. Thus, Leonski was committing symbolic matricide. With his mother far away, he needed to find some substitutes to kill. Wertham also contended that Leonski's fascination for the victims' voices referred to his mother's voice—in the sense that an infant feels that their mother's voice is for them alone.

Another theory proposed by an unnamed Australian psychiatrist posited that Leonski was influenced by the popular 1941 feature film *Dr. Jekyll and Mr. Hyde*. In it, Hyde chokes a girl as she sings to him, saying, "You have a marvelous voice. I want to hear that voice. I want that voice." Leonski had actually said almost the exact same thing in his confessions and had referred to the story in his talks with his friend Anthony Gallo.

The board of review at the Leonski trial suspected a sexual motive in the murders, but it was difficult to directly establish one. There was no evidence of sexual interference with the victims and no record of any traces of semen in or around the bodies.

It is likely however, that the rage Leonski expressed in beating and strangling his female victims was in some way an expression of intensely repressed sexual desire. It is significant that in his extensive descriptions of the crimes, Leonski never made any reference to the obvious beatings he gave his victims. This tends to suggest that he felt some semblance of shame over these actions and would rather pretend they never occurred. He was happy to talk at length about the actual strangling, even to make a joke of it, but he never spoke of using his fists on the women before or after death.

Ivan Chapman noted that Leonski allegedly made a bizarre confession to another of his superior officers shortly before the trial. Lieutenant Ira C. Rothgerber claimed that Leonski told him he had killed all three women and committed necrophilia with one or two of them. He also allegedly described to the Lieutenant his vivid hallucinations about extinguishing the voices of his victims. Whether this represents a genuine indication of delusion or a cleverly worded ploy to suggest insanity is open to conjecture.

Leonski went to the gallows at Melbourne's Pentridge Prison on November 9, 1942. His body was first interred in an unmarked grave at Springvale Botanical Cemetery and later removed to a military cemetery in Hawaii.

That Eddie Leonski left a deep psychological imprint on Australian society is attested by the art he inspired: the aforementioned feature film *Death of a Soldier*; a factional novel *Leonski: The Brownout Murders* by Andrew Mallon (1979); and he was also immortalized on canvas by Albert Tucker in his "Images of Model Evil" series in a painting entitled *Memory of Leonski* (1943).

The Man in Black and the Silver Screen:
The Life and Crimes of Peter Moore

MARK FRYERS

"The most evil man to ever set foot in Wales" was the headline that heralded the trial of Peter Moore, the so-called "Man in Black" who physically and sexually assaulted countless men in a reign of terror that lasted more than twenty years. His crimes culminated in a killing spree in the winter of 1995, which ended the lives of four men unfortunate enough to fall under Moore's perverse vision. It was fitting for a man who owned and ran several cinemas in the area, and acted like a film star at his trial, to claim it was not he who committed these outrages but a phantom lover nàmed Jason, after the masked homicidal killer in the *Friday the 13th* film franchise. Some critics and analysts believe that cinema enacts the features of scopophilia—the pleasure of watching is chiefly voyeurism, sexual pleasure gained from watching others who are unaware. But Moore, the cinema owner, was not content with just watching, and those he was watching were painfully aware of his presence.

THE MAN IN BLACK

Of the countries of the British Isles, Wales is possibly the least-known internationally. Indeed, its stunning green fields punctuated by its mountains and slate-lined valleys, often shrouded in mists and gentle rain, offer a country equally veiled in history, folklore, and romance. This is compounded by its Gaelic heritage and unique national language that adds a further layer of mystery to the place. Wales is perhaps best recognized for its proud tradition of rugby; singing (Tom Jones, Shirley Bassey); the mystical fables of the Mabinogion; and mining communities depicted in such films as *The Proud Valley*, featuring Paul Robeson, and John Ford's Oscar-winning epic *How Green Was My Valley*.

The film of Peter Moore's existence would be the antithesis of the community depicted in Ford's gentle evocation of simple village life and bears more resemblance to the slasher films he alluded to in his futile attempt to wriggle free from justice at his trial.

Moore's upbringing embodies several of the serial killer pathologies endlessly reiterated in films, television, and writings about better known individuals such as Ted Bundy, Jeffrey Dahmer, or Ed Kemper. He was born in North Wales in 1940 and was to spend the rest of his non-incarcerated life in the same area. His association with the seaside was to continue too, but it was not to be of the carefree levity and pleasure-seeking of the traditional seaside resort: for Peter Moore, the beach was to embody the liminal space of death.

His family was financially secure, his father being a local businessman who owned a hardware store in Kinmel Bay. The family lived above it in a grand edifice dubbed Darlington House. As tends to fit the profile for a deranged killer, much has been made of Moore's relationship with his mother. Edith Moore was in her forties when she bore Peter, despite being practically resigned to never having children. She therefore regarded him as her "little miracle," a title that would be hard to live up to or would make it hard to do anything wrong. It seemed the latter applied in little Peter's case. She doted on Moore—loved him unconditionally to the point that he was known as a "mummy's boy" and likely appeared spoiled to the other children, who could not afford to live in the lifestyle afforded him. But Mrs. Moore was also a domineering presence, pulling the strings behind the scenes, as it were. His introverted nature at an early age was in part due to this—she wanted to keep him as her little boy, and he was likely forced to live a Peter Pan-like existence until he could struggle free from this closeted world. The boy who grew up was a dark doppelganger to the introverted little boy.

The "mother's boy" murderer has passed into popular culture thanks mainly to Norman Bates in Hitchcock's influential *Psycho*, but the film was based on the figure of Ed Gein and several other high-profile killers including Ed Kemper, who were driven by rage or maternal obsession to commit their atrocities against women. For Moore, this duality between life and the cinema screen was to mark his existence. Like Norman Bates and Gein himself, Moore kept his mother's room intact after she died, as though a shrine to her existence, while the rest of the house bore lurid testimony to his crimes. Moore kept a black truncheon by his bed for his own sexual pleasure among a collection of stuffed animals, suggesting how there was little distinction between two very different objects.

By contrast, Moore's relationship with his father, Ernie, was far from harmonious. Allegedly a hard man and strict disciplinarian, Ernie's relationship with his son was agitated by the young Peter's relationship with his mother and his suspicions that Moore was homosexual. Moore was alleged to have received a physical beating from his father on numerous occasions. Ernie's sour temperament was compounded by his struggles with alcohol, with former customers of the hardware store noting that he took solace in regular nips from a whiskey flask during working hours and that he was often *non compos mentis* by the middle of the day.

There was probably another reason for Peter's closeness to his mother, as Peter began to realize that he was "different" to others, drawn to the boys in his school while they liked the girls. Like Jeffrey Dahmer, this possibly led the young Moore to feel alienated from the rest of society. The upside of living in a small community in an underpopulated area is the sense of community and belonging this can foster. The downside is that everyone knows your business, and, if you are "different," it can be a harsh and unforgiving place. However, it should be borne in mind that this is not an ameliorating factor in the crimes that Moore committed and certainly not a direct or causal link to sadism and murder.

Profilers are therefore faced with a compelling killer's profile that echoes numerous other famous killers whose crimes are said to at least be partly explained by their upbringing, especially through unhealthy or abusive relationships with parents or parental figures. This is further underlined by the fact that three of his victims were either men of a certain age, had imbibed alcohol, or were known to frequently imbibe alcohol, something Moore came to hate in his father and generally. Additionally, his dark lifestyle was something he especially kept from his doting but controlling mother, whose death hastened Moore's leap from assault to murder.

THE SILVER SCREEN

Film was a constant in the life of Moore. At a young age, his parents bought him a cine camera, a rare acquisition in those days, and Moore would make little films of himself and his mother—peculiar romantic affairs featuring him running toward the camera with flowers in the manner of an advertisement or declaring his love for her. Blessed with wealth inherited from his parents, Moore found a way to be an important and even respected part of the community. Again, cinema was the conduit through which this was achieved. Bagillt had not had a cinema for many years when Moore reopened the Focus Cinema in 1991 in a converted chapel. It is easy to underestimate how important the cinema was to small towns in the age before multi-platform media and Internet streaming. The cinema was a place to escape—a little shining beacon of warmth and excitement in what would have been long, dark winter months in North Wales when the tourist industry drew to a standstill. Locals remember the excitement at the arrival of the new cinema, and the first film screened there, the 1991 Kevin Costner blockbuster *Robin Hood: Prince of Thieves*.

Moore went on to run three cinemas in the area; the Empire at Holyhead was followed by the Wedgewood in Denbigh. Therefore, Moore was not only seen as a respected local businessman, but also fulfilled a yearning for entertainment in the area. Local residents could even drop their children off at the cinema for the Saturday-morning matinee, knowing they were in safe hands. The tall man who dressed in black shirts and black ties even took on avuncular duties. He was also, unlike other sadistic serial killers, very deferential to women. His neighbor, George Marland, recalled that "he treated women like he would have liked women to treat his mother." Difference and idiosyncrasy could be forgiven or overlooked, it seemed, if the purveyor provided a useful function or provided a public service.

Yet underneath the façade of community server and local businessman, Moore was living a double life; the impetus toward pain and murder that was to overcome his desires found an outlet in his clandestine, nocturnal activities. Again, the moving image played its part. Moore would peddle pornographic videos on the side: a flipside to the Hollywood product screened in his cinemas. The French film director Jean-Luc Godard once claimed that cinema is truth, at twenty-four frames a second. For Moore, it was death at the same rate. His mother passed away some nineteen months before the murders were committed, and he increasingly threw himself further into the sadomasochism underworld he frequented, seemingly unshackled from his mother's apron strings or looking for a way to forget her passing. The death of his mother was swiftly followed by several pets—his two Alsatians, his cat, and the fish in his pond. Moore became convinced he was haunted by death; it "literally just seemed to start following me," he claimed.

More intense than distributing pornography, he would meet up with other gay men, probably having to shield their activities from disapproving neighbors and relatives. Moore seemed to take full advantage of the fact that these sessions would by necessity be clandestine, using them as a training ground to dip his toes into the world of sadistic depravity. He was in control—inflicting pain and humiliation on those unlucky enough to succumb to him. Some of these sessions were performed in his cinemas, suggesting a literal double life in front of the screens.

His activities became more extreme, but his appetite for inflicting pain would remain unsated. Moore, in common with a number of notorious serial killers from the British Isles—most famously Ian Brady—was fascinated with the iconography of the Third Reich. While the rest of Britain basks in the comforting nostalgic glow of World War II myths that celebrate the defeat of an insidious evil, the insidious evil still holds a seductive allure for others. Moore dressed in a black leather outfit styled on those of the SS during both his sadomasochistic sex sessions and his nocturnal homicidal excursions. This was what helped earn him the sobriquet "The Man in Black." His weapon of choice was a specially purchased combat knife, a sinister birthday present to himself procured from a shop in Rhyll. At the time of his arrest and trial, the press seemed to focus on the price paid for this weapon—twenty-five English pounds, as if a higher price would somehow have justified its intended use.

Not content with willing volunteers, Moore advanced to sexually assaulting unsuspecting victims in the Conwy area, reported at the time of his sentence to be possibly more than fifty. It was another grim stepping stone toward the ultimate outrage—taking a life. Many of his victims were men walking home alone from the pub late in the evening a little inebriated. He would beat them unconscious and either masturbate or defecate on them. The rules of masculinity dictated that there would be too much shame for these heterosexual men in reporting these crimes, so they invariably went unnoticed. One man suffered brain injuries so severe that he was confined to a wheelchair and relied on care for the rest of his life. Again, Moore's trajectory mirrors those of other serial killers forged in the pursuit of gaining sexual gratification purely through the infliction of pain on others.

However, both darkness and shame shrouded his activities, leaving him to go undetected for so long in a reign of terror that presumably would have sated his desire, albeit temporarily. Due to this, the discovery by police officers of the body of Anthony Davies on Pensarn beach on December 18, 1995, was initially a mystery.

MURDER

For most, the beach is a place of freedom and abandonment—a carefree and transient place where the anxieties and constrictions of everyday life can be forgotten, at least for a short while. Before the

THE BEST NEW TRUE CRIME STORIES: SERIAL KILLERS

days of cheap international travel, the seaside holiday or day trip was an unofficial national institution in Britain, woven into the fabric of everyday life. It was a practice first started by the monarchy in the eighteenth century, lending it a certain democracy—something enjoyed by royals and commoners alike. Indeed, the economy of North Wales is heavily predicated on this notion, with the beaches and resorts at Llandudno, Rhyl, and Colwyn Bay all geared toward the pleasure principle, equipped with piers, promenades, and pleasure palaces to accommodate the eight-million tourists who pass through Wales each year.

Beaches and coastal areas can also be grim and unforgiving environments, especially out of season, and no more so than in North Wales where the harsh winters disrupt the tourist flow, and the bitter winds blow through the piers and the shutters that protect the tourist sites during the off-season.

For the unfortunate Anthony Davies, the beach at Pensarn was a harsh and unforgiving place, and not only the place where he breathed his last, but where he was subject to a final, post-mortem outrage. His trousers were around his ankles, and his buttocks had been slashed. Davies had been looking after his aunt after she had broken her leg. He told his family he was going to drive to check on her and was not seen alive again. His car was found parked near the beach. His brother helped the police in the search and was witness to the unhappy discovery. As they searched the beach, the tide came in, and a police officer noticed a shape in the shallow water and evidence of a struggle—blood stained the pebbles on the beach nearby. Davies had been stabbed in the chest five times.

Pensarn beach was rumored to be a gay meeting point, but it was also a site of danger for those on the literal and figurative margins. A history of brutal attacks on the beach were rumored to be carried out by a mysterious tall man in black clothing who assaulted and robbed people. This "man in black" remained at large for more than twenty years, but the murder meant that this dark affair had to finally be brought into the light. A large collection of watches and wallets were later found at Moore's house, trinkets of his dark escapades and trophies of his power over his victims.

Dave Morris was the lead investigative officer assigned to the case tasked with finding the perpetrator of a seemingly motiveless crime, with no murder weapon and in an area quite unused to murder. However, it was not the isolated incident it first appeared to be.

The body of Henry Roberts, a retired railway porter, was found facedown outside his house on September 22, 1995. Roberts was viewed as an eccentric recluse, a loner who lived with his mother until her death a few years previously. He was rumored to be gay but was also seen as harmless with no known enemies. Much of this parallels Moore's life, and they seemed to share a less savory passion—that of Nazi paraphernalia. A Nazi flag owned by Roberts was found at Moore's house, clearly purloined as one of the many mementos of his crimes.

Roberts lived alone with his pet dog in the dilapidated property where he had lived with his mother before her death. His daily visits to the local pub were almost as regular as clockwork, and he was noted for always having plenty of cash about him, eating out constantly and taking taxis regularly. Thus, it was also initially speculated that his murder was prompted by robbery, a hypothesis also supported by the piles of cash discovered squirreled away in different parts of his house. The only other clue authorities had was a report that a van was seen parked on Robert's driveway in the days before his body was found.

Suspicion fell on those who may have known that Roberts had unexplained wealth. Nigel Owens, a taxi driver who regularly transported Roberts to venues and eateries in the nearby town of

Holyhead, was initially arrested on suspicion of the murder and
remained in custody for three weeks until police pieced this murder
together with those of Davies and another. Owens must have seemed
a less likely suspect, considering the manner in which Roberts was
found and killed. Roberts was stabbed twenty-seven times. As with
Davies, his buttocks were slashed, and forensics discovered that
he had been made to suffer, with the final, fatal blow somewhat
prolonged. Renowned psychology professor Louis B. Schlesinger
speculated that this would have given Moore arousal, a prolonging of
the act that signified Roberts's life was in his power.

The deaths of Roberts and Davies proved that Moore was an
opportunistic killer, striking in darkness and in isolated areas on
victims either on the periphery of society, as with Roberts, or far away
from the safety of their loved ones, as with Davies. This followed on
from his previous activities—targeting men who would apparently be
too embarrassed or frightened to report their assault for fear of being
ostracized for their sexual proclivities.

Moore's final victim, Keith Randles, fits this profile only for the
fact that he was temporarily on the margins. Randles was a very well-
liked and popular traffic safety officer who happened to be working
away from home on a roadside construction site in late 1995. He
was temporarily based in a caravan on the site. One evening, after
bringing some chips back to the caravan on the way back from the
pub, he received a knock on the door. When he opened it, he was
confronted by the tall figure of Moore, who proceeded to attack him
with his combat knife. Detectives claim Moore admitted to them that
Randles had begged for his life for the sake of his grandchildren. He
also asked why he was doing it. "Fun" was the reply Moore allegedly
gave. Such was his cold approach that he even drove back to the scene
of the crime to reclaim one of his signature bow ties supposedly lost
in the struggle. Randles's body was found in the morning by his work

colleagues—a grim discovery that was matched by clear signs of a struggle on the ground outside and which pointed to a protracted and brutal encounter. Police were confronted with signs of a recurring *modus operandi*.

The signs were perhaps there for the keen-eyed, but, until there was a body, a person to file a complaint against Moore, a smoking gun of sorts, there was no reason to link Moore to much untoward. A flatmate of Moore's, a projectionist at one of his cinemas invited to share a room with him, remembers him, like many others, as being kind and helpful. In hindsight, he also recalled a lot of what might be described as suspicious activity that hinted at a double life. Moore would disappear at night and return in the early hours. He was constantly changing his wallets and watches, always renting vans, and, most alarmingly of all, constantly washing them out as if he was on the run from an imaginary assailant or removing the vestiges of a heinous crime. Moore diversified his business interests by selling gas to customers, often late at night, which necessitated Moore driving to remote locations (a gesture that was appreciated by customers). This, along with the fact that he would travel between his cinemas at Bagillt, Holyhead, and Denbigh, offered the man in black a perfect alibi for his transitory lifestyle.

Police and neighbors noticed it too, with whispers of illicit, lascivious activity at Darlington House. Police officers who investigated instances of shoplifting at the department store Moore inherited found his staff, many of whom were involved in a relationship with Moore, very quiet and unwilling to talk much, as though they had been intimidated into not doing so.

Another individual recalls a terrifying encounter with Moore that occurred in one of his cinemas. He was a regular visitor to the cinema at Bagillt, as it was cheaper than the multiplex in nearby Chester by virtue of only showing films after their initial runs (and likely available on video by that stage). As such, he recalls that it was always eerily empty when he visited with his father during the day. He remembers Moore as a friendly and jovial man who would often chat with his father before the screening, but one unscheduled meeting with the man in black highlighted his dark doppelganger. Visiting the toilets during one of the screenings, which were only accessible down some stairs and in a dark hallway, the boy walked out of the toilet to see the silhouette of Moore in the dark hallway—he had clearly vacated the projectionist's booth specially (it was a one-man show at this stage due to the dearth of paying customers). Moore was just staring at him blankly and blocking his route back to the screen. After a few moments of this terrifying scene, the boy finally summoned the courage to push past the dark figure and ran back to his seat. The fact that this cinema was a converted chapel positioned the man in black as some perverted priest of darkness. On another occasion, Moore blatantly chased a young customer from one side of the auditorium to another, apparently without explanation. Maybe Moore was trying to intimidate him—appearing as the dark, silent killer of the *Friday the 13th* films he so venerated. Either way, this encounter pointed to Moore's "Jekyll and Hyde" character, with his gratification in scaring and intimidating people and his propensity to use darkness to cast a veil over his crimes.

APPREHENSION

Moore was finally apprehended and taken for questioning at Llandudno police station, where he initially denied any involvement. This was in part due to a tip-off from one of his former victims, who bravely recounted being taken back to Darlington House and viciously assaulted. His descriptions led them back to the scene of his torment. A search of the property revealed several mementos of Moore's murders, including Henry Roberts's Nazi flag and video recorder nestled among his own Nazi trinkets and leather fetish gear. A grim accessory to these was the murder weapon that had traces of the blood of several individuals, as well as blood spatters on the walls as testament to his sex crimes.

In custody, Moore, as with many of a similar profile, seemed to revel in the attention and notoriety. This is most likely what prompted him to reveal the murder of a fourth victim, Edward Carthy, that the police had not yet uncovered. Unlike his other victims, Carthy was a young drifter of twenty-eight and was picked up by Moore in a gay bar during a sojourn to the English city of Liverpool, which lies near the border with North Wales. Moore offered to drive Carthy back to his home, but instead drove him to Cerrigydrudion woods and stabbed him to death. He allegedly told detectives that Carthy "just collapsed in a heap… I stuffed him behind some trees." He tried to justify his crimes in other ways, telling police on one occasion that he had "yellow flashes in his eyes" during the crimes, but on another blaming them on the mysterious associate he called "Jason." The judge, jury, and prosecution were to concur that this last fantasy was "a figment of Moore's warped imagination."

His trial began at Mold Crown Court in the fall of 1996. Throughout, Moore appeared adorned in trademark black shirts, trousers, and ties and reveled in the attention. For the cinema tycoon and film lover, this was his moment of fame, and he acted like a film star throughout. This behavior was an affront to the victims who saw him in court and who often found the blank and remorseless visage of Moore staring back at them. He would also glare straight into the cameras as he was ferried to and from court, a grim smile on his lips. He corresponded with the local press, discussing his business plans after his release.

Moore even had the nerve to send a letter to Carthy's niece, protesting his innocence. It was a further act of intrusion for the family. She was only fourteen at the time she received a letter from the man she'd never met who was responsible for killing her uncle. She was faced with his greeting: "Dear Katie."

Prosecuting barrister Alex Carlile alluded to Moore's imagined celebrity when he described "the man in black—black thoughts and the blackest of deeds" and informed the jury that Moore was planning further killings, including that of his bank manager. Capital punishment was abolished in Britain in 1965, so justice for the families hinged on whether "life meant life" imprisonment and no chance of freedom. The jury deliberated for the comparatively short period of two hours and thirty-five minutes before a unanimous "guilty" verdict was passed. In the sentencing on November 29, 1996, Justice Maurice Kay described Moore as "as dangerous a man as it is possible to find" and that his crimes were "killing for killing's sake." Noting that Moore had not shown the "slightest remorse or regret," he sentenced him to life imprisonment with the recommendation to the Home Secretary that parole never be considered. "Scum!" yelled some of the relatives of his victims, and in the vernacular appropriate to Wales, "I hope you die in hell, boy."

A question often asked about serial killers after they are caught and convicted is—could there have been more victims? Often narcissistic, boastful, and attention-seeking, killers will often dangle tantalizing hints that they hold the key to other unsolved crimes. It is another way to hold power over victims and authorities. Cold cases are reopened and investigated, but usually there is only speculation to consider, especially after many of the alleged perpetrators have passed away or are executed, taking their dark secrets to the grave. Peter Moore is no exception to this tendency, and several unsolved murders and other crimes have been linked to the Man in Black's reign of terror.

The skeletal remains of a man were discovered in woodland near Cerrigydrudion in 2015. Incarcerated Moore subsequently sent a letter to police claiming to know the identity of the then-unidentified victim, who was found near the spot where the unfortunate Edward Carthy was left. However, as the dates did not add up with Moore's crime spree, police discounted it, and the mystery remains unsolved.

Moore's sentencing was the cause of a larger project of self-reflection for many in Britain, coming two years after the grim discovery of the "House of Horror" in Cromwell Street, Gloucester, the scene of Fred and Rosemary West's sexually motivated killings, and in the same year that Thomas Hamilton killed seventeen children and teachers in a massacre in Dunblane, Scotland. Bernard Levin, writing in *The Times*, concluded that "we are living in an age that is unshockable." Levin quoted politician Frank Field in blaming an unemployable underclass of young men—"new barbarians" who grow up to commit unspeakable atrocities. But unlike the louts and thugs who'd never had any advantages in life, Moore was clearly lavished with material welfare. However, the link the author made was that there appeared to be a number of crimes without obvious motive, prompted by Moore's admission during his trial that he committed murder for "fun." It is hard to reconcile Moore's life with the idea that these were not, at least in part, motivated by a perverse sexual pleasure derived from killing. Similar to serial killers John Wayne Gacy, Jeffrey Dahmer, and Dennis Nilsen, Moore's victims were exclusively male; the fact that his earlier sex sessions had led to increased instances of sadism and the victims' slow and violent demise further supports this theory.

Moore has been active in jail, perhaps hoping for another chapter or sequel to his notoriety. He successfully sued for loss of earnings against a neighbor who sold some of his possessions post-incarceration and launched a bid to do the same against his former accountant. Moore allegedly forged a friendship with fellow killer Harold Shipman while the pair were in prison together. For all his boasting and lack of remorse, Moore was adamant he would not spend the rest of his life in prison, as was dictated by his life sentence, a decision subsequently upheld by successive Home Secretaries. Alongside other convicted lifers Jeremy Bamber and Douglas Vinter, Moore sought to overturn this decision at the European Court of Human Rights (ECHR) in Strasbourg. They claimed that such a sentence was tantamount to "inhuman and degrading treatment," something his victims were subjected to with absolute certainty. Edward Carthy's family voiced their concern and disgust at the move, arguing his release would further degrade them as victims of his crimes. Families of his victims therefore undoubtedly breathed a collective sigh of relief when the ECHR upheld the verdict of the British judiciary in 2013. Moore will spend what remains of his life behind bars.

For many, the lives, crimes, and trials of killers are a little like a movie—morbid curiosity turns our attention to the spectacle of the lurid details of the crimes, the trial and conviction provides the satisfying finale, and the details of these as well as forensic examinations into the killers' childhoods are endlessly replayed and revisited as ghastly flickering shadows of a misspent life. However, there is no denouement for the victims and their families and certainly no happy ending. Public and media scrutiny keep the memories of the victims alive, but they are forever cast as the tragic victim—their lives indelibly defined by their sad encounter with the killer and destined to be endlessly replayed as such. Rightly, their families would prefer to remember them in life, not in death, as we should too.

THE FINAL CURTAIN

Life slowly returned to normality in North Wales. Darlington House is now a thriving motorcycle business bearing little resemblance to its former utility and looking like a more placid venue than its history suggests. The cinemas did not survive. Bagillt reopened for a few weeks under new management before succumbing to the competition of multiplexes at Llandudno and other towns as did Denbigh, whose house lights went up permanently in 2008.

As the end credits roll, the projector splutters off, and the lights raise to end this unhappy chapter in the story of North Wales. Hopefully those whose lives were darkened by the man in black can finally feel a sense of closure. One hopes that the script will be changed the next time, and another individual with such dark proclivities will not be allowed to satisfy his or her debased urges under the cover of darkness, but instead that light prevails.

Jolly Jane and the Deacon

RICHARD O JONES

Oramel Abraham Brigham had known Jane Toppan since she was a little girl and was adopted into the family he had married into.

Captain Abner Toppan and his wife Ann founded a boarding house in Lowell, Massachusetts, an industrial town known as "Spindle City," so named for its proliferation of textile mills. Ann ran the boarding house since Captain Toppan, a seafaring man, was away most of the time (he died at the relatively young age of forty-five). Their only daughter Elizabeth married Oramel Brigham in 1862 while both were in their early thirties. They set up their home in the widow Toppan's stately Georgian house on Third Street.

Brigham was a well-respected member of the Lowell community. He worked for the railroad, first as a conductor, then later as the station master of the Middlesex Street Station of the Boston & Maine. But perhaps of more importance to his social standing, he was a deacon at the First Trinitarian Congregational Church. He was so associated with the position, the people of Lowell referred to him as "Deacon Brigham." In photos of him in the newspapers, he appeared portly and distinguished, with massive sideburns and a convivial expression that seemed on the brink of a chuckle.

Two years after her daughter's marriage and the addition of Deacon Brigham into the household, Ann Toppan took into their home young Nora Kelly, an indentured seven-year-old girl who, with an older sister, had been abandoned by her derelict father at the Boston Female Asylum. Although never formally adopted, the widow renamed her Jane Toppan, but most people called her "Jennie."

Despite an impoverished early childhood, young Jane was bright, active, and "blessed with marked exuberance of spirits," her childhood friends would later recall. She made up vivid and impossible stories, insisting they were true. One of her favorites she told the Brighams was a tale about having discovered long-lost sisters and how she was in some way to inherit several thousands of dollars.

In 1874 Jane turned eighteen and received fifty dollars from the Widow Toppan as stipulated by the indenture agreement. Though released from her obligation, she remained with the family for nearly a decade as a servant. At twenty-five, Jane expressed a wish to become a nurse. Deacon Brigham and other Lowell dignitaries gave her letters of recommendation to the training school of the Massachusetts General Hospital. She was accepted but told she'd have to wait a year, during which time she worked at a hospital in Cambridge, where she returned for a time after finishing her studies. Eventually, she got enough work as a private nurse with much better pay, having recommendations from the best-known physicians in Cambridge and Boston to care for some of the most prestigious families.

Although many were put off by her tall tales, she was quite well-liked and earned the nickname "Jolly Jane" around Cambridge, Boston, Somerville, and in Cataumet on Cape Cod, where she took working vacations. Acquaintances described her as "agreeable," "vivacious," "generous and warm-hearted"—and "a prevaricator" (liar). One schoolmate said that if Jolly Jane were at a party, no other entertainment was necessary. No one suspected that she was addicted to any kind of drug, though she did have a fondness for candy, and, as the years passed, her girth increased.

By most accounts, Jane's "storytelling" was her greatest flaw, as
her murderous mania was yet to be revealed. Much of the time, she
simply spun fanciful tales. She once declared she was engaged to
a Cambridge theological student, a few weeks later saying she had
broken the engagement in order to marry a millionaire resident of
the Back Bay who'd fallen in love with her. But she also aroused the
ire of people whom she considered friends by making up stories and
spreading them like gossip.

Although vivacious and sociable, Deacon Brigham said Jane
"mingled little in the company of men." "At one time, she was
engaged to a young man of this city. She was a young woman at that
time. He lived in Lowell but went away to Holyoke where he married
the daughter of a woman with whom he had boarded. The news of
this unfaithfulness was a blow to Miss Toppan. The young man had
given her a ring that had a bird engraved upon it. Miss Toppan always
had a superstition on this account that we regarded as very peculiar.
She always hated the sight of a bird after that, believing it to be a bad
omen for her."

Jane left the Brigham/Toppan house on Third Street in 1885
but, for the next fifteen years, even while moving to various parts of
Massachusetts for work, returned as a frequent visitor and welcomed
guest. Even after the death of Mrs. Toppan in 1891, her foster sister
Elizabeth promised that Jane would always have a place in the
Brigham home. When in Lowell, Jane stayed in her old room and
never exhibited the animosity against Elizabeth that smoldered inside
her. Relations with her foster sister had always been cordial, if not
friendly, and there never seemed to be any serious conflict between
them. But Jane later confessed that she harbored a long-seething
hatred for Elizabeth, looking upon her as spoiled and privileged—
feelings exacerbated by jealousy over Elizabeth possessing the one
thing Jane wanted most in life: a husband.

So, nothing seemed particularly out of order when Jane invited Elizabeth to Buzzards Bay in the summer of 1899 for a relaxing vacation at the little village of Cataumet in the city of Bourne. Jane had been vacationing there for several years in a cottage owned by the eccentric Alden P. Davis and his family. Although in excellent physical condition for a woman of sixty-eight, Elizabeth had been suffering from a mild but persistent case of "melancholia," so Deacon Brigham encouraged her to go. She left Lowell on August 25 in fine fettle, but, two days later, the deacon received a telegram from Jane saying that his wife was dangerously ill. He made straight for Cape Cod, but by the time he reached Elizabeth's bedside, she was already in a coma.

Jane told him that the day after Elizabeth arrived at Cataumet the two of them enjoyed a picnic of cold corned beef at Scotch House Cove. They had a wonderful time, but the exertion proved too much for Elizabeth, so she retired early. She failed to respond to a call to breakfast the following morning.

What Jane didn't tell the deacon but confessed two years later when the scope of her murderous deeds was revealed, is that Elizabeth was the first of her many murders that had been committed out of hatred and vindictiveness. She liked her previous victims and was sincere with her loving care, at least in her own mind. But when Jane brought her sister a tumbler of Hunyadi water, a bitter mineral water imported from Hungary renowned for its digestive effects, it was laced with morphine and spite.

"I let her die slowly, with gripping torture," Jane said. "I held her in my arms and watched with delight as she gasped her life out."

Even though Elizabeth had no history of heart disease, the unwitting physicians, based on Jane's reports as opposed to any authentic postmortem, gave the cause of death as cerebral apoplexy when Elizabeth died on the morning of August 29, 1899.

Deacon Brigham would later recall that as he was gathering up his wife's belongings to take back to Lowell, he noticed she had but five dollars in her pocketbook although—and he distinctly remembered discussing how much cash to take with her—she'd left Lowell with more than fifty dollars. He questioned Jane but could only dismiss his suspicions, if he had any, when she told him that was all the money she had seen her sister carrying. Then Jane told him that his wife's dying wish, just before she slipped into the coma, was that Jane be given her gold watch and chain for a keepsake. That was so like Elizabeth, he thought, and gladly gave her the timepiece without hesitation. He never saw Jane with the watch in the subsequent two years, but among Jane's possessions at the time of her arrest was a stack of pawnshop tickets. Kleptomania was apparently another of her secret sins.

As he made the sad trip back to Lowell, Deacon Brigham was not aware that his wife's death was preceded by at least twenty others in the notorious career of his foster sister-in-law, nor that it was the first step in the nurse's devious matrimonial plan. Jane Toppan, now in her early forties, was craving a husband, and she was determined that Deacon Brigham, though nearly thirty years older, would be that groom.

The second phase of her plan was accomplished that winter when Jane came to Lowell for the holidays. Soon after her arrival, the housekeeper Florence Calkins fell ill. Jane, ever helpful, gave Florence an abundance of loving care along with frequent tumblers of Hunyadi water, alternately laced with morphine and atropine. Florence died on January 15, 1900. Unaware of Jane's practiced hand at murder, Dr. William Bass, one of the oldest physicians of Lowell, attributed her death to heart failure. Lowell people marveled at how fortunate it was that a trained nurse should be visiting the Brigham home at the time Florence fell ill. Jane later said that she poisoned Miss

Calkins because she considered her a rival for the desired affections of Deacon Brigham.

In April 1901, Jane asked Brigham for a loan of six-hundred dollars to make a final payment on a house at Cataumet that she wanted to buy to run as a boarding house.

"Some months later, she came to me in an excited condition and told me she had indorsed a note of $800 for a Boston merchant who lives in Cambridge, that he could not pay it and as indorser she had to meet it," Brigham said. "I gave it to her and took her note. I found recently by talking with the Boston merchant that she never indorsed a note for him. I owed Jennie Toppan $200 on the bequest of my wife to her, but when she owed me $1,400 I thought of holding it until she made some payments."

When a reporter asked about Miss Toppan's finances, he replied, "Well, if you can tell me what she has done with her money, I should like to have you do so. She has been earning $21 a week as a nurse for the last dozen years or more, but I don't know what use she has made of it. She borrowed money off me, $1,400 in all, $600 to pay as she said on the Ferdinand cottage at Cataumet but on which she never paid a cent, and $800 to cover an indorsement on a note. Here was $1,400 that went somewhere, but only Miss Toppan seems to know. However, I never pressed her for payment. I haven't the slightest idea what she could have done with all of her money. She was pretty constantly engaged in nursing ever since she left the hospital, yet when she came to the house, she was destitute."

During her visits and with Elizabeth out of the way, Jane frequently approached the subject of marriage with the deacon, but, ever the gentleman, he gently put her off. "It was generally understood that she did [want to be married to him], but I never proposed to her nor she to me. I suppose she wanted to get the money Mrs. Toppan left, and if she married me, and I was out of the way, of course it would be hers."

At the same time, Deacon Brigham, a robust seventy years old, was showing interest in another member of the congregation, the never-married Miss Martha Cook, a younger woman of sixty-five. Murmurs of a union seemed to further inflame Jane's frustrated passion (if that's really what it was) for the deacon, and they had more than one stormy scene over the matter.

To others in Lowell, perhaps part of a misguided ploy to make the deacon jealous, she frequently spoke of her intention to go to Australia, where she'd heard that wives were scarce. She went around bidding friends goodbye, saying that her ticket was bought and all arrangements made for her departure.

Whether she really was in love with her dead foster sister's husband, she simply wanted the security of a home for her declining years, or the master plan included herself becoming a widow at some point to receive the property she felt due her was known only by Jane herself. Deacon Brigham was so overwhelmed by her expressions of desire to marry that he went to his pastor to confide that he felt he "lived a life of persecution." Jane refused to allow her suit to be summarily dismissed. At one point, she insisted he fire the housekeeper who replaced Miss Calkins and give her the job. Brigham refused.

Deacon Brigham would later tell reporters about "the champion of Miss Toppan's many fables" that debuted during the April visit. She told several of her friends that she expected to go to Russia that fall as a member of the Tsar's household and receive a fabulous salary. She said the Tsar had heard much of the skill of American-trained nurses and wished to secure one for attendance on the Tsarina.

She went neither to Australia nor Russia but to Cambridge, where she connived her way into a job as a housekeeper for her landlords, the Beedles, and then a short, fateful stay at the Davis cottages in Buzzards Bay before returning to Lowell for her last visit there in late August.

Jane was dismayed to find yet another female in the Brigham house; and although she was in no way a competitor to matrimony, Jane was consumed with jealousy. Deacon Brigham's seventy-seven-year-old sister, Edna Bannister of Tunbridge, Vermont, was combining a family visit with a journey to the Pan-American Exposition in Buffalo, New York. She'd arrived a few days before Jane came on August 24. Although elderly, she was a strong and vigorous woman, but, two days later, after lunch, she complained of dizziness and retired to her room. Jane immediately brought her a tumbler of Hunyadi water, and, during her brief illness, citizens of Lowell once again marveled at how fortunate it was to have an experienced nurse on hand. The elderly woman slipped into a coma that evening. Although Dr. Bass came early the following morning, he could not revive her and she was dead before lunch.

Miss Toppan's strange behavior at Mrs. Bannister's funeral began to arouse the suspicions of the Reverend George F. Kenngott. She was extremely nervous, and her mourning did not seem sincere. The deaths of the Davis family in Cataumet had started making the news, and Reverend Kenngott knew she had attended the four members of the family as their nurse. The sudden death of Mrs. Bannister seemed to be part of that string, but he said nothing to Brigham.

It was just one day after Mrs. Bannister's funeral that state detective General Jophanus H. Whitney visited Jane at the Brigham home with questions about the deaths in the family of Alden P. Davis. If the deacon had yet to have any suspicions that his foster sister-in-law had been a mass murderess, his presence at this first interview between Jane Toppan and the police would certainly have put him on his guard.

•••

When Nurse Toppan returned to Cambridge to work, she went to board with Melvin and Eliza Beedle at 31 Wendell Street. She was at the Beedle house at the beginning of the summer of 1901, an unusual brutally hot season in the northeast, when Jane received an unexpected visitor, Mary "Mattie" Davis, who ran a resort on Buzzards Bay with her husband, Alden P. Davis. Jane had been vacationing there for the past five summers and owed them five hundred dollars. Sixty years old and diabetic, Mattie had come to collect the debt in a frazzled state, collapsed after dinner, and died during the night despite Jane's copious administration of Hunyadi water.

The body was taken back to Cataumet for the funeral, which Jane attended, staying on to attend to the grieving Alden Davis and his married daughters Minnie Gibbs and Genevieve Gordon. Genevieve took ill and Jane remained by her side until she died during the early morning hours of July 27. The official cause of death was listed as "heart disease" by Dr. Leonard Latter, but everyone attributed her demise to grief and a broken heart over the loss of her mother.

"Grief" struck again two weeks later on August 9 when Alden Davis, after returning home exhausted from a business trip to Boston and chugging down a big glass of Hunyadi water offered him by his nurse, went to his bed to die during the night. Dr. Latter put down "cerebral hemorrhage" as the cause of death.

Then, Minnie fell ill while preparing for a morning carriage, and even though Jane was on the spot with a glass of Hunyadi water, she died the next day.

The proximity of the deaths seemed more than suspicious to Captain Paul Gibbs, Minnie's father-in-law, so he made some visits and pulled some strings; police were informed and bodies exhumed.

When Jane Toppan got on a train to Lowell in the last week of August, she was followed by state detective John Patterson, who took a room with a view of the Brigham home.

•••

Shortly after the demise of Mrs. Bannister, Detective Whitney questioned Jane Toppan in Deacon Brigham's parlor about the Cataumet deaths; she repeated what the doctors had decided: that Mrs. Davis died of exhaustion—"all worked out," she said—and that grief had taken her husband and daughters.

At Nurse Toppan's trial, Whitney testified that Deacon Brigham was present when he suggested the "propriety" of having autopsies done on the Davis family. "If these people died from natural causes, it would be better for all parties concerned," he said. "Don't you think it would be better?"

Instead of directly answering him, Jane turned to the deacon: "What do you think, Mr. Brigham?" Mr. Brigham replied that he thought it would be better to have the autopsies, which would settle the matter, to which Jane replied, "I don't know that it would."

Jane was still under surveillance, Detective Patterson following her every move about Lowell, and Whitney's visit was meant to put her on guard in the hope she'd give up her murderous ways and no more lives would be lost before the test results were finished on the exhumed organs of the Davis family. Jane apparently didn't get the hint. Although Mrs. Bannister would be the last person to die at the nurse's hands, she wasn't yet done poisoning.

"I returned from church one Sunday [September 15], accompanied by Jane Toppan," Deacon Brigham later said, "and did not eat much dinner. I suffered extremely from headache during the afternoon."

The next day, the Reverend George F. Kenngott, pastor of the First Trinitarian Congregational Church, was surprised to receive a letter from Nurse Toppan informing him that Mr. Brigham had been taken suddenly and seriously ill. His previous discussion with the deacon regarding Jane's desire to be wed and now the mysterious death of a family that was under her care certainly on his mind, Kenngott went in haste to the house on Third Street and closely questioned the sick man and Miss Toppan.

On returning home, he sent a messenger to warn Dr. Lathrop: "Watch Jennie Toppan. She is trying to poison her patient." The next morning, the clergyman telephoned the physician to make sure he got the message and would heed it. Together, they made sure Miss Toppan was never alone with Brigham. In a few days he'd recovered enough to take a five-day trip into the White Mountains on doctor's orders—without Nurse Toppan. It was just what he needed.

"I did not consider Mr. Brigham suffered from arsenical poisoning," Dr. Lathrop said. "I was not aware Miss Toppan was under suspicion at the time I attended her, or I would have saved samples of spring water and aromatic mixtures of rhubarb I found in bottles. Detective Whitney expressed regret that I did not save any samples."

"When I was prostrated by illness," Brigham later reported, "I did not attribute it to any of Miss Toppan's actions but…I have never known a day's sickness until that time. My housekeeper told me when I came home…that Miss Toppan had been acting very badly. She was so nervous that she could not stay still."

Home from the mountain retreat, Deacon Brigham told Jane she would have to leave the house. That was September 27. Two days later, Miss Toppan made the first of two suicide attempts.

"I called Miss Toppan to dinner on Sunday," Brigham said, "and she said she did not care for any. The housekeeper went up to see if anything was the matter. Miss Toppan told her that she had taken poison and requested that a lawyer be sent for as she wished to make her will. We soon had a physician and later got a nurse to care for her."

Dr. Lathrop found Miss Toppan in an extremely drowsy state caused, he surmised, by some form of opium. He gave her an injection of apomorphine and she rallied but refused to tell him what she'd taken. Given her experience in administering morphine, it seems certain Jane never meant to kill herself, but to take just enough of a dose to be convincing.

"Why didn't you let me die?" she moaned. "I am tired of life. No one cares for me. People talk so about me that I am sick of living."

On Monday morning she appeared better, so the hired nurse went downstairs to get her some breakfast. When she returned, her patient was again in a stupor. Fortunately, Dr. Lathrop was just then coming to check on her. This time, she was much nearer death than the night before. He gave her another injection of apomorphine and, he said, "She threw off the poison. But for prompt treatment, she would have died. Upon regaining her senses, she made the same replies to questions as the day before. I am of the opinion she was insane."

While Jane was in the Barnstable jail prior to her trial, Deacon Brigham told reporters, "I don't know as I knew it then, but now I come back to look at the time Jennie was living with me, there were many queer things about her. I guess she's insane fast enough."

He was now convinced she was a morphine addict on top of whatever other trouble she'd gotten herself into, and again told Jane that when she had partially recovered, she would have to leave the house.

On September 1, she checked into Lowell General Hospital, where she stayed for most of the month. She then went to New Hampshire to visit an old friend, Sarah Nichols.

"It was probably to work on my sympathies," said Deacon Brigham to the newspapers about the alleged suicide attempts. "[A]nd when she found that I did not even then come around to her way of thinking, she made the second attempt, this time really desiring death.

"While I suppose that I cannot deny that she wanted to marry me, you can be assured that I'm very glad that she didn't. If I had married her, I don't believe that I would be alive today. Jennie certainly did tell queer stories, and many of them were undoubtedly done to injure me, although I always treated her like a sister."

The determined Detective Patterson, who'd been living quietly in a boarding house across the street from the Brigham house, reported, "Since then, up to the night of the arrest, I have kept her in sight, and in fact became acquainted with Miss Toppan and was quite intimate with her, accompanying her frequently on trips to the post office, etc. Her mail was examined and every effort made to find the evidence that was sought for."

He went so far as to feign illness to get a room in the same part of the hospital so he could keep an eye on her there. "On leaving the hospital in Lowell, Miss Toppan proceeded to Amherst, New Hampshire, ostensibly to visit a sister of George L. Nichols of that town. I followed her to Amherst, both arriving there October 14."

On October 29, General Whitney came to the Nichols home with a warrant and was shown to Jane's room.

Jane later told the alienists that if Whitney hadn't arrived as he did, she probably would have poisoned George and Sarah Nichols too.

•••

Jane seemed to take the arrest in stride and in her own jolly fashion. She was formally charged only with the murder of Minnie Gibbs, but, as the story began to unfold through Whitney's investigation, Jane's confessions to her lawyers, and the court alienists assigned to the case, the number quickly advanced to at least thirty-one at the time of her trial, but there is no official body count.

At first, Jane denied all the charges and gossip against her. Her first public statement was delivered to the press two days after her arrest:

"I know nothing about the poisoning either of Mrs. Gibbs or any members of the Davis family. I suppose they all died from natural causes. I'm willing to tell all about these cases. I have nothing to conceal. I am sorry that Doctor Latter is dead. Were he alive I would not have the slightest difficulty in clearing my skirts. The officers knew where I was all the time. I was not hiding and could have been found at an hours' notice. Such talk as my hiding from arrest is absurd."

Her lawyer, James Stuart Murphy, appended the statement with his own personal testimony. "I have known her for twenty years, and I am positive that she has no such thing as a mania. She is a bright, intellectual woman, mentally and morally pure. The story about her wanting to get married is absolutely absurd. I never saw her in the company of a man or ever heard her speak of a man. I know she had nothing to do with them. Any friend of Miss Toppan will vouch for her very excellent moral character. I am convinced of Miss Toppan's innocence. I've known her since her childhood and never has the finger of suspicion been lifted against her. We will admit nothing. Let the state go ahead and prove its case."

At her arraignment later that day, a little group of curiosity-seekers in front of the jail watched Jane step out of the door arm-in-arm with Murphy in the journey to the courtroom. At the sight of the prisoner, a murmur of surprise came from those who'd seen her first appearance a week before. Her face was pale. She walked with faltering steps and her eyes cast on the ground through the lane of spectators to the courthouse a few yards away. Once inside the courtroom, she sat on the seat near the door to await the perfunctory request for a continuance from Murphy. With head bent forward, Miss Toppan listened to the requests of her counsel. She was attired in the usual black dress, but she looked unkempt, her black hair, shaded with gray, sticking straight out from beneath her black bonnet. A carelessly tied large white ribbon encircled a wide front collar. Her eyes, with ever-shifting glances about the room, were sunken with dark, deep-lined circles showing beneath. She appeared nervous, pale-cheeked, and hollow-eyed. Trembling with emotion and seemingly on the verge of collapse, she stood before the court and pleaded "not guilty" to the charge of murder. She looked like a hunted animal at bay, the newspapers said. She clasped her hands together to stop the trembling, little beads of perspiration glistening on her brow. Then, her lips quivered, and she bit them nervously until a tiny drop of blood turned them a brilliant crimson.

She was in court only four minutes, yet she seemed to go through a thousand emotions before she turned to leave. She then faltered as if in danger of falling, seizing Murphy's arm for support. She kept her lips tightly shut as though restraining herself by great effort. Her step was slow, and she walked with seeming difficulty, a pronounced stoop rounding her shoulders. The strain of confinement, the seriousness of the charges against her, and her name and picture all over the newspapers seemed to sap her strength. She was like a woman without hope.

Searches of the Brigham home and her room in Cambridge revealed a cache of letters Jane had written to various persons. If there had been doubt about her skills as a liar and storyteller, the letters put it to rest. In some instances, Miss Toppan had written letters on two consecutive days to the same person exactly contradictory of each other. The stories she told bordered on the marvelous with an absolute disregard of the truth. Some told of the fabulous wealth left to her, others of a marriage soon to take place with a prominent man, and yet another anticipated a trip around the world on a private yacht with some young man who was infatuated with her. There seemed to be no benefit to spreading these fanciful stories, so the doctors opined they were purely the product of a disordered mind.

Being captured and having to publicly face her crimes added an element of paranoia to her mental maladies. One physician said she was rapidly developing a suspicious nature she didn't possess when arrested. When asked about certain things, she assumed an air of extraordinary cunning and returned evasive answers. He therefore predicted there would never be a real confession. But he was wrong about that. She revealed to two of her attorneys and the three alienists appointed by the court to examine the details of her murders a cool frankness and an "utter calmness" that equaled the deliberate and thoughtful way she carried them out, shaking all concerned—perhaps even herself—to the core.

"No doubt," one of the alienists told a reporter, "the ordinary citizen would unquestionably pronounce Miss Toppan insane when talking with her. She shows no evidence of her malady save to one who has made that branch a special study. She talked and even laughed with us and did not seem greatly concerned about her fate. But even this was abnormal. An ordinary woman placed in her position would have done her best to counterfeit insanity as soon as she became aware of the identity of her visitors, but Jane Toppan did nothing of the sort. She seemed perfectly at her ease."

The confessions revealed a tale of cleverness and daring, glee over outwitting doctors, and the sexual lure of causing and witnessing the deaths of both men and women. She played with the lives entrusted to her like a cat with a mouse, and it was rarely, she said, that those who once came under her charge arose from their beds of sickness; when the patient lay helpless and insensible, she exulted in her power and kissed and caressed them as they drew nearer and nearer to death.

"You see," she said to one of her attorneys, "I am not insane. I remember it all or at least most of the last few years. Those whom I killed in the hospitals, of course, I didn't know. I can't tell their names nor how many—perhaps ten, perhaps twenty, fifty-five."

She showed no remorse and expressed her own concern over that. She told one alienist, "When I try to picture it, I say to myself, 'I have poisoned Minnie Gibbs, my dear friend. I have poisoned Mrs. Gordon. I have poisoned Mr. Davis and Mrs. Davis.' This does not convey anything to me, and, when I try to sense the condition of the children and all the consequences, I cannot realize what an awful thing it is. Why don't I feel sorry and grieve over it? I cannot make any sense of it at all."

Corroboration of some of the sordid details of Jane's *modus operandi* came from a former patient at the Cambridge Hospital who came forward to tell of her own experience. Mrs. Amelia Phinney had been in the hospital for an operation on her uterus. After surgery, Nurse Jolly Jane gave Amelia some bitter-tasting medicine to help with her pain. As she slipped in and out of a morphine haze, the friendly nurse who'd been caring for her got into the bed, kissed Amelia all over her face, and stroked her hair, cooing, then suddenly stopped and hurried out of the room. Groggily recalling the bizarre event the following morning, Amelia talked herself into believing it was all a dream. But when the news broke of Jolly Jane's crimes, she realized she could have been another of the nurse's unfortunate victims had the sensual poisoning not been interrupted.

•••

It was warm and sunny in Barnstable, Massachusetts on June 23, 1902, a beautiful day compared to the oppressive heat of the previous summer. Citizens wandered about the jail grounds as early as seven, hoping for a glimpse of the prisoner Jane Toppan on her way to meet her fate in a court of law. The prisoners of the jail generally awakened at six, but on this day the jail matron made an exception. A long, hard day was before the prisoner, and the kind-hearted matron gave her an extra hour to sleep before gently waking her. Jane roused, sporting a big, friendly smile, a bit of the old Jolly returning for a moment. After breakfast, Jane and the matron spent a half-hour deciding on her wardrobe for the day even though the choices were limited to two dresses and three shirtwaists. Every waist, every skirt was put on and taken off at least a dozen times, and still she was not pleased. When her attorney called to accompany her to court, she was still confounded and made a hasty decision of a black dress, white waist, and a wide-brimmed black hat profusely trimmed with forget-me-nots.

While Jane agonized over her wardrobe, the crowd in front of the courthouse swelled until they were elbow-to-elbow. Promptly at nine, the little gallery at the rear of the courtroom was thrown open and in ten minutes was packed to the dome. At ten, Jane walked slowly in and took her place in the long prisoner's dock. She shot quick glances here and there at the crowd, the little gallery, the reporters, and at the sheriff and his assistants, the forget-me-nots in her hat bobbing up and down continuously. At first, she kept her heavy veil over her face, but, when her interest in the proceedings increased, she pushed it impatiently away.

Jolly Jane Toppan's fate was settled a mere six hours later. Impaneling the jury took only thirty-one minutes, and the jury required a mere twenty-seven minutes to agree on a verdict. The reading of the indictment consumed twelve minutes—twelve minutes during which Jane Toppan was forced to hear four times those terrible words of "poison," "kill," and "murder." Her emotion increased at each recital by the shaking voice of the aged clerk, and at one time it seemed as if she was about to faint. With a gasp, her head fell forward onto the railing, and until the reading was finished, she kept her face buried upon her arm.

All of the witnesses were escorted from the courtroom with the exception of the three alienists—doctors Stedman, Jelly, and Quinby, upon whose opinion Miss Toppan's fate would be determined. They sat directly in front of her.

The central testimony came from Dr. Henry R. Stedman, who said Jane Toppan told him in the presence of other medical experts that she had killed Mrs. Gibbs by giving her a poisonous dose of atropine and morphine, that she administered the drugs in the form of tablets or pellets, and that more than one dose was given. The two other physicians concurred that Jane Toppan was insane on August 13, the day of Mrs. Gibbs's death, and was still suffering from "a form of degenerative insanity having defective control of an irresistible impulse." In short, she was not responsible for the crime with which she was charged.

There were no witnesses for her defense. Her attorneys relied entirely upon the insanity plea, and the alienists who testified fully agreed that the woman was insane. Neither the counsel for the defendant nor the prosecutors desired to address the jury.

When the defense rested, the judge turned to Miss Toppan and said, "You have the privilege, if you see fit, to exercise it to address the jury in your own behalf. You are not obliged to do so, and may, if you choose, leave your defense upon the basis where it had been placed by your counsel. No inference will be drawn against you from your omission to say anything to the jury in your own behalf. Do you desire to say anything?"

The defendant said, "I do not."

The jury found her not guilty by reason of insanity. The district attorney suggested she be sent to the Taunton Hospital for the Insane and the defense agreed.

Back at the jail, a reporter asked her if she was feeling well. She said, "Oh, never better. I feel just grand."

"Do you dread your new life?" he asked.

"Oh, no," she replied. "I'll be all right again in a few years. They'll let me out the way they did Freeman," (the zealot who Alden Davis defended. He, too, was sent to Taunton, released after seven years).

Even in jail and in the insane asylum, Jolly Jane never lost her propensity for exaggeration. By the time she arrived at the state mental hospital in Taunton, her confession had grown to a total of eighty-four victims.

One newspaper wag asserted, "It is thought that unless her imagination be curbed, she might claim or confess to the murder of half the inhabitants of the state."

"There was just eighty-four," she insisted to a reporter. "I was going to make it an even hundred and then stop."

In an update two years later, she was claiming ninety-one victims, and her paranoia had grown to extreme proportions. She had stopped eating for fear of being poisoned, and her plump figure had begun to waste away. Her keepers went to "heroic measures," the report said, to keep her nourished, including force-feeding her through a tube.

"One look at this weak, incapable woman sitting in her cell in the hospital is sufficient to convince the visitor that some share of the vengeance, which delusions induced from horrible realities can inflict, has been meted out to her," the *Boston Post* reported.

By the time of her death in 1938 at the age of eighty-one, she claimed to her keepers, "I killed at least one-hundred persons."

•••

Postscript: Oramel Brigham married Martha Cook in May 1902 while Jane Toppan awaited trial in the Barnstable jail. He died in Lowell in 1920 at eighty-nine years old.

The Bluebeard of Rome

Deirdre Pirro

A heavily built, well-dressed balding man with a robust mustache swore and sweated profusely as he lugged two heavy suitcases to the nearby station. He was already tired. He had spent an hour that morning finishing the job. For the rest of the day, he cleaned up the mess his handiwork had made in the rented apartment. To add to his bad mood, almost as soon as he boarded the train, he was fined for carrying overweight baggage. When the conductor questioned him about what was in it, he simply replied, "Salted meat."

The cold day after, on November 16, 1932, the two suitcases were found abandoned at the Naples Central Station in southern Italy. They arrived on Train No. 5 coming from Turin's Porta Nuova Station. Once opened, out tumbled the severed head and other parts of a woman's body wrapped in newspaper. The station master fainted. The next day, the rest of the body turned up in another suitcase at Rome's main station.

At that time, Italy was still in its honeymoon period with Benito Mussolini, the country's fascist dictator. In late October 1922, Mussolini had seized power after the March on Rome, and he would hold his grip on it for the next twenty-odd years. To help promote the idea of the ideal state the regime wanted to portray, Mussolini imposed rigid censorship. Crime was to be reported as little as possible in film, on radio, and in print, and when that was impossible, it was to be heavily downplayed. The aim was to give the populace a false sense of security and boost confidence in its new leaders.

But nothing could keep the lid on a story like this. The newspapers splashed the lurid details of the discovery of the unidentified woman's body all over the front pages. To try to stem the outcry, two experienced inspectors from Rome's police headquarters were assigned to the case. Both were already working on a similar case though so far without success. In November 1930, decapitated and mutilated remains of another nameless woman had washed up on the shore at Santa Marinella, not far from Rome.

The break came when a waitress named Olga Melgradi turned up at the police station after reading about the case in the newspapers. She told officers that she might know the woman in the suitcases. Her friend, Paola Gorietti, had gone missing. Originally from Umbria, Paola, who walked with a limp, was a twenty-nine-year-old spinster who worked as a domestic servant in Rome.

Before her disappearance, Paola told Olga she'd met a fascinating man after she answered a lonely-hearts ad in a magazine. It read: "Pensioner, 450 lire a month [then a considerable sum], would like to meet a single woman with means. Preferably to get to know each other with the idea of marriage." Her friend described him as a retired army officer who'd been wounded in World War I. A short time after meeting her, he had, Paola said, asked her to marry him and help him manage a small boarding house in La Spezia on the Ligurian coast. But after Paola had accepted and left to begin her new life, Olga heard nothing more from her.

Based on this information, the inspectors took Olga and Gino, her friend's brother, to Naples, where they identified Paola Gorietti as the victim. Olga also recognized one of the suitcases; she had loaned it to the unfortunate betrothed for her trip. Investigations were already concentrating on La Spezia after a child had found a bloody butcher knife in an alley near the station, but it was Olga who informed police that, although the prospective groom had ordered Paola not to tell a soul about the romance until after they were married, she couldn't resist. Bursting with joy, she'd told Olga that her suitor's name was Cesare Serviatti.

Fifty years old and a snappy dresser with a persuasive banter, Serviatti was born in Rome to unknown parents on September 24, 1880. He grew up in the care of foster parents in a nearby town. Known to have a quick and vicious temper, he was fired from his job as a nurse at a local hospital for mistreating patients. He then did a series of low-paid odd jobs. At one time, he had wanted to be a butcher, but in truth he was indolent and had little desire to work. When short of money, he often traveled to La Spezia to help out at a friend's boarding house.

Vain and greedy, Serviatti was convinced of his prowess in captivating and defrauding women. The police traced the unemployed Serviatti to his home in Rome and took him to police headquarters for questioning. After four days, Serviatti confessed to Paola's murder. He told police they had a violent argument the morning after they arrived at the apartment in La Spezia. He said he'd been shaving when Paola tried to grab the straight razor out of his hand. To defend himself, he kicked her in the stomach and she fell backward onto the floor, hitting her head. He rushed out of the building and did not return until evening, finding the body where he'd left it. Panicking, he dismembered it and disposed of it in the suitcases. Unconvinced, police arrested him, certain his motive was to rob his victim of her life savings.

Given the similarities in the crimes, detectives were persuaded that Serviatti had also killed the woman found on Santa Marinella beach. After further questioning, he admitted to throwing the severed remains of a woman, Bice Margarucci, into Rome's Tiber river. The tide did the rest, washing her body up farther down the coast. A middle-aged, thickset woman who worked as a maid, Bice had just returned from visiting her brother in America. She brought back with her jewelry, elegant underwear, and a sizable sum of money. Employing his usual stratagem, Serviatti had her sign her bank book over to him.

If he had killed two women in the same way, police surmised that he had probably killed other women too. To fit his *modus operandi*, Serviatti's victims would be lonely, single, vulnerable women who were no longer young, but still in search of love. They would do anything for him, even abandon their families and friends, leaving them without news of their whereabouts just to be with him. By isolating the women, Serviatti was sure he could easily beguile, rob, and kill them with little chance of ever being caught.

Once news spread that Serviatti had perpetrated the second murder, the press began calling him the "Landru of the Tiber," since his case was like that of French serial killer Henri Landru, known as the "Bluebeard of Gambais." Between 1915 and 1919, Landru had used lonely-hearts' messages to lure eleven unsuspecting women to his isolated home in the country, where he had them sign their money over to him. He then strangled them, cut up their bodies, incinerated the pieces in his kitchen stove, and sprinkled their ashes over the surrounding fields. This was probably the model Serviatti copied, believing he would be more successful than its inventor, who was tried and decapitated by guillotine in 1922.

Further inquiries brought to light that there was no trace of yet another woman Serviatti had been in contact with. In 1928, the tall, slim, well-off blonde widow Pasqua Bartolini Tiraboschi had mysteriously disappeared from the boarding house in La Spezia where Serviatti worked (and pretended to own). She, too, had met him through a newspaper ad, but he claimed he had thrown her out of the boarding house with her dog when she became too insistent about wanting him to marry her. Her dog was found wandering the streets, but there was no sign of its mistress.

In December 1932, the police, doubting his story, searched the boarding house and dredged the cesspool. They found the carved-up remains of the hapless Pasqua, Serviatti's first quarry. Faced with this discovery, Serviatti could do little other than confess to this crime too. In all, he confessed to killing five women, but never revealed the names of the final two or the locations of their bodies. Instead, investigators were convinced he had killed at least ten women and perhaps more but were unable to prove it.

In the meantime, forty-eight-year-old Angela Taborri, Serviatti's wife of two years, was arrested. It soon became clear she knew little of her husband's crimes, though she did know that the money he gave her came from illicit sources. Serviatti's lover, Anna Morsiani, who lived with both him and his wife, was also arrested as an accomplice. This *ménage à trois* caused a huge scandal when the papers reported about it, confirming the depravity of the man in the public's eyes.

In late December 1932, all three accused were sent to the jail in Sarzana. Before the trial, the two women were released, and only Serviatti's wife faced the court. Many curiosity-seekers waited outside the courtroom when, on June 16, 1933, the couple made their appearance. The accused, dressed in black, was arrogant and walked with a cocky swagger, a smirk on his face, while Angela Taborri appeared subdued, fearful, and on the verge of tears.

As soon as the judges were seated, the defense lawyers called for an examination of Serviatti to ascertain his psychological condition, which they argued was affected by a syphilis infection he'd been treated for in the past. They maintained that, given the repeated pattern of his crimes, he was a psychopath but, because of his weakened mental capacity, he did not deserve the death penalty. After five hours of deliberation, the court denied the defense's request. Angela Taborri's lawyers argued that she, too, was a victim of her evil husband and should not be on trial.

Twenty days later, the court delivered its verdict:

"In the name of His Majesty, the King of Italy…this Court, recognizing the full responsibility of Cesare Serviatti, condemns him to life imprisonment for the homicide of Pasqua Bartolini, widow Tiraboschi; to life imprisonment for the homicide of Bice Margarucci; and the death penalty, by firing squad, for the homicide and vilification of the body of Paola Gorietti."

Serviatti's wife was acquitted.

On October 3, 1933, Serviatti appealed to the Supreme Court to have the death sentence commuted on the grounds that his plea of mental infirmity had not been properly taken into consideration by the lower court.

Criminal psychology in Italy, which dates back to the 1870s, was greatly influenced by the theories of physician and psychiatrist Cesare Lombroso, who founded the Italian school of criminology or, as we know it today, criminal anthropology. In his trailblazing works, especially the five editions of *L'uomo delinquente* (*Criminal Man*), first published in 1876, Lombroso classified criminals into categories. One of the main categories was "born criminals"—criminals who, in his opinion, had no choice but to commit crimes. Their physiological and physiognomic nature was influenced by hereditary factors or mental disorders, thereby diminishing their responsibility. These, Lombroso explained, were demonstrated by the shape of a criminal's skull and other parts of the body, like a club-shaped nose, proximity of eyes, jutting ears, limited facial hair, prominent canine teeth, sloping shoulders, long arms, and pointy fingers—all similar to those of primitive or atavistic man.

Although the "scientific" methods Lombroso employed are considered flawed according to modern standards, criminal anthropology still plays a role in the study of social and forensic psychology. With the translation of his books, his theory of the "born criminal" dominated European and American thinking during the late nineteenth and early twentieth centuries. With this in mind, Serviatti's lawyers argued in their appeal that he was demented due to a sexual fixation. His sadistic sexual manifestations, they contended, resulted from severe infections caused by tuberculosis and advanced syphilis. These were aggravated by a head injury Serviatti suffered in his youth. Furthermore, he was left-handed, and one of the pupils in his eyes was bigger than the other, so, as a "born criminal," he was compelled to do what he did. Therefore, an expert should be called to carry out a proper psychiatric assessment of his true condition.

The Supreme Court rejected these conjectures and found that the evidence showed that at the time he committed the crimes, Serviatti was perfectly sane, intelligent, and calculating. His intention was clearly to rob his victims and dispose of their bodies to avoid being caught; he therefore deserved no mercy. On the same grounds, the king also refused to grant Serviatti a pardon.

In the early morning of October 13, 1933, Serviatti was awakened and told his pardon had been denied and he would be executed. Just as dawn was breaking, he was taken from the prison to the rifle range in Sarzana, where a crowd of more than six thousand people had been waiting for hours to catch a glimpse of him. Dressed in a white shirt, wearing flashy yellow shoes, and with a priest by his side, he was blindfolded and tied onto a chair with his back facing a firing squad of twenty-four policemen. Hit by a deafening burst of rifle fire, Serviatti was pronounced dead. His body was taken to Sarzana cemetery for burial. No headstone marks his grave.

Serviatti's last words in a letter to his wife were, "When you receive news of my death, drink to it and get drunk."

References

Buxom Belle: Her Own Story

Female Killers. "Belle Gunness Documentary." YouTube video, 14:20. Posted by Female Killers, August 7, 2016. https://youtu.be/vWwj-OrM-Jo.

Most Notorious. "Indiana Serial Killer Belle Gunness with Harold Schechter: A True Crime History Podcast." YouTube video, 1:06:05. Posted by Most Notorious, March 8, 2018. https://youtu.be/fDl2_efbW_E.

Rosewood, Jack. *Belle Gunness: The True Story of The Slaying Mother.* True Crime by Evil Killers (Book 14), 2016. Kindle.

Schechter, Harold. *Hell's Princess: The Mystery of Belle Gunness, Butcher of Men.* New York: Little A, 1018, Kindle.

"Serial Killer—Belle Gunness Only Belle Full Documentary." YouTube video, 1:27:14. Posted by Ertwer Hertyas, May 28, 2015. https://youtu.be/wtC-kcdSsog.

Unidentified person. "Coroner's Inquisition" on bodies exhumed from the farm of Belle Gunness, La Porte, IN. Transcription prepared by Andrea Simmons, 2006.

"Ye Should Nae Kill": Glasgow's Bible Bashing Serial Strangler

Brady, Ian. *The Gates of Janus: Serial Killing and its Analysis, by the "Moors Murderer," Ian Brady.* Los Angeles: Feral House, 2001.

Durkheim, Emil. *The Division of Labor in Society.* Mansfield Centre: Martino, 2012.

Durkheim, Emil. "The Normal and the Pathological." *Criminological Perspectives: Essential Readings,* 2nd Edition. E. McLaughlin, J. Muncie & G. Hughes (Eds.) London: Sage, 2003.

Durkheim, Emil. *The Rules of Sociological Method.* New York: MacMillan, 1982.

Durkheim, Emil. *Suicide: A Study in Sociology.* New York: Simon & Schuster, 1979.

Harrison, Paul. *Dancing with the Devil: The Bible John Murders.* Skipton: Vertical Editions, 2013.

Wilson, David & Harrison, Paul. *The Lost British Serial Killer: Closing the Case on Peter Tobin and Bible John.* London: Sphere, 2012.

The Kičevo Monster

Andonov, Zoran. "Murder, He Wrote," *Mail & Guardian.* June 23, 2008.

Bilefsky, Dan. "Macedonian Murder Suspect Found Dead in Cell." *The New York Times,* June 24, 2008.

Bilefsky, Dan. "Murder Mystery in Macedonia." *The New York Times,* June 23, 2008.

Jovanovic, Dragana. "Murder He Wrote: Chilling Death Details." ABC News, January 8, 2009.

Kenarov, Dimiter. "The Mask of Sanity: On the Trail of a Serial Killer in Macedonia." *The Virginia Quarterly Review,* Vol. 85, no. 2, Spring 2009.

"Murder He Wrote: Vlado Taneski," *Evil Up Close.* S.1. Ep.9. FirstLook TV. Directed by Robert Murray. 2012. Stratford-Upon-Avon, UK A&E Television Networks.

Smith, Helena. "The Shocking Story of the Newspaper Crime Reporter Who Knew Too Much." *The Guardian,* June 23, 2008.

Testorides, Konstantin. " 'Serial Murder' Journalist Commits Suicide." *Independent,* June 24, 2008.

"The Strange Case of a Journalist with a Killer Deadline." *The Irish Times*, June 28, 2008.

Watson, Philip. "Murder, He Wrote." *Esquire* (UK). January 2009.

The First of Criminals

Smith, Janet. *The Shipman Inquiry*, Crown Copyright (UK). 2002-2005.

Whittle, Brian, and Ritchie, Jean. *Prescription for Murder*. London: Warner, 2000.

The Man in Black and the Silver Screen: The Life and Crimes of Peter Moore

Barker, Rhodri. "The First Victim of 'The Most Dangerous Man Ever to Have Set Foot in Wales.'" *The Daily Post*, July 28, 2010.

Crump, Eryl & Bona, Emilia. "The Man in Black: How Killer Cinema Owner Peter Moore Struck Fear in the Heart of Merseyside's Gay Community." *Liverpool Echo*, August 26, 2018.

Evans, Owen. "Police Still Need Your Help to Solve Forest Mystery Three Years After Grisly Find." *The Daily Post*, November 16, 2018.

"Ex-Flatmate of Flintshire Serial Killer Peter Moore Says He Should Never Be Released." *The Daily Post*, March 31, 2011.

"Gay Serial Killer Should Never Be Let Out of Jail, says Judge." *The Times*. November 30, 1996.

Levin, Bernard. "Growing Up as Killers." *The Times*, December 20, 1996.

"Mother's Death Gave Free Rein to Sadistic Fantasies of 'Miracle Son.'" *The Times*, November 30, 1996.

"Peter Moore: The Man in Black." *Born to Kill*. S.7, Ep.4. Directed by John-Pierre Newman. 2015. London, England. Two Four Productions. Channel 5.

"Serial Killer Moore Sues His Accountant." *The Daily Post*,
    April 20, 2013.

Shrouded Hand. "My Encounter with a Serial Killer." September 18,
    2016. YouTube. https://youtu.be/9sjJ4kFHTek.

"The Man in Black: Peter Moore." *Evil Up Close*. S.1, Ep.10. Directed
    by Robert Murray, 2011. FirstLook TV. Stratford-Upon-Avon,
    UK A&E Television Networks.

"Victim's Family 'Disgusted' at Peter Moore's Bid for Release." *The
    Daily Post*. March 7, 2011.

War, David. "Gay Killer Should Never Be Free—Judge." *The
    Guardian*. November 30, 1996.

Jolly Jane and the Deacon

All direct quotes have been taken verbatim from the following:

"Agree That She's Insane." *Boston Globe*, April 6, 1902.

"Government's Case Against Jane Toppan." *Boston Post*,
    November 9, 1902.

"Jane Toppan an Imbecile." *Boston Globe*, July 10, 1904.

"Jane Toppan Declared Insane." *Boston Post*, March 28, 1902.

"Jane Toppan Sent to Taunton Asylum for Life." *Boston Post*,
    June 24, 1902.

"Jane Toppan Thinks She Murdered 84." *Boston Post*, July 3, 1902.

"Jolly Jane, Poisoner, Dies." *The Mason City Globe-Gazette*,
    August 18, 1938.

"Marriage and Money." *Boston Globe*, November 1, 1901.

"Miss Toppan Will Force the Fight." *Boston Herald*,
    November 1, 1901.

"Poison in Stomach." *Boston Globe*, October 30, 1901.

"Woman Suspected of Many Murders." *Boston Post*, October 31, 1901.

About the Editor

Mitzi Szereto (mitziszereto.com) is an author and anthology editor whose books encompass multiple genres such as crime, gothic fiction, horror, cozy mystery, satire, parody, science fiction and fantasy, erotic fiction, general fiction, and non-fiction. Her novels, short stories, and anthologies have been translated into several languages. She's appeared internationally on radio and television and at major literature festivals and has also taught creative writing around the world, including at several UK universities. A story from her British crime anthology *Getting Even: Revenge Stories* received a Highly Commended from the Crime Writers Association's Silver Dagger Awards, and she has the added distinction of editing the first anthology of erotica to include a Fellow of the Royal Society of Literature. She's the creator and presenter of the London-based web TV channel Mitzi TV and also plays herself in the pseudo-documentary British film *Lint the Movie*. Her blog of personal essays can be found at *Errant Ramblings: Mitzi Szereto's Weblog*. Follow her on Twitter @MitziSzereto.

About the Contributors

Mike Browne is creator, writer, producer, and host of the popular, independently produced *Dark Poutine Podcast*, which focuses on true crime, dark history, and mysteries in Canada. Mike is also president and CEO of Dark Poutine Media Inc., which is responsible for content creation across various mediums. You can listen to his weekly show at darkpoutine.com.

Martin Edwards's latest novel is *Gallows Court*, set in 1930. He received the CWA (Crime Writers' Association) Dagger in the Library in 2018 and is president of the Detection Club, consultant to the British Library, and former chair of the CWA. His whodunits include *The Coffin Trail*, which was shortlisted for the Theakston's Prize for best crime novel. *The Golden Age of Murder* won the Edgar, Agatha, HRF Keating and Macavity awards, while *The Story of Classic Crime in 100 Books* won the Macavity. He has also received the CWA Short Story Dagger, the Margery Allingham Prize, and the Poirot Award "for his outstanding contribution to the crime genre."

Anthony Ferguson has published more than forty short stories and non-fiction articles in magazines and anthologies in Australia, Britain, and the United States. He authored the nonfiction book *The Sex Doll: A History* (McFarland & Co., 2010), and edited the short story collection *Devil Dolls and Duplicates in Australian Horror* (Equilibrium Books, 2011). A committee member of the Australasian Horror Writers Association (AHWA) and editor for *Andromeda Spaceways Magazine* (ASM), he has judged and been shortlisted as a finalist in the AHWA Awards, Australian Shadows Awards, and Aurealis Awards on several occasions.

Dr. Mark Fryers is a freelance writer and academic who has worked in the television industry, providing research for true crime drama-documentaries for October Films, including *The Killer Beside Me* (Discovery ID, 2018). He has numerous articles, chapters, and peer-reviewed publications to his name including from John Libbey Publishing, Vernon Press, Manchester University Press, and IB Tauris.

Vicki Hendricks is the author of noir novels *Miami Purity*, *Iguana Love*, *Voluntary Madness*, *Sky Blues*, and *Cruel Poetry*, an Edgar Award Finalist in 2008. Her short stories are collected in *Florida Gothic Stories*. She currently lives in central Florida, the rural locale of her most recent novel *Fur People*.

Richard O Jones gave up the grind of daily journalism after twenty-five years as an arts and culture writer for his hometown newspaper and turned to a life of true crime, first as an author of two books about historical murders (*The First Celebrity Serial Killer in Southwest Ohio: Confessions of the Strangler Alfred Knapp* and *Cincinnati's Savage Seamstress: The Shocking Edythe Klumpp Murder Scandal*), and then as the host of the podcast *True Crime Historian*, where he presents tales of the scandals, scoundrels, and scourges of the past as told through historic newspaper accounts in the golden age of yellow journalism.

Danuta Kot, who also writes as Danuta Reah, has published eight novels and several short stories. She won the Crime Writers' Association Short Story Dagger for her story "No Flies on Frank," and was Highly Commended for her short story "Glazed." She is a regular academic speaker at conferences and literary festivals and has appeared on radio and television. Her latest book, *Life Ruins*, is published by Simon & Schuster.

Dr. Lee Mellor is a writer, scholar of homicide and sex crime, cold case consultant, offender profiler, and singer-songwriter. He is the author of the Canadian bestseller *Cold North Killers: Canadian Serial Murder* and its companion piece *Rampage: Canadian Mass Murder and Spree Killing*, as well as contributing chapters and entries to *The Crime Book: Big Ideas Simply Explained*, and the academic textbooks *Understanding Necrophilia: A Global Multidisciplinary Approach* and *Homicide: A Forensic Psychology Casebook*. Lee hosts the popular true crime podcast *Murder Was the Case*, where he has spoken extensively about the Bible John case and divulged a profile of the killer he created for his doctoral dissertation. Follow him on Twitter @dr_mellor.

Deirdre Pirro, author of *Italian Sketches: The Faces of Modern Italy* and *Famous Expats in Italy* (The Florentine Press), is an international lawyer who lives and works in Florence. She is also a columnist with *The Florentine*, the English-language newspaper in Florence. Her writing focuses on Italy, its people, its history, and its customs. Follow her on Twitter @dp_in_florence.

Craig Pittman is a native Floridian. Born in Pensacola, he graduated from Troy State University in Alabama, where his muckraking work for the student paper prompted an agitated dean to label him "the most destructive force on campus." Since then he has covered a variety of newspaper beats and quite a few natural disasters, including hurricanes, wildfires, and the Florida Legislature. Since 1998, he has covered environmental issues for Florida's largest newspaper, the *Tampa Bay Times*, winning state and national awards. He is the author of four books, including *The Scent of Scandal: Greed, Betrayal, and the World's Most Beautiful Orchid*, which is the only book ever classified as "True Crime/Gardening," and *Oh, Florida! How America's Weirdest State Influences the Rest of the Country*, which won the gold medal for Florida nonfiction from the Florida Book Awards.

Marcie Rendon is a citizen of the White Earth Nation. Her novel *Girl Gone Missing* (Cinco Puntos Press) is the second in the Cash Blackbear series. The first, *Murder on the Red River* (2017), won the Pinckley Women's Debut Crime Novel Award, 2018 and was a Western Writers of America Spur Award Finalist 2018 in the Contemporary Novel category. She curates community-created performance such as *ART IS… CreativeNativeResilience*, which features three Anishinabe performance artists on Twin Cities Public Television (2019). Diego Vázquez and Rendon received the Loft's 2017 Spoken Word Immersion Fellowship for their work with women incarcerated in county jails.

Francesca Roe was born in Leeds and lived in Italy and Germany before returning to England, where she gained a doctorate in cultural history. In 2018, she moved back to Leeds and has been exploring the landscapes and history of the north of England through her writing, which has been featured in *CityMetric* and *The Conversation*. She is also a keen artist and printmaker and enjoys walking and the outdoors.

Joe Turner is a freelance writer specializing in the true crime and crime fiction genres and is the author of the Alex Rainer series of detective novels. He is a criminal psychology graduate and a Lovecraft obsessive and spends most of his time researching obscure serial killer cases. He lives with his wife and children in the West Midlands, United Kingdom.

Stephen Wade has written widely on true crime and also worked as a writer in prisons. His most recent books are *Murder in Mind* (Scratching Shed Publishing) and *The Count of Scotland Yard*

(Amberley Publishing). He also writes Westerns (his favorite crime fiction) under his pen name, Frank Callan.

James Young is a Northern Irish writer, translator, and journalist. He lived in Brazil between 2005 and 2017 and has written about the country for *Rolling Stone*, *Sports Illustrated*, *The Guardian/ Observer*, *The Independent*, ESPN, and other publications and sites. His short fiction has appeared in a number of literary journals, and he recently completed a blackly comic literary crime novel set in Recife, Brazil, for which he is seeking representation at the time of this collection's publication.

Mango Publishing, established in 2014, publishes an eclectic list of books by diverse authors—both new and established voices—on topics ranging from business, personal growth, women's empowerment, LGBTQ studies, health, and spirituality to history, popular culture, time management, decluttering, lifestyle, mental wellness, aging, and sustainable living. We were recently named 2019's #1 fastest growing independent publisher by *Publishers Weekly*. Our success is driven by our main goal, which is to publish high quality books that will entertain readers as well as make a positive difference in their lives.

Our readers are our most important resource; we value your input, suggestions, and ideas. We'd love to hear from you—after all, we are publishing books for you!

Please stay in touch with us and follow us at:
Facebook: Mango Publishing
Twitter: @MangoPublishing
Instagram: @MangoPublishing
LinkedIn: Mango Publishing
Pinterest: Mango Publishing

Sign up for our newsletter at www.mango.bz and receive a free book! Join us on Mango's journey to reinvent publishing, one book at a time.